HITLER
—— AND THE ——
HABSBURGS

HITLER

—— AND THE ——

HABSBURGS

The Vendetta
Against the Austrian Royals

JAMES M. LONGO

DIVERSION
BOOKS

Diversion Books
A Division of Diversion Publishing Corp.
443 Park Avenue South, Suite 1004
New York, New York 10016
www.DiversionBooks.com

For more information, email info@diversionbooks.com

First Diversion Books paperback edition July 2020.
Paperback ISBN: 978-1-63576-650-9
eBook ISBN: 978-1-63576-475-8

Printed in the U.S.A.
1 3 5 7 9 10 8 6 4 2

For my wife, Mary Jo Harwood, and
HSH Princess Sophie de Potesta of Hohenberg

CONTENTS

CONTENTS

HITLER

AND THE

HABSBURGS

CHAPTER ONE
HITLER AT THE HOTEL IMPERIAL, 1938

"I resolved that night that someday I would come back to the Imperial Hotel and walk over the red carpet in that glittering interior where the Habsburgs danced."   —ADOLF HITLER

At five thirty on the evening of March 14, 1938, Adolf Hitler's gray and black Mercedes-Benz limousine slowly drove past Schönbrunn Palace to the Hotel Imperial in the heart of Vienna. The forty-eight-year-old native son was returning to conquer the city, and the country, that once conquered him. Twenty-five years earlier, Hitler had been a homeless vagrant on Vienna's streets, a hungry dreamer sitting on a park bench in Schönbrunn's public gardens. Ten years later, he was sent to a German prison for treason. By the spring of 1938, he was the undisputed dictator of both nations.

Schönbrunn Palace and Vienna had once been home to the Royal and Imperial Habsburg family, rulers of an empire stretching across Europe and around the globe. The seeds of Hitler's remarkable rise to power, his Faustian rags-to-riches story, could be traced to his hatred of the Habsburgs and their multinational vision for the future of Europe.

Hitler's sleek, heavily armored convertible needed no bulletproof windows or armor that day. Hours earlier his army of one hundred thousand German soldiers had seized his Austrian homeland without a shot fired. Thunderous cheers greeted him as he stood erect and unsmiling for all of Austria and the world to see. Many unbelievable political and military victories would soon be his, but none was sweeter than this one. His greatest dreams since childhood were to unite Austria with Germany, and to destroy everything the Habsburg Empire represented to him. Everything else grew from these dual ambitions. On that deceptively mild March afternoon, he had achieved half of his goals. The second half would kill millions and destroy much of Europe.

Adolf Hitler could have stayed in any of Vienna's magnificent palaces but insisted on staying at the Hotel Imperial. It held a powerful attraction for him. Two decades earlier when he was a failed art student reduced to earning money by shoveling snow, a crystalizing experience occurred right on that hotel's doorsteps. The occasion was a reception honoring the Habsburg heir to the throne, Archduke Karl, and his wife, Archduchess Zita. The evening Hitler triumphantly returned to the city that had rejected him, he shared only one story with his entourage about his five fateful Vienna years. The memory he shared was of that bitterly cold night:

> I could see the glittering lights and chandeliers in the lobby, but I knew it was impossible for me to set foot inside. One night, after a bad blizzard which piled up several feet of snow, I had a chance to make some money for food shoveling snow. Ironically enough, the five or six of us in my group were sent to clean the street and sidewalk in front of the Imperial Hotel. I saw Karl and Zita step out of their imperial coach and grandly walk into this hotel over the red carpet. We poor devils shoveled the snow away on all sides and took our hats off every time the aristocrats arrived. They didn't even look at us, although I still smell the perfume that came to our noses. We were about as important to them, or to that matter to Vienna, as the snow that kept coming down all night, and this hotel did not even have the decency to send a cup of hot coffee to us. I resolved

that night that someday I would come back to the Imperial Hotel and walk over the red carpet in that glittering interior where the Habsburgs danced. I didn't know how or when, but I waited for this day and tonight I am here.

His rapt listeners applauded his story of the once forgotten man who had turned the world upside down. Few people in history had come from so little, or risen so high, in such a short period of time. Now, on the evening when Adolf Hitler united his adopted country of Germany with his Austrian birthplace, his thoughts turned not to celebrations, but to vengeance. They were not directed toward Karl, who died in 1922, or Zita, who lived in Belgian exile. Instead they fell on the royal orphans of Archduke Franz Ferdinand, the man whose 1914 assassination sparked the First World War. Shortly before Hitler arrived at the Imperial Hotel, Duke Maximilian Hohenberg, the Archduke's oldest son, his wife, and five children fled the same hotel to go into hiding.

Within hours of Hitler's return to Austria, the Duke would go from being the human face of the state to being denounced as an enemy of the state, and exchange his palace home for a Nazi prison. His fall from grace was as dramatic as Hitler's rise to power. Adolf Hitler and his Nazis had an enemies list of thousands of Austrians to be liquidated. Within weeks, seventy-nine thousand arrests were made, but the first two men the Gestapo arrested, deported to Germany, and imprisoned at Dachau were not Jews, Czechs, or the foreign immigrants Hitler denounced and demonized. The night of his greatest triumph, the first two Austrians the Führer ordered arrested were Maximilian and Ernst Hohenberg, the sons of Franz Ferdinand. He told Herman Goering and Heinrich Himmler to show them no mercy, a challenge the competitive rivals readily embraced.

Following Austria's seizure, Hitler also ordered the Gestapo to undertake a more clandestine mission. Gestapo agents were told to help the Jewish doctor who cared for his late mother in her last fatal illness to immigrate to the United States. Two Jewish officers he served with in the First World War were also provided his personal protection. Like his family doctor, they were allowed to escape the Holocaust he would soon unleash on Europe's Jews. Hitler's infamous anti-Semitism could be selective, but he was unwilling to show mercy to Franz Ferdinand's sons. The hatred directed toward them was more personal than Hitler's animosity toward their dead parents or his aversion to the millions of innocent victims about to die in his name.

Yet even as the arrests of the Hohenberg brothers made headlines in Europe and America, the women who loved them would fight back. Their wives, sister, and female allies would wage an unrelenting guerilla war against the Nazis in Vienna, Prague, and Berlin to free them. Hitler and his Gestapo would be up against the intelligence, strength, and resilience of women motivated by love as much as the Nazis were motivated by hate.

———————

The seeds for Adolf Hitler's vendetta against the vanished Habsburg Empire, the dead Archduke, and his royal orphans were planted even earlier than his snowy encounter with the Habsburgs at the Hotel Imperial.

Shortly before Hitler's birth in the Austrian border town of Braunau am Inn, Crown Prince Rudolph, the thirty-year-old charismatic heir to the Habsburg throne, died by his own hand, or by assassination. The government's clumsy cover-up made the truth elusive. England's Ambassador spoke for many when he exclaimed, "It is all mystery, mystery, mystery." The Habsburg Empire, the lynchpin of central Europe for six hundred years, never fully recovered. Emperor Franz Joseph had only one son—Rudolph. No daughter or female relative could inherit the throne. To fill the dangerous vacuum created by Rudolph's death, the Emperor reluctantly selected his oldest nephew,

Archduke Franz Ferdinand, as his successor. It was not a popular choice. The Archduke was thought to be a dead man walking, a sickly introvert no one expected to live. The abrupt disappearance of the popular Crown Prince from the public stage thrust Franz Ferdinand into a role not suited for his brittle personality. Stefan Zweig, Austria's most famous novelist, wrote that Franz Ferdinand lacked the thing most valued by the Viennese—charm.

No one could have imagined that this obscure, tiny, half-dead Archduke, born miles away from Vienna in a rented palace, might someday be Emperor. He was rejected by his own mother within minutes of his birth. As he struggled for each elusive breath, she shouted, "Take it away. If it can't live, I don't want to see it." Rejection followed throughout his life. Poor health, poor school grades, a nervous personality, and a quick temper made him the least popular Habsburg of his generation. In a family known for its mastery of foreign languages and equestrian skills, he struggled with both, inheriting none of the handsomeness or gracefulness his sorely missed cousin Rudolph epitomized. Only his piercing blue eyes marked him as a Habsburg, but most people found them impenetrable.

Yet hidden deep beneath them and his rough exterior was a first-rate mind and a vision for Austria and Europe no other statesman seemed able to imagine. In reserve he held a wry sense of humor and abundant charm when he chose to use it. But he and all of Austria lived under the melancholy shadow of the dead Crown Prince. Few celebrities of the day had been as loved, idolized, or charismatic as Rudolph. Some believe the burden and high expectations he engendered drove him to the brink of insanity and his premature death. The shock, scandal, and void he left behind did nothing to make Franz Ferdinand's life easier.

Adolf Hitler's late father, Alois, a fierce supporter of the Habsburg dynasty, worshipped Austria's elderly Emperor Franz Joseph the way a younger generation worshipped Rudolph. He could not remember a time Franz Joseph had not sat on the throne. His Imperial and Royal Apostolic Majesty had been Emperor since 1848, stubbornly outliving five younger heirs. In the modern world of constant change, he represented stability and permanence.

Alois Hitler's entire career was spent as a customs official in the bureaucratic labyrinth of the Habsburg's Ministry of Finance. In a lifetime devoid of successes, it was his only claim to fame. That tenuous link to the Imperial Habsburg dynasty empowered him to become a haughty tyrant at work and a bullying martinet at home.

He religiously celebrated Franz Joseph's birthday, wore his whiskers "modeled on those of his supreme master the Emperor," and regularly intimidated, mocked, and beat his children. The people and values Alois Hitler cherished, his son Adolf rejected. As a young schoolboy, Hitler found a kindred spirit in his favorite high schoolteacher. Dr. Leonard Pötsch, an obscure racist, rabid German nationalist, never tired of mocking the Habsburgs and their multinational Empire. Hitler later wrote of Pötsch, "His dazzling eloquence not only held us spellbound but actually carried us away... we sat there, often aflame with enthusiasm, and sometimes even moved to tears... it was then that I became a little revolutionary."

In reality, Hitler had been a rebel since primary school. He bullied other children and regularly battled with his religion teachers, especially Father Sales Schwarz. The highly ritualized Catholic Church and Habsburg monarchy of his childhood were seen by most Austrians as interchangeable. Father Schwarz lectured him, "In your heart you should have ideals for our beloved country, our beloved house of Habsburg. Whoever does not love the Imperial Family does not love the Church, and whoever does not love the Church, does not love God." Hitler only laughed. The priest told his mother her son was a "lost soul." Like most Austrians Adolf Hitler, the soulless revolutionary, believed revolution not possible as long as the old Emperor lived. Reformers and revolutionaries alike believed change only possible after Franz Joseph joined his son and 112 ancient ancestors in Vienna's Imperial burial vaults. Even the Emperor privately worried revolution would follow him. He did not think his nephew, Franz Ferdinand, could prevent it. Adolf Hitler feared the opposite. He saw the Archduke as someone who would *lead* a revolution—one antithetical to him—by selling out German Austria to its ethnic inferiors.

Following Rudolph's death, Franz Ferdinand offered few clues where he would take central Europe's greatest multicultural empire, but his 1900 marriage provided a hint. The blue-blooded Habsburg could have married any German princess from the royal and imperial courts of Europe. Instead he married a Slav, a Czech Countess whom the rabidly racist Hitler saw as an Untermenschen, a subhuman Trojan horse from the Empire's largest ethnic minority. To him, the marriage was an abomination, an example of the escalating mongrelization, miscegenation, and the assimilation threatening Austria's Germans. Reinforcing Hitler's mistrust, the Archduke preferred living outside of Prague with his family in the Bohemian homeland of his wife rather than the many Austrian palaces at his disposal. To Hitler, Franz Ferdinand was a traitor to his German roots, too tolerant of the ethnic and religious groups poisoning Austria.

For six centuries the Habsburgs had expanded their empire not by the Prussian swords and wars glorified in Dr. Pötsch's lectures, but in the wedding bed. The result could be found in the twelve distinct nationalities, hundreds of ethnic groups, countless religious traditions, and over fifty million citizens ruled by Franz Joseph. No empire on earth was more diverse.

Franz Ferdinand's uncle was saluted as the head of state in over a dozen languages in thousands of classrooms across central Europe. Austrians recognized him as their Emperor. In Hungary, Bohemia, Croatia, Slovenia, Dalmatia, and Galicia he was their King, in Cracow their Grand Duke, in Transylvania their Grand Prince, and in Lorraine, Salzburg, Styria, Carinthia, Silesia, and Modena their ruling

Duke. Whether it was the title, history, traditions, or family ties, personal loyalty to Franz Joseph united the diverse pieces of his Habsburg tapestry into one of the world's largest, wealthiest, most powerful empires on earth. The open borders and diversity Franz Joseph and Franz Ferdinand championed within the Habsburg Empire, Hitler reviled. To him, immigrants were a cancer stealing his future and destroying Austria. Their social and economic success personally stung him as his own dreams for a career as an artist or architect collapsed. It was during his years in Vienna that he came to believe immigration was engulfing and overwhelming the German people, language, and culture. To Hitler, the mixing of races, cultures, languages, and religions threatened to marginalize Austria's German population, making them a minority in their own homeland. His roommate remembered, "His fury turned against the state itself, this patchwork of ten to twelve, or only God knows how many nations this monster of Habsburg marriages built up."

Habsburg Vienna convinced Hitler only a political earthquake or war could save German Austria from a tide of immigration and assimilation. Emperor Franz Joseph seemed blind to the danger, but at least he had married a German, a good Bavarian princess. Not so his unpopular heir. Franz Ferdinand's marriage to a Czech Countess made him the Habsburg most hated by Adolf Hitler. Decades before he displayed any trace of the anti-Semitism that devoured him in Vienna, Czech classmates, not Jews, were the object of his youthful scorn. In his mind, the Archduke's marriage confirmed his worst suspicions: Franz Ferdinand and his Czech wife were the architects behind the Slavization, marginalization, and destruction of German Austria.

The Archduke was a member of a conservative, tradition-bound family, an unlikely reformer, and an even more improbable peacemaker. He was a military man infamous for slaughtering hundreds of thousands of animals during his travels on four continents. Yet he had a vision for peace, and a plan to achieve it. The Archduke was one of the few royals to travel to America. He saw the ethnic diversity there as a strength, studied and recognized the genius behind the United States' federal system of government, and, along with his wife, had close personal friends who were Americans. In the speech he planned to give at his accession to the throne, he wrote:

> We desire to treat with equal love all the peoples of the monarchy, all classes and all officially recognized religious faiths. High or low, poor or rich, all shall be held in the same before the throne.... Just as all people under Our scepter shall have equal rights of participation in the common affairs of the monarchy, equality requires that each of them be guaranteed its national development within the framework of the monarchy's common interest, and all nationalities, all classes, all occupations shall, where this is not yet done, be enabled by just electoral laws to protect their interests.

A longtime aide of the Archduke wrote, "Something about Franz Ferdinand raised him above all Habsburgs, the old Emperor included; he had freed himself from the traditional channels... took up problems on his own... looked at new questions... appealed to competence and experience wherever he found them, in or out of office."

Many outside of Austria saw Franz Ferdinand as representing a hopeful, peaceful future. Among them was the Emperor of Germany, the nation Adolf Hitler most admired. Princess Viktoria Luise, daughter of Kaiser Wilhelm II, wrote that her father could never understand why many Austrians could not see the wisdom of Franz Ferdinand's religious and political tolerance in meeting "the various nationalities" of his "multinational State" at least "half way."

Across the English Channel, William Cavendish Bentick, the Duke of Portland, a member of the British Government's Privy Council and a cousin of Queen Mary, wrote of his Austrian friend:

> From 1900 to 1910 an incessant struggle continued within the country, during which the Archduke put up a tremendous fight in

order to achieve a rejuvenation of the State... gradually these ideas prevailed in Austria, and the Archduke found enthusiastic followers to help him remodel the old State in such ways that every nation within its boundaries be given a "place in the sun"... his one aim in life was peace, his policy eminently constructive, and his greatest joy embellishing everything with which he came into contact. His unalterable determination was to strive for a higher standard of living for all people and to bring about internal peace by dealing with the utmost fairness to all.

Franz Ferdinand was not an idealist, but a realist who recognized the rising tide of nationalism could unleash ethnic furies and "Rassenkrieg"—an apocalyptic race war pitting ethnic groups against one another. Such a war would destroy not only the Habsburg Empire, but all of Europe.

Adolf Hitler's bitter years in Vienna convinced him a race war was not only inevitable, but cleansing and desirable. To him, the sooner the war came the better. Only when Austria was destroyed, Germany free of foreign influences, when those he dismissed as inferior were expelled, enslaved, or destroyed would Germany achieve its full greatness. When Hitler learned of the assassination of the Archduke on June 28, 1914, he fell on his knees, thanked God, and wept out of happiness. Almost no one at the time thought the assassination in Sarajevo would spark a war. But Hitler was certain the war he had prayed for was at hand. He believed that the death of the peacemaker whom he hated above all others made war inevitable. The war came one month to the day, and to the hour, of the assassination.

CHAPTER TWO
THE ARTIST, THE ARCHDUKE,
AND THE EMPEROR

"I lived in palaces of the imagination."   —ADOLF HITLER

"Shhhh! Be quiet. The Emperor is dead, but he doesn't know it."
                          —A POPULAR VIENNESE JOKE
               at the beginning of the twentieth century

"I have an indomitable affection for Vienna, but I know her
   abyss."   —SIGMUND FREUD

Adolf Hitler was an eighteen-year-old high school dropout when he
boarded a train in 1907 from his hometown of Linz. Despite the speed
and efficiency of the Imperial Royal Austrian State Railway, his trip
was leisurely. It was a milk train, loading and unloading milk, pro-
duce, and people to towns and villages along the meandering Danube
River. Hitler was in no hurry. He brought with him suitcases full of
books, and dreams of becoming a successful artist or architect. There
was no doubt in his mind success waited for him in the capital of the
mighty Habsburg Empire.

   Fifty miles short of his destination, the steam engine slowed and
stopped at the small village of Pöchlarn. On a nearby hilltop sat Artstetten Castle, the childhood home of forty-three-year-old Archduke
Franz Ferdinand d'Este, heir to the Royal and Imperial Habsburg

throne. Hitler was unable to see the Archduke or his stunning castle from his third-class compartment window. The frenetic Archduke was seldom there, anyway. He was relentlessly on the move, a man who loved speed in an age of speed, a traditionalist who embraced modernity. Gas, electric, and steam-driven cars all competed to break speed records. It was no coincidence Franz Ferdinand's onetime chauffeur was Ferdinand Porsche, a winner of speed records across Europe and the designer of the first hybrid petroleum and electric automobile.

Not everyone embraced the modern times. Like an ancient, finely tuned clock, the legendary Emperor Franz Joseph left Schönbrunn Palace on the outskirts on Vienna at exactly 7:00 a.m. He then rode in a horse-drawn carriage along Mariahilfstrasse, Vienna's main shopping street, to perform his public duties at the Hofburg Palace. At half past four, he returned to his palace home where he had been born seventy-seven years earlier. There he worked late into the night reading dispatches and signing papers.

Eight perfectly synchronized snow-white Lipizzaner horses pulled his gold-gilded green carriage. Each had a regal, erect gait, much like the Emperor himself. Franz Joseph and his horse-drawn carriage were images from another century. It took England's King Edward VII to persuade Austria's Emperor to take his one and only ride in an automobile. Franz Joseph declared of his 1908 adventure, "It stank, and one couldn't see anything." If the words were truly his, it was one of the few times Franz Joseph revealed honest thoughts from the man behind the public mask.

The monarch—surrounded by the dazzling pomp, ceremony, and etiquette of his court—projected a grandfatherly image of stability, permanence, and continuity. The image was carefully orchestrated by a palace public relations apparatus second to none. It may have been the only modern thing about him. Franz Joseph's royal façade allowed the aging monarch to cling stubbornly to his routine and to maintain power after nearly sixty years on the throne. Adolf Hitler, no fan of the Habsburgs, begrudgingly recognized, "Monarchy instituted something extremely useful. It artificially created the idol. All that fuss, the whole shebang, did make sense in a way." Liberal social reformer Joseph Maria Baernreither, a member of Franz Ferdinand's inner circle, might have been speaking for the frustrated Archduke when he wrote, "The powerfully surging life of our times scarcely reached the ear of the Emperor as distant rustling.... He no longer understands the times and the times pass on regardless."

Franz Joseph's pace stood in stark contrast to that of his restless nephew and heir. When Franz Ferdinand was in Vienna, his large Austrian-built Graf & Stift automobile raced and careened in and out of Schönbrunn's gravel driveway from his nearby home and office at Belvedere Palace. The contrast between the Emperor and Archduke was available for all to see. One seemed to have ice water in his veins, the other burning oil. The resulting steam made it impossible to clearly see and understand each other.

Once Hitler arrived in Vienna, money inherited from his father allowed him to rent a tiny back room in a crowded tenement in the heart of the city. It provided him privacy, but proximity to the great Ringstrasse Boulevard and Franz Joseph's 2,600-room Hofburg Palace to the north, Schönbrunn Palace and gardens to the south, and Franz Ferdinand's Belvedere Palace to the east. Museums, parks, theatres, and magnificent architecture and monuments were within easy walking distance.

There was no escaping the Habsburgs in Vienna. The first postcard Hitler sent home to his one and only friend, August Kubizek, pictured the city's Karlsplatz and Karlskirche, a famous plaza and church named after a long-dead Habsburg Emperor. On it he scribbled, "I find everything very beautiful." Later he told him in person, "For hours I could stand in front of the Opera, for hours I could gaze at the parliament; the whole Ring Boulevard seemed to me like an enchantment out of *The Thousand and One Nights*."

He was initially captivated by the cosmopolitan city. Hitler later reminisced about Habsburg Vienna to his Nazi inner circle:

> Dazzling riches and loathsome poverty alternated sharply. In the center and in the inner districts you could really feel the pulse of this realm of fifty-two million, with all the dubious magic of the national melting pot. The Court with its dazzling glamour attracted wealth and intelligence from the rest of the country like a magnet. Added to this was the strong centralization of the Habsburg monarchy itself. It offered the sole possibility of holding this medley of nations together in any set form.

Perhaps more than any other European metropolis at the dawn of the twentieth century, Vienna was a magnet for thinkers, dreamers, artists, and schemers. Pioneering psychologists Sigmund Freud and Hermine Hug-Hellmuth, best-selling author Stefan Zweig, painter Gustav Klimt, philanthropist Adele Bloch-Bauer, composer Gustav Mahler, cigar-smoking aristocratic confidante Anna Sacher, and the first woman to win the Nobel Peace Prize, Bertha von Suttner, claimed the city as their home. Father of Zionism Theodor Herzl, director-filmmaker Fritz Lang, singer-actress Lotte Lenya, inventor-movie star Hedy Lamarr, revolutionaries Joseph Tito, Leon Trotsky, and Joseph Stalin also lived there at one time. Austrians liked to brag the modern world was born in Vienna.

Vienna in 1907 was a dramatically different city than the one Hitler's father had found fifty years earlier as a thirteen-year-old runaway. Different, too, than the one Hitler's mother, twenty-three years younger than his father, experienced during her visit as a girl. Only the Emperor remained the same. Immigration had expanded Vienna's population fourfold to nearly two million people, bringing with them a living tapestry of languages, religions, foods, music, dress, and traditions. At its center was Franz Joseph, the linchpin holding it all together. The immigrants did not come for the Emperor, but for the upward mobility his Empire offered.

That upward mobility eluded Adolf Hitler. He was stunned when he failed to pass the Academy of Fine Arts' entrance exam. Years later he wrote that the rejection struck him "like a bolt from the blue.... Downcast, I left [the] magnificent building in the Schillerplatz, for the first time in my young life, at odds with myself."

A second blow brought him back to Linz. His beloved mother was dying of cancer. He returned home to care for her, but she died five days before Christmas. The holiday was forever ruined for him. Within months the world he had known and the world he had imagined were shattered. Eduard Bloch, the Jewish doctor who cared for Hitler's mother during her last illness, later wrote of him:

> He was tall and pale and looked older than his age. His eyes, which he inherited from his mother, were large, melancholic and thoughtful. To a very large extent, this boy lived within himself. What dreams he dreamt, I do not know.

With his father already dead, Hitler returned in February 1908 to wintry Vienna as an orphan. The small inheritance from his father and an orphan's pension from his mother provided him enough income to stay in Vienna one year. He was certain he would pass the Academy entrance exam on his next try. Until then he often slept in his room until noon. Waking hours were spent in warming rooms and coffeehouses where he could read and draw before exploring the city's museums. Evenings were reserved for the opera. Hunger became part of his life, but he would rather feed his dreams with music than his body with food.

The young Hitler made no friends in Vienna and had only one in Linz. Two years earlier, he had met August Kubizek in the standing room gallery of the Linz regional theatre. They discovered a shared love of music and poetry, had similarly poor grades in school, and had no other friends. Their mothers had each lost three other children. Both boys were survivors.

Kubizek had never lived anywhere but Linz. Meanwhile, following Hitler's birth in the Austrian-German border town of Braunau am Inn, his restless father moved the family seven times. After attending five different schools and flunking twice, Hitler quit school without graduating at the age of fifteen. Perhaps what attracted him most to Kubizek was that his solitary friend was a listener. Hitler was a talker without a regular audience, a leader in search of followers. In Kubizek and Linz he found his first disciple whom he quickly tried to persuade to attend Vienna's famous Music Conservatory. He wrote him from his tiny rented room, "The whole of Vienna is waiting for you!" Whether he believed that of his friend or not, he certainly believed it for himself.

August's parents were fiercely opposed to having their only son leave Linz. When Hitler returned to care for his dying mother, he took the opportunity to change their minds. His surprising victory was early proof of his persuasive verbal skills. August Kubizek soon arrived at the same train station that had brought Hitler to Vienna. The crush of people and the sights, sounds, and smells of the city nearly overwhelmed him. But he quickly recognized Adolf in the teaming crowds wearing a handsome dark overcoat, a matching hat, clasping an ivory-tipped ebony walking stick.

The illusionary magic Hitler momentarily spun quickly disappeared when August saw the "wretched shabby" room where his friend lived. A quick fifteen-minute walk to the magnificent Opera House, the Ringstrasse, and St. Stephen's Cathedral revived his spirits. Unable to find a place of his own, he and Adolf agreed to split the rent and moved into a slightly larger room offered by Hitler's landlady. August applied and was quickly admitted into Vienna's Conservatory of Music. Hitler did not tell his friend about his own rejection and talked as if he were taking art classes. Once winter retreated, Hitler spent his days not in school, but in hiking the city and sitting in the gardens of nearby Schönbrunn Palace. It was there on a favorite bench and table he drew and sketched buildings he had seen, and dreamed of rebuilding Linz and Vienna.

When he again failed his entrance exam, Hitler's personality darkened. August knew his friend was troubled but had no idea why. In Linz, the slim, deathly pale Hitler had always been somber. August remembered, "He was capable of loving and admiring, hating and despising, all with the greatest seriousness." But in Vienna he suddenly seemed "unbalanced." Hitler's gaunt appearance, sleepless pacing back and forth, and hour-long rants made an already gloomy room a claustrophobic prison cell. Finally, late one night, Hitler angrily offered August his own raging version of the truth. "The Academy is a lot of old fashioned civil servants, bureaucrats, devoid of understanding, stupid lumps of officials. The whole Academy ought to be blown up." Then, and only then, did he share his secret. "They rejected me. They twice turned me down."

August was stunned; but his friend's dismissal of the Academy faculty was telling. Hitler bitterly associated "civil servants" with his father, who proudly, some would say arrogantly, served as a customs official for the Habsburg government. Hitler projected his father's martinet personality on any annoying bureaucrat he felt disrespectful to him. Following the outburst, Kubizek wrote that his roommate seemed "at odds with the world. Wherever he looked he saw injustice, hate, and enmity. Nothing was free from his criticism. Nothing found favor in his eyes." Everyone around him seemed to be getting ahead, even the shy roommate he had brought from Linz.

In April 1909, Hitler received another shock. A letter informed August he was being called into military service. If possible, he was more upset than Kubizek, protesting that his friend was a musician, not a soldier. Franz Joseph's government expected all young men in the Empire to serve in his army. Hitler, one year younger, was scheduled to be inducted the following year. He insisted August not serve, telling him the "moribund Habsburg Empire did not deserve a single soldier."

The army motto, "Inseparable and Indivisible," reflected the Habsburg philosophy of having all ethnic groups of the Empire serve side by side in the army. Personal loyalty to the Habsburg Emperor through shared military service, not religion, not language, and not nationality, united the polyglot Austro-Hungarian Empire. To the Habsburgs, the army was the foundation of the Empire, but to Hitler the thought of mixing different "races" together was an abomination. He urged August to flee to Germany.

August wavered, but a trip home to Linz, his father's words, his mother's tears, and the advice of his Viennese music instructors convinced him to join the army reserves. His decision disappointed Hitler, but it shortened August's military obligation, kept him from becoming a fugitive, and allowed him to finish the semester at the Conservatory. It was the first time Hitler had not bent his friend to his will. Kubizek did not realize it at the time, but the days of their friendship were numbered.

CHAPTER THREE
CAN THIS BE A JEW?

"The vitriol of hate began to creep through his body. The grim realities of the life he lived encouraged him to hate the government, the labor unions, the very men he lived with. But he had not yet begun to hate the Jews."

—DR. EDUARD BLOCH,
the Hitler family's Jewish doctor

"I no longer wandered like a blind man through the city."

—ADOLF HITLER

"All that he later became was born of this dying imperial Vienna."

—AUGUST KUBIZEK,
Hitler's childhood friend and Viennese roommate

That spring Emperor Franz Joseph's Diamond Jubilee, celebrating six decades on the throne, briefly distracted Hitler from his unhappiness. Emperor Wilhelm II and other German royalty from Württemberg, Saxony, and Bavaria traveled to Vienna to celebrate the anniversary. Hitler loved all things German. The visit of Wilhelm II allowed him a fleeting respite from his frustrations and growing anger.

Along with thousands of others, Hitler cheered as the German Emperor and his royal delegation drove in open carriages to Schönbrunn Palace. Newspapers reported that the royals gathered in the palace's Marie Antoinette room just as a horrendous thunderstorm broke over the city. The room took its name from a large tapestry of Marie Antoinette and her children, a gift from France's Napoleon III. No royal personage had the temerity to mention the tragic fate of the French queen born a Habsburg Archduchess, or the misfortune that befell her children.

Wilhelm II used the occasion to salute Franz Joseph as the living embodiment of "three generations of German princes." Austria's Emperor, sensitive to cooling the flames of Pan-Germanism among his subjects, praised the peaceful goals and high ideals of "monarchial principles." Franz Joseph's refusal to embrace his German heritage revealed the tensions beneath their military alliance. Hitler hated the alliance. This peace and the Habsburg's multi-ethnic empire were threats to German nationalism, unification, and expansion. Looking back years later with bitterness regarding the alliance and Germany's defeat in the First World War, he wrote:

> This mummy of a state allied itself with Germany, not in order to fight a war to its end, but for the preservation of an eternal peace which could astutely be used for the slow but certain extermination of Germanism in the monarchy. This alliance was an impossibility for another reason; because we could not expect a state to take the offensive in championing national German interest as long as it did not possess the power and determination to put an end to the process of de-Germanization on its own immediate borders. If Germany did not possess enough national awareness and ruthless determination to snatch power over the destinies of ten million national comrades from the hands of the impossible Habsburg state, then truly we had not the right to expect that she would ever lend her hand to such farseeing and bold plans. The attitude of the old Reich on the Austrian question was the touchstone of the conduct in the struggle for the destiny of the whole nation.

In June of 1908, twelve thousand marchers, four thousand horses, and thousands of colorfully dressed soldiers, singers, dancers, and musicians gathered on the Ringstrasse to honor Franz Joseph's Diamond Jubilee. The three-hour procession under a scorching sun saluted the historic multi-ethnic, multicultural rainbow of the Habsburg Empire. The Emperor was addressed by the honorary parade marshal who declared, "All of Austria's nationalities thank you, Your Majesty, that they may pass loudly cheering in a parade, conscious to form a united Austrian people and to be the loyal subjects of an exhaustingly kind ruler and emperor." Newspapers reported the cheering of dozens of nationalities "in their own mother tongues."

Among the most fervent celebrants were the city's Jewish population. Publicly and privately they praised Franz Joseph's religious tolerance and the legal protections he afforded them. Many affectionately saluted him as their "guardian angel, custodian, and patron saint." The loyalty of Vienna's Jews was not shared by everyone. Many Hungarian, Czech, Croat, and Italian nationalists refused to participate in the parade for political reasons. But thousands of others from across the Empire happily watched the spectacle wearing their distinctive hats, colors, and regional folk costumes. Hitler was horrified by the "exotic dress and appearance" of the revelers. Patriotic demonstrations by any group celebrating the Habsburg Emperor triggered his anger and ethnic paranoia.

Even hearing foreign languages or dialects on the street ignited his short fuse. His roommate remembered Hitler tightly grabbing his arm when he heard other languages, especially Czech. He complained bitterly, "There you have your German Vienna!... Was Vienna, into which streamed from all sides Czechs, Magyars, Croats, Poles, Italians, Slovaks, Ukrainians, and above all Galician Jews still a German city?" August Kubizek wrote of that time:

> In the state of affairs in Vienna, my friend saw a symbol of the
> struggle of the Germans in the Habsburg Empire. He hated the Ba-

bel in the streets of Vienna, this "incest incarnate" as he called it....
He hated this state which ruined Germanism and the pillars which
supported this state; the reigning house, the nobility, the capitalist
and the Jews.

Hitler himself later wrote, "The view of life in the streets of Vienna
provided me with invaluable insights. The time came eventually when
I no longer wandered like a blind man through the city, but with open
eyes saw not only the buildings but also the people."

Franz Ferdinand served as host of many of the Diamond Jubilee
events due to the Emperors' advanced age. His wife, Sophie, who
had been given the title the Countess of Hohenberg, was nowhere
to be seen. Her fourth pregnancy provided a convenient excuse
for her absence. Aside from Adolf Hitler, perhaps the only people
more repelled by the Archduke's Czech marriage were his Habsburg
relatives.

Sophie, Countess Chotek of Chotkova und Wognin, was not of
royal blood. Her name was nowhere to be found on the approved list
of brides supplied by the Habsburgs to the Catholic courts of Europe. She descended from a distinguished family of Czech nobility,
but her blood was not blue enough for them. What was worse for the
caste-conscious Habsburgs was Sophie's former station in life. When
the Archduke met his future bride, genteel poverty had forced her to
take a position as a female companion, a lady-in-waiting to his cousin,
a Habsburg Archduchess.

For Franz Ferdinand to remain heir to the throne, his uncle the
Emperor had to formally approve his choice of a marriage partner; but
His Imperial and Royal Apostolic Majesty, His government, and the
Archduke's own family did not approve. To them, Sophie Chotek could
never be accepted as a royal wife after being a mere servant. Romantics
found their upstairs-downstairs romance a fairy tale. The Habsburgs
did not. To them it was a nightmare, an affront to their own miserable

dynastic marriages. The famously overdressed, over-jeweled, overweight Archduchess Isabella Hedwig Habsburg, Sophie's former employer, bitterly complained, "That's how this scheming girl rewards us, with her Slav deceit, for our kindness!"

Crown Prince Rudolph's widow, Princess Stephanie of Belgium, wrote of the sad reality that most royals were unhappily married to their own cousins and detested any semblance of a normal family life. She confided to her friend Countess Bertha von Suttner, "The Emperor has no heart. He can't help the fact that he is stupid, but he has no feelings."

Dynastic marriages were traditionally based on pedigree, politics, and money. Stephanie was an expert on the subject. After her husband passed his syphilis onto her, he died next to his seventeen-year-old mistress in a public scandal that shook the Empire to its core. Emperor Franz Joseph also reportedly passed syphilis onto his own wife, Empress Elisabeth, who then suffered a debilitating nervous breakdown. Their marriage never completely recovered. Elisabeth, perhaps for her own sanity, selected a new mistress for the Emperor. The actress Katharina Schratt remained his companion for the rest of his life.

Franz Ferdinand needed to look no further than his younger brother Otto to see the tragic end of court-arranged marriages. Once considered the handsomest Habsburg of them all, his public and private debauchery resulted in a slow, painful, syphilitic death. After deserting the wife he loathed—his nose, larynx, and reputation gone—only his mistress, his confessor, and his loyal stepmother remained at his side when he died.

After three years of threats, turmoil, struggle, and endless maneuvering, the Archduke finally won the right to marry the woman he loved, but he and Sophie were made to feel the full wrath of the Emperor's disapproval. On June 28, 1900, he was forced to swear an Oath of Renunciation deeming the marriage morganatic. It was an ancient term allowing Sophie Chotek to legally be his wife, but to never be accepted as his equal in any public ceremonies connected with the Imperial court. She and children born of the marriage would never be Habsburgs. They were given the last name of Hohenberg, a name taken from an extinct branch of the Habsburg family tree. Franz Ferdinand could still become Emperor, but his wife would never be an Empress or a Queen, and their children could never inherit the throne. The Archduke's family were condemned to remain outsiders in the greatest family of royal insiders in Europe.

The humiliating "Oath of Renunciation" that legally permitted the marriage took place in the ornate red, white, and gold Privy Council Room in the innermost chambers of the Hofburg Palace. Franz Ferdinand made his "irrevocable" verbal and written pledge standing alone before the frozen faces of Emperor Franz Joseph and fifteen stiff and scowling Habsburg Archdukes. Among the blue-blooded Archdukes were murderers, pederasts, philanderers, wife beaters, sexual predators, and the Emperor's recently exiled, infamous cross-dressing youngest brother. The highest echelons of the Empire, one hundred carefully selected civic, government, and religious leaders, also served as witnesses. No attempt was made to spare the Archduke's feelings. The palace released every demeaning detail of the elaborately orchestrated ceremony to the press.

Three days later, the happy but embittered heir married the impoverished Czech Countess he loved. The entire Imperial family boycotted his wedding, except for his loyal stepmother, Archduchess Maria-Theresa, and two younger stepsisters. The fearless Archduchess hosted the wedding at her summer castle miles from Franz Joseph's Vienna. Her stepson proved himself to be a formidable opponent of the establishment. He had forced his will on the rigid Emperor and his calcified court. But he had made powerful enemies in the process.

The past, present, and future personal problems, feuds, and scandals of Franz Joseph's quarreling family did not interest Adolf Hitler, *except* in this Habsburg marriage. He came to see it as an attempt on Franz Ferdinand's part to forge a "strong Catholic–Slav bloc" that would erode German influence in Austria, and eventually dominate Europe. To Hitler, the marriage between an Austrian and a Slav was a racial abomination. It combined his hatred of the Habsburgs with his deep-seated bigotry against Czechs.

Four Habsburg Archduchesses had more personal reasons for resenting the marriage. Archduchess Isabella Hedwig never forgave the Archduke for marrying her lady-in-waiting rather than one of her eight less than attractive unmarried daughters. He had also repeatedly rejected the Archduchess Maria Josepha as a marriage partner before she unhappily married Otto, his philandering brother. Archduchess Marie Valerie, the Emperor's youngest and favorite daughter, fiercely took her father's side in all family disputes. She, more than anyone, knew how bitterly the Emperor opposed, resented, and fought the Archduke's choice of a marriage partner. Crown Prince Rudolph's only child, Archduchess Elisabeth Marie, resented the man who took her father's place as heir to the throne. If the Habsburgs permitted a woman to inherit the throne, she would have been Empress. The four angry women bonded. Individually and collectively, they did everything within their powers to undermine and destroy Franz Ferdinand and his wife.

Perhaps the only people unaware of the scandal that preceded their births were the three young children born of the Archduke's marriage. At the time of the Emperor's Diamond Jubilee, their age and invisible status allowed them to participate in the celebrations blissfully unaware of the court intrigues surrounding them. On May 21, 1908, eight-year-old Princess Sophie, six-year-old Prince Maximilian, and four-year-old Prince Ernst joined the eighty-two thousand schoolchildren on the lawn of Schönbrunn Palace to see, serenade, and salute their Emperor. Franz Joseph seemed deeply moved. He addressed his youthful audience, telling them, "The older I get the more I like children."

The comment must have pained Franz Ferdinand. Although he had been heir to the throne for two decades, his own children had never met the Emperor. Later in the year, the younger members of the Habsburg family were invited to present a tableau at the private theatre in Schönbrunn Palace for Franz Joseph. To the Archduke's surprise and pleasure, his children were included. Poems were to be read, songs sung, and flowers presented. Sophie, Max, and Ernst rehearsed for weeks. Special costumes were created for them. Franz Ferdinand was so pleased he commissioned a portrait of his children to commemorate the event. The afternoon activities went off smoothly, but his sons and daughter were not introduced to Franz Joseph before, during, or after their performance.

The Archduke was not the only one disappointed during the celebrations. Much to Hitler's annoyance, the Diamond Jubilee kept him from visiting his favorite bench in Schönbrunn's public gardens. As the day approached when August Kubizek would leave Vienna, the two spent weekends exploring the countryside outside the city. There they could avoid the crowds of invading "foreign" tourists and Hitler could crystallize his thoughts and vent his rage. Kubizek later wrote:

> This Habsburg state, Hitler felt, must fall, and the sooner the better, for every moment of its continued existence cost the Germans honor, property, and their very life. He saw in the fanatical internecine strife of its races the decisive symptoms of its coming downfall. He visited parliament to feel, so to speak, the pulse of the patient, whose early demise was expected by all. He looked forward to that hour full with impatience, for only the collapse of the Habsburg Empire could open the road to those schemes of which he dreamed in his lonely hours.

Shortly before his roommate left for military training, Hitler came across a Hasidic Jew selling ribbons, thread, and buttons on the street.

Some street merchants skirted the Viennese law against begging by aggressively selling small trinkets easily hidden from the police. The panhandler wore the distinctive heavy boots, long dark robes, thick beard, and braided dreadlocks of eastern European Jews. Hitler was horrified. He never forgot his initial repulsion:

> "Can this be a Jew?" was my first thought. They don't look like this in Linz. I threw the man a few sidelong glances but the more I stared at his foreign face and examined his features one by one, the more my first question took on another aspect. "Is this a German?"

The Jews in Hitler's hometown of Linz, including Dr. Bloch who cared for his dying mother, looked like every other citizen. They seemed fully assimilated into Austrian society. In Hitler's mind, his encounter with the poor Hasidic panhandler unmasked the truth behind the Jewish veneer. A police officer arrested the man for begging. Hitler quickly agreed to act as a witness against him. When the "poor" beggar was searched, three thousand Kronen, a considerable sum of money then, was discovered underneath his caftan. With his own funds increasingly depleted, the evidence of the duplicity of Jews was reinforced in Hitler's mind. This proved to be one of the major turning points in his life. He told and retold the story to his roommate for hours on end.

The two friends agreed to continue as roommates when August returned from his eight weeks of military service. Hitler walked him to the train station repeating "for the hundredth time how little he wanted to be alone." The rejected art student took the hands of the successful music student, squeezed them, spun around, and vanished into the crowd. August received several postcards from Hitler complaining of his "hermit"-like existence. Then on October 7, 1908, Franz-Joseph's government made an announcement that stunned Adolf Hitler, Franz Ferdinand, and most of Europe.

As a Jubilee gift to the Emperor, with his approval, his own Foreign

Minister announced that the Balkan territories of Bosnia-Herzegovina would be annexed by Austria into the Habsburg Empire. Vienna had administered the two former provinces of the disintegrating Ottoman Empire for thirty years. Recent revolution in Turkey seemed to offer an opportunity to keep them forever. The annexation brought nearly two million Slavs into what was already the most diverse multicultural nation in Europe. Hitler saw the move as a concrete example of the "Slavization of Austria." He believed the "anti-German ruling house" had once again sold out its German citizens. Franz Ferdinand was also angry, but for other reasons. He had courted the friendship of Nicholas II, the Czar of Russia, for over a decade and feared the annexation would antagonize Russia. Austria's colossal neighbor to the east was home to the largest concentration of ethnic Slavs and Eastern Orthodox Christians in Europe. Nicholas viewed himself as the champion and natural protector of Balkan Slavs. Expansion by the Catholic Habsburg Empire, his centuries-old political and religious rival in the region, threatened war. The Archduke wrote to one of his military aides:

> What would be the point of fighting Russia? Not even Napoleon could succeed. And even if we beat Russia—which to my mind is totally out of the question—a victory like that would still be the greatest tragedy for the Austrian monarchy.

Franz Ferdinand was the public face of the Austro-Hungarian Empire's military might. Friend and foe alike recognized him as the man who brought the Emperor's army into the twentieth century, and almost single-handedly created its modern navy. Few outside the Habsburg inner circle knew he was also the leader of the government's peace party. The Archduke fiercely opposed the annexation of Bosnia-Herzegovina, prophetically writing, "A war with Russia will finish us! Are the Emperor of Austria and the Czar to knock each other off their throne to pave the way for revolution?"

Hitler imagined Franz Ferdinand the mastermind and evil catalyst behind the annexation. But, in fact, the Empire's ambitious Foreign Minister, Baron Alois von Aehrenthal, and his own former protégé, Army Chief of Staff Conrad von Hötzendorf, prevailed against his vehement arguments. In response, the Archduke angrily left Vienna, taking his family to St. Moritz, but he remained livid and sleepless until weeks of delicate diplomacy prevented war. The immediate crisis passed, but mistrust, fear, and poisonous political fallout from the event lingered in the capitals of Europe. Germany's Emperor, Wilhelm II, felt personally compelled to offer an explanation and reassurances to his cousin Nicholas II, the Russian Czar. Addressing him as "Dearest Nicky," he wrote:

> The annexation of Bosnia and Herzegovina was a genuine surprise for everybody, but particularly for us as we were informed about Austria's intentions even later than you.... Of course... these small states are an awful nuisance.... The slightest encouragement from any quarter makes them frantic... I do hope with all my heart that notwithstanding the numerous and serious difficulties that have to be surmounted a peaceful solution will be arrived at; anything I can do in that direction will certainly be done. Take my word for it! ... Ever your true and devoted cousin and friend, Willy.

This was the tense political atmosphere August Kubizek found when he returned from his reservist training to Vienna on November 20, 1908. Hitler had agreed to meet him at the train station, but never appeared. August walked to their apartment at No. 29 Stumpergasse, but found it had been rented to someone else. Their landlady, Frau Zakreys, told him Hitler had moved with no forwarding address. August rented another room, returned to complete his studies at the Conservatory, and continued searching for his friend. Hitler had not left Vienna, but carefully avoided any of their former haunts.

It would be years before August discovered what became of him. In thinking back to their time together, Kubizek later wrote, "The old imperial city with its atmosphere of false glamour and spurious romance, and its now evident decay was the ground on which his social and political opinions grew. All that he later became was born of this dying imperial Vienna."

CHAPTER FOUR
THE LION AND THE LAMB

"Vienna was and remained for me the hardest most thorough school of my life."   —ADOLF HITLER

"She was the ideal partner for such a high strung man and she knew how to handle him."   —ARCHDUCHESS ZITA
on Franz Ferdinand's wife

On December 2, 1908, Archduke Franz Ferdinand hosted the culminating events for Emperor Franz Joseph's Diamond Jubilee celebration. The glittering afternoon soiree at the Hofburg Palace was attended by all the Habsburg Archdukes and Archduchesses. His own wife had not been seen in Vienna since delivering a stillborn son in early November. He and his family deeply grieved over the loss, but the tragedy was ignored by the Habsburg court.

That same evening, a musical concert titled *The Emperor's Dream* was presented at Vienna's opera house. Rapturous ovations greeted Franz Joseph as he entered and left the event. The tableau featured an actor portraying the thirteenth-century founder of the Habsburg dynasty, Rudolf, dreaming of Austria's coming greatness. Showcased were scenes from the 1515 royal wedding that brought Bohemia and Hungary under the Habsburg crown, the 1683 defeat of the Ottoman Turks before the gates of Vienna, Empress Maria Theresa and her children listening to a 1762 recital by Amadeus Mozart, the 1815

Congress of Vienna, and other glorious triumphs in the Empire's long history.

The female narrator representing the "Future" predicted, "What you have planted, you see blossom again... love binds people and ruler." Actors dressed as the nationalities united under Franz Joseph's crown proclaimed a "vision of the monarchy as a harmonious mosaic of peoples and cultures moving into the future with confidence, guided by the experience of the sacred House of Habsburg." The culmination of the evening was a merging of all the voices on the stage "with the collective singing of the state hymn."

To outward appearances, the Habsburg dynasty seemed at the pinnacle of its power and glory, but beneath the luminescent surface were deep fissures. At the conclusion of the pageant, the Emperor was discreetly handed a coded message from Prague. Fighting between Czech and German nationalists had forced authorities to declare martial law there. The stone face the monarch displayed throughout the evening betrayed no hint of the dispatch's contents.

The next day, a front-page article in the *Prager Tagblatt* stated, "Of all the Emperor's dreams, the dream which he had harbored since his youth of creating peace among his peoples materialized the least and had become the most cruelly destroyed." Franz Joseph dreamed of a peaceful future, even as the foundations of his restless Empire shifted beneath his throne. If Adolf Hitler had not been in such a downward spiral, he might have celebrated the schism between the Habsburg Emperor and his Czech subjects. He no longer lived in the apartment he once shared with August Kubizek because he could no longer pay the rent. Unwilling to face his friend, he moved into a cheaper room, but poverty and hunger followed. He relocated to poorer and poorer neighborhoods, unable to escape the frustrations, anger, and despair dogging him. Along the way, Hitler was forced to sell his overcoat, his ivory-tipped walking stick, most of his books, and even his art supplies. Finally, unable to make the smallest rent payment, he became homeless.

Hitler came to the city to receive an education, and received one in its slums. He later wrote of this time, "I had been so busy with my own destiny that I could not concern myself much with the people around me." Once park benches and doorways became his bed, it was the invisible people he had ignored who taught him how to survive, and much more. The experience did not increase his empathy, but it gave him a rare insight into the thinking, feelings, and anger of the underclass.

Hitler had always scorned what he dismissed as "bread and butter jobs," but the police, drunks, rain, and an early winter convinced him to take a job as a construction worker. "I looked for work only to avoid starvation, only to obtain an opportunity of continuing my education." His fellow construction workers, many of them socialists, communists, and trade unionists, tutored him in their worldview:

> These men rejected everything: the nation as an invention of the "capitalistic" classes (how often I was forced to hear this single word!); the fatherland as an instrument of the bourgeoisie for the exploitation of the working class; the authority of law as a means of oppressing the proletariat; the school as an institution of breeding slaves and slaveholders; religion as a means of stultifying the people and making them easier to exploit; morality as a symptom of stupid, sheep-like patience, etc.

Hitler asked himself:

> Are these people human, worthy to belong to a great nation?... If it is answered in the affirmative, the struggle of my nationality really ceases to be worth the hardships and sacrifices which the best of us have to make for the sake of such scum; and if it is answered in the negative, our nation is pitifully poor in *human beings*.

Heated political arguments with his coworkers and threats of "terror and violence" convinced him to return to the ranks of the unemployed. Hitler wrote, "A few of the spokesmen on the opposing side forced me to either leave the building at once or be thrown off the scaffolding." Free time allowed him to spend hours avoiding Vienna's harsh weather by sitting in the warmth of the parliament building and listening to the cacophony of debates and multitude of dialects and languages there. The sights and sounds of the Empire's "liars and sneaks" provided him a link to his emerging favorite villain. "Only the Jew can praise an institution (such as parliament) which is as dirty and false as he himself." To Hitler the parliament was worthless. Debates were allowed in ten languages with no interpreters. To him, it was multiculturalism gone mad, one more example of the Habsburg government's failure to protect and champion the German language and German people.

Life on the streets drove Hitler to seek asylum in a large homeless shelter in the city's poor working class Meidling neighborhood. The shelter sat literally on the other side of the tracks behind the massive South railway station. Franz Ferdinand's Belvedere Palace stood on a nearby hilltop. Many, including Hitler, considered it the most beautiful palace in Vienna. It must have seemed a taunting mirage to him.

The tiny space Hitler once shared with August Kubizek was luxurious compared to the overcrowded shelter where he came to live. Men, women, and children lined up early in the day hoping to be given a five-day pass to be admitted there, but despite its large size, there was never enough room for the homeless. In the winter, guards turned hundreds away. Newspapers regularly reported the grisly discovery of frozen bodies near its locked entrance. The Emperor was the asylum's royal sponsor, but its upkeep was paid by ennobled Jewish philanthropists. When Hitler had first moved to Vienna, he often walked past the five-story Ringstrasse mansion of a benefactor of the shelter. He could have never imagined as a finely dressed, newly arrived opera patron that he would one day be living in a homeless asylum paid for by the Jewish nobleman whose mansion he admired.

It was in the Meidling dormitory that Hitler found a new friend who helped him navigate the underbelly of Viennese society. Reinhold Hanisch was a Sudetenland German who had traveled throughout Germany and Austria. Hanisch taught him to "never approach a drunk," where to find food, and how to earn money. Mornings they walked to the Sisters of Mercy Convent where the nuns served warm soup to the homeless. Midday they walked two-and-a-half hours to another charity sponsored by a Jewish philanthropist. The soup and bread they received there was often their last meal until the next morning. Hitler earned tips carrying luggage for passengers arriving at the rail station, but his slight size and unkempt appearance caused most travelers to avoid him. People were quick to reject the scruffy porter wearing thin layers of clothes that failed to protect him from the dropping temperatures. As Christmas 1909 approached, Adolf Hitler looked like hundreds of other Vienna tramps with long dark hair hanging over his frayed collar, scraggly facial hair, and outstretched hand.

It was that winter when he found himself shoveling snow outside the Hotel Imperial, a night he never forgot. The reception inside the magnificent hotel was for Archduke Karl Habsburg, Franz Ferdinand's nephew and heir. Since Franz Ferdinand's marriage was morganatic and his sons were not legally Habsburgs, they could not inherit the throne. His nephew Karl was his designated successor and would become Emperor after him. Despite Hitler's hatred of the Habsburgs, at times he was dazzled by the pomp and ceremony of their court. That night was not one of those times. As he shoveled snow in the freezing cold, he watched in silent contempt as the twenty-two-year-old Prince entered the hotel to warm applause and cheers. Karl, only two years older than Hitler, seemed to have the world at his feet.

———

During the Christmas Hitler spent at the crowded homeless shelter in Vienna's slums, Franz Ferdinand's nearby Belvedere Palace sat empty.

He and his family had many houses where they might enjoy the holidays. None was more stunning than Belvedere. The palace had been built for the French-Italian emigrant Prince Eugene of Savoy who became a famous Austrian general, diplomat, and statesman. Sophie affectionately referred to it as "Our Belvedere" after their son Max was born there. Yet Konopiste Castle, thirty miles southeast of Prague, was where she and her family traditionally celebrated Christmas. It was where the couple had honeymooned, began their married life, had their first child, and retreated for family holidays. Most importantly, Konopiste was the only home where she could be the hostess and undisputed mistress of the house.

Sophie was not permitted to be her husband's hostess at Belvedere. An empty place setting and chair could be set for her, but court protocol forbade her to use it. When the Archduke left the palace for more than a few hours, its guards and gatekeepers were withdrawn. Since no member of the House of Habsburg was present, they were recalled to their barracks until the heir returned. Franz Ferdinand's children were delighted at their absence. In the magical thinking of childhood, it gave them an opportunity to play in the empty guardhouses.

Max, Ernst, and Sophie Hohenberg were never told about the significance of the absent guards or why two sets of carriages were kept in Belvedere's stables. Those trimmed in gold were reserved for their father as a member of the royal and imperial family. When they rode in a carriage with him, they were driven by a coachman dressed more elegantly than many field marshals. If they joined him in his huge chauffeured Graf and Stift automobile, gentlemen doffed their hats and ladies and children bowed. When they rode without him in simpler carriages, they were ignored.

Nine years after the only genuinely happy marriage in the Habsburg family, the court continued keeping the Archduke's wife completely isolated from his public life. The Oath of Renunciation permitting him to marry their mother was no secret to his children.

Franz Ferdinand told his daughter it was his gift to her and her brothers. The Oath would allow them to marry for love, just as he and their mother had done. Sophie, named for her mother, later recalled:

> We never asked our parents about the problems they were facing, and I can never remember them sitting down and explaining any of the difficulties to us. The situation was just unmentioned, as though it didn't exist. But of course we knew it. We were always nervous at being taken to court because we sensed we were in a different category.

Their mother was permitted to attend court functions, but not allowed to enter or exit with their father, sit or share a court meal with him, or be seen with him when he reviewed military units or received their salute. Much to his frustration, Franz Ferdinand was even forbidden from using the term "My wife and I" during any public event or address.

The Archduke protected his family in a gilded cage that obscured most of the insults and harassment directed at them. Whenever possible he took them on endless holidays to escape the snobbery and rejection of the Habsburg court. During January and February, the height of Vienna's Winter Carnival season, they enjoyed winter sports at St. Moritz. In March they celebrated the Duchess's birthday at Miramar Castle on the Adriatic Sea. The Belgium coast was visited in June, cool Carinthia during the heat of August, Eckartsau and Blühnbach for fall hunting. Depending on the court social calendar, and hunting, Vienna was generally avoided. Only Konopiste remained home. To Hitler and other critics, the arrogant Archduke snubbed Vienna—the largest German-speaking city in Europe. To the Archduke, he was protecting his family from the antagonism of the Habsburg family and Imperial Court. Few people understood the dynamics and truth behind his marriage. One who did was Archduke Karl's wife, Zita.

Franz Ferdinand's family loved music, but they were forbidden to use the Imperial Box at Vienna's Opera House. He kept a private box next to it so he and his wife, Sophie, could entertain guests there. Shortly after their wedding, Karl and Zita were invited to join them at the opera. When Sophie entered their box, Zita rose to kiss her hand, but her aunt fled into the shadows. She whispered to her niece, "Please, you must never again do that in public." Zita was shocked and said, "But I always kiss my aunt's hands when greeting them." Franz Ferdinand's wife explained she had received hate mail, even death threats, over such simple gestures. That event at the opera, more than any other, provided Zita an insight into the straitjacketed life her Aunt Sophie lived in Vienna. She later wrote of her:

> Aside from her striking good looks and very feminine charm, it was her air of quiet calm which made her so irresistible. She was the ideal partner for such a high strung man and she knew how to handle him. She could nearly always make him relax, and whenever he had one of his angry outbursts, she would quiet him by simply pressing his arm and saying, "Franzi, Franzi."

The Archduke's wife took on the role of Androcles to his long-suffering lion. She became adept at soothing his pain and calming his explosive outbursts. In appreciation, he presented her with a small lamb broach set with exquisite diamonds and pearls. When his volcanic temper erupted, she gently stroked the broach, which she wore over her heart. The simple gesture more than words usually pacified him. For the rest of their married lives, he regularly gifted his wife with small ceramic lambs kept in a glass case at Artstetten Castle. The lion and the lamb became a symbol of their love, but the public and private restrictions, slights, and petty snubs continued.

Konopiste remained their refuge. Franz Ferdinand had bought the castle as a young man after inheriting a huge fortune from a distant cousin named Este'. Adding Este' to his name kept it from becoming extinct and provided him a lifetime of financial security. It took him five years to repair, restore, and modernize the seven-hundred-year-old castle, installing indoor plumbing, electricity, telephones, central heating, a dozen hot and cold running baths, and the first electric-powered elevator in central Europe. Hunting trophies, antiques, and mementos from his childhood filled the eighty-five-room palace. One entire wing was devoted to the collection of mediaeval armor inherited from his cousin Este', but more than anything else, it was a family home.

The Archduke saved the crumbling fortress and rebuilt it into a modern, comfortable, peaceful citadel. Its ancient foundation and façade had been saved, but within its walls he created a model of all that was new and good in the twentieth century. He hoped to do the same for the Habsburg Empire.

The castle held a special place in his heart unlike any other. After his childhood lung problems erupted into the tuberculosis that claimed the life of his twenty-eight-year-old mother, he spent a lonely Christmas sailing on the Nile River seeking the warmth of the Egyptian sun. Only a small evergreen sent from Konopiste eased his homesickness.

His health dramatically improved following his marriage and he made Konopiste a shrine to the shared interests of his wife, children, and himself. Family portraits and photographs hung on every wall. The fifteen-hundred-acre estate was surrounded by heavily forested woods, lakes, and a five-hundred-acre rose garden. He claimed to know every plant and tree on the grounds, telling his estate manager, "I can rebuild roads and houses, but trees are irreplaceable. Someday these woods will belong to my children. I won't cut down their inheritance." The Archduke relished his good health, his wife, his family, and the home he shared with them at Konopiste. Twice they spent Christmas elsewhere, but both times their Christmas trees came from Konopiste.

Despite his ongoing frustrations with the court, Franz Ferdinand found much to celebrate as 1909 drew to a close. His close friend

Prince Konrad Hohenlohe had received a warm and positive response in St. Petersburg to his personal appeal for peace and dynastic solidarity with Russia. In October, the Emperor begrudgingly gave his wife the title Duchess of Hohenberg, elevating her status in the Empire and abroad. Only the Habsburg Archduchesses now ranked above her at court. Sophie had even been given the public honor of christening the Empire's newest battleship. Earlier in the year, he and Sophie made a triumphant trip to Rumania where she was warmly accepted by the Rumanian royal family. The success of that trip seemed to have forced the Emperor's hand.

An equally successful trip to Berlin followed. There in the capital city of Austria's closest ally, the Archduke and Duchess were entertained in grand style by the German Emperor and Empress. The Kaiser had initially opposed their marriage, confiding, "If I give way, I'll find my sons one day marrying a lady in waiting or even chambermaids." But political reality prevailed. King Edward VII of England predicted sooner or later the royal families of Europe, including the Habsburgs, would have to "face facts" and accept Sophie.

Times were changing. Shortly after the birth of their second son, Ernst, in 1904, the Archduke had written his devoted stepmother, Archduchess Maria-Theresa. She had been instrumental in finally persuading Emperor Franz Joseph, through the personal intervention of Pope Leo XIII, to permit their marriage:

Dearest Mama,

…How happy I am with my family, and how I can't thank the good Lord enough for my happiness! And next to the Lord I must thank *you* who did so much to bring this happiness about. The *best thing* I've done in all my life was to marry my Soph. She is everything to me, wife, advisor, doctor, companion—in a word, my whole happiness. We're in love after four years as on the first day of our marriage, and not for one second has our happiness been dimmed.…

And you, dearest Mama, were the only one not to forsake me when
I was down; that I am so happy was all your doing.

———

The week before Christmas 1909, Franz Ferdinand celebrated his
forty-sixth birthday. His health had never been better. During his
sickly childhood, adolescence, and early adulthood, he was painfully
thin and tubercular. For the first time in his life, he looked healthy,
even plump, surrounded at Konopiste by the family he loved. Much
to the disgust of enemies in and out of court, his marriage had made
him a modern Lazarus, a man back from the dead. Following years
of snubs, slights, and vicious gossip, his wife was also finally being
accepted in the capitals of Europe. The Archduke prayed acceptance
there would earn her respect and acceptance in Vienna.

He also believed he had finally found an ally among the vipers of
the Habsburg court, his nephew and political heir, Karl. Franz Ferdinand had stood as Karl's godfather at the time of his birth and became
his legal guardian when Franz's scandalous brother, Otto, died. They
enjoyed each other's company, hunted together, respected each other's
opinions, loved their wives, and had unusually happy marriages, a rar-
ity in the Habsburg family. Lastly, they shared similar political views
on the future of the Empire.

As Christmas 1909 came and passed, Franz Ferdinand was as
happy as Adolf Hitler was miserable. The Habsburg Archduke whom
Hitler hated above all others celebrated the holiday surrounded by his
family in the Czech countryside outside of Prague. Hitler, hungry,
homeless, and defeated in Vienna, was at the lowest ebb of his life.

He never could have imagined any Christmas worse than the one
he had spent two years earlier. Then, next to the tiny family Christmas
tree, he watched his mother die a slow, painful death from cancer.
Klara Hitler had always been his champion, the only person whose loyalty and faith never wavered. Her bed had been moved to the kitchen

because it was the warmest of the three small rooms in their apartment. The tree was there in a futile attempt to cheer the melancholy scene. After Klara's death, she was buried next to her late husband. Hitler spent Christmas Eve alone at his mother's freshly dug grave in the Catholic cemetery outside of Linz.

On the second anniversary of his mother's death, Adolf Hitler found himself in a Viennese homeless shelter surrounded by the sights, sounds, and smells of failed lives. At times, his only escape from the suffocating reality of his failed dreams was found in reading. German writers Goethe and Schiller comforted him, but he returned again and again to the writer he considered their superior, William Shakespeare. The English bard translated into German had become his favorite wordsmith, *The Merchant of Venice* his favorite play, and Shylock his favorite villain.

That winter, the winter of 1909 when he shoveled snow for the Habsburgs at the Hotel Imperial, the Christmas he spent invisible and alone in a crowded Vienna homeless shelter as Franz Ferdinand's star rose and his own star fell, it could have been the opening lines of Shakespeare's *Richard III* that haunted him. It was the winter of his discontent.

CHAPTER FIVE
THE GRANITE FOUNDATION

"He validates Vienna's lower class in all its qualities, in its lack
of intellectual wants, in its distrust of education, in its tipsy
silliness, in its love of street songs, in the adherence of the
old fashioned, in its boisterous smugness; and they rave, they
rave blissfully when he talks to them."

—AUSTRIAN AUTHOR FELIX SALTER

Franz Ferdinand needed time. The heir to the Habsburg throne
had wealth, health, and a family he loved, but to fulfill the rest of
his dreams he needed time. He worried that the growing threat of
nationalism would destroy the Empire and the peace of Europe. To
prevent the restless ethnic groups from devouring each other, he also
needed ideas and allies. During his 1909 trip to Rumania, he met
with representatives of the Empire's ethnic minorities, including Aurel
Popovici, a Hungarian exile. Popovici's controversial book, *The United
States of Greater Austria,* proposed federalizing the nation-states of
the Habsburg Empire into sixteen units along the lines of the United
States. Although the Hungarian authorities labeled him a traitor, the
Archduke recruited him to join his staff at Belvedere. Popovici's book
became their bible.

As a young man, the Archduke had sailed around the world. He
was impressed with the United States, a nation of immigrants, and
the federal government holding them together. He believed Popovici's

ideas could serve as a model not only for Austria, but all of Europe. His embrace of Popovici, his willingness to meet with ethnic minorities, and the diverse staff of visionaries he assembled at Belvedere Palace further alienated him from the Emperor's tradition-bound court, the elites of Austria, the oligarchs of Hungary, and Adolf Hitler.

The Archduke's dreams for his two sons and daughter were on a less grand scale. He told one of their tutors, "Please bring it home to my children that to rule and wear a crown is a heavy burden imposed from heaven and that one should never yearn for such things. My children are destined to become simply large Bohemian landlords." His secretary recalled:

> Franz Ferdinand seemed to envy his children their tranquil future. In the entire education he prepared for them, there was nothing which might be construed as a preparation for eventual succession to the throne. He wanted his boys to enjoy the untrimmed existence of country squires and not the artificial life imposed by court. He had similar intentions for his daughter. He believed she would be a thousand times happier at the side of a socially suitable partner who she loved rather than be subjected to those marriages of convenience—which so often went wrong—entered into by a princess of the royal house.

The Archduke was a private man surrounded at court by enemies, by a calcified bureaucracy threatened by change, and by family members who disliked, even hated him. He kept his thoughts, hopes, and plans to himself. Many believed Crown Prince Rudolph's openness regarding the need for political reforms led to his untimely death. Conspiracy theorists whispered his "suicide" had been staged by reactionaries within the government or by members of the Habsburg family themselves. Franz Ferdinand and Rudolph had been close in life, and perhaps closer in death. He would not make the fatal mistakes his cousin had made by writing and openly talking about reforms, but the diverse staff of reformers he surrounded himself with at Belvedere revealed the direction of his thinking. To Adolf Hitler, they reinforced his worst fears about the future of German Austrians.

In February 1910, one of the family members Hitler referred to as a "Philistine" sent him enough money to relocate to a poor working-class neighborhood north of the city center. The district surrounding his new residence, the Mannerheim Men's Hostel, was peopled by immigrants, Jews, and foreign dialects, but the rent was cheap, a single room was available, and he could have both the privacy—and the audience—he craved. The shelter had been built in 1905 by the Franz Joseph Anniversary Foundation for Public Housing and Charitable Institutions. The Emperor himself had visited, but Baron Rothschild and other Jewish philanthropists paid for its construction.

There in a third-floor, five-foot by seven-foot room, the frustrated dreamer attempted to regain control over his life. The four large suitcases he had brought from Linz had been reduced to a thin summer jacket and pants faded by wear, a single pair of socks, and worn scuffed shoes. Unlike most of the hostel's five hundred residents, Hitler did not smoke, drink, or look for a job. Although he claimed Jews were "a different race" with a "different smell," he befriended many Jewish residents, and they befriended him. His usual verbal targets of choice were rooted in his middle-class childhood years in Linz: the Czechs, the communists, and politically meddling Jesuit priests. His newly found dependence on Jewish friends at the hostel may have tempered his anti-Semitism.

Its ground-floor common room afforded him a space to read, a view of the hostel garden where he could paint, and a less-than-enthusiastic audience of listeners. He and Reinhold Hanisch, who had moved to the hostel with him, formed a business partnership. Hitler would paint watercolors from postcards and Hanisch would sell them to frame dealers, saloon patrons, and Jewish junk shops. They split the profits 50-50. Hanisch was a self-promoter who made a better impression as a salesman than the shabbily dressed antisocial artist. It took three years of communal living at the Mannerheim Hostel to socialize Hitler.

Marriage, meanwhile, had polished Franz Ferdinand's own brusque introverted social skills. He had no childhood memories of being touched, held, or embraced by his ill mother who died of tuberculosis when he was seven. Nearly everyone assumed he would soon follow her to the grave. To their surprise, the infant survived a rambunctious but sickly childhood and adolescence, and tenaciously reached adulthood. His late overbearing father, Karl Ludwig Habsburg, younger brother of Emperor Franz Joseph, isolated him from his healthier younger brothers and sister, and smothered him with prayers, doctors, nurses, and Jesuit priests.

Like Adolf Hitler, the Archduke was a poor student. But unlike the son of a provincial customs official, he was not allowed to quit school. From the age of six until nineteen, when not confined to his sickbed, he spent eleven hours a day, six days a week, at his school desk. Twenty minutes were allowed for meals. His nervous energy, restless mind, impulsivity, distractibility, and hyperactivity brought him into constant conflict with the rote memorization and endless recitation demanded by his teachers. He became the most physically disciplined of any Habsburg of his generation. Franz Ferdinand remembered his early schooling with bitterness, telling his daughter:

> Everything was mixed together from morning until night one hour after the other. We were allowed to go outside only once between lessons, holding the hands of the chief of the household for short walks. The outcome of such an education was that we were pushed to learn everything and at the end knew nothing.

The Archduke, like Hitler, devoted the rest of his life to learning about what he had not been taught. Hitler supplemented his own sketchy education with his love of opera, passion for architecture, and voracious reading. He later wrote, "Since my early youth I tried to read in the right way and supported in the best way possible by memory and understanding. Looked at in that manner, my time in Vienna was especially fruitful and valuable."

Schiller, Dante, Carlyle, and composer Richard Wagner's political tracts on race, politics, and religion supplemented the newspapers Hitler read each morning at the hostel. He returned time and again to novelist James Fennimore Cooper's tales of heroes and villains, and Karl May's fictional western novels filled with racial stereotypes of American cowboys and Indians. May's sixty books were among Hitler's favorites as a child, read "by candlelight and with a large magnifying glass by the light of the moon." To Hitler, the Germans were the cowboys, and everyone else the Indians. He regularly quoted Shakespeare, but Goethe's *Faust* was another favorite, which he claimed "contained more than the human mind could grasp."

Although his paintings and watercolors finally provided Hitler an income, he preferred spending his time talking politics. His hatred of the Habsburgs, the heir to the throne, and his Czech-born wife were favorite topics. Austria's 1867 constitution proclaimed, "All ethnic groups in the nation have equal rights, and each ethnic group has an inalienable right to preserve and cultivate its nationality and language." The Habsburg embrace of ethnic groups, their religious tolerance of Jews and non-German Aryans, and the Czech marriage of Franz Ferdinand agitated and continually fueled his self-righteous indignation.

Adolf Hitler regularly shared his anger with his fellow hostel inhabitants. He seethed that there were more Czechs in Vienna than in Prague, more Croats than in Zagreb, and muttered more Jews than in Jerusalem. He had begun wearing a long dark overcoat and a greasy derby hat that made him look like the Bohemian immigrants he hated. His appearance did nothing to win over his listeners, who enjoyed baiting and mocking him. Jokers sometimes tied his coat to the back of his chair. When he jumped up to emphasize a point, the chair would loudly follow, accompanied by the laughter of his tormentors. Hitler gritted his teeth, waved his arms, and screamed at them. Supervisors at the hostel were forced to intervene, but even his detractors began to take notice that he was becoming very good at making speeches.

Vienna offered him a menu of demagogic role models to emulate. The editorial offices of George Schönerer's Pan-German newspaper were located doors from the room he and Kubizek once rented. For months the newspaper's stridently pro-German banner headlines must have been the first news greeting him every morning. Although Schönerer's star had set by the time Hitler moved to the city, the newspaper he founded continued trumpeting his bigoted views. Schönerer proclaimed himself Führer of the Empire's German-Austrians, incorporated Richard Wagner's music into political rallies, urged the expulsion of Jews, Gypsies, Czechs, and other Slavs from the Empire, and campaigned for the union of Austria with Germany. Hitler found much to like, and much he would use in the future, in Schönerer's rhetoric.

Shortly before his death, Crown Prince Rudolph condemned Schönerer and his anti-Semitic rhetoric. Pan-German attacks on Vienna's newspapers by his rabid supporters resulted in his being arrested and expelled from parliament. Schönerer's prestige and movement were further damaged when he ordered followers to convert to the Protestant faith. Many viewed his "Away with Rome" crusade as a step toward annexation by Germany. In the heart of Catholic Austria it was a step too far. Franz Ferdinand declared, "Away with Rome means away from Austria." The Archduke sealed Schönerer's fate by rallying religious and politically loyal Catholics against him. His role in Schönerer's downfall provided Hitler another reason to hate the heir to the Habsburg throne.

Karl Lueger, the anti-Semitic mayor of Vienna, provided an even more charismatic tutor for Hitler. As immigration to the city reached an all-time high, so, too, did Lueger's popularity. He masterfully presented himself as the champion of Austrians fearful that their place in society was being overtaken by foreigners. His motto—"We must help the little man"—spoke to the heart, soul, and concern that their language, culture, and political dominance were threatened. Felix Salten, a popular Austrian writer at the time, wrote of Lueger:

> He surrenders everything that intimidates and confines the masses. He throws it down, stomps on it laughing. The cobblers, the tailors, the coachmen, the green grocers and shopkeepers rejoice. They roar with enthusiasm.... He validates Vienna's lower class in all its qualities, in its lack of intellectual wants, in its distrust of education, in its tipsy silliness, in its love of street songs, in the adherence of the old fashioned, in its boisterous smugness; and they rave, they rave blissfully when he talks to them.

Karl Lueger thundered, "The soil on which the old imperial city stands is German soil and will remain German soil. Vienna is not in any position to make any concessions to the Slavic elements who are pouring into the center of the Empire, but on the contrary it is up to the Czechs, etc., who accept Vienna's hospitality, to foreswear any conspicuous display of their tribal affiliation and to get accustomed to the German environment."

When Hitler first heard the demagogic mayor speak, he found his political and oratorical mentor. The same anti-Semitic rhetoric that attracted Hitler had put Lueger on a collision course with Franz Joseph. The Emperor stubbornly refused to accept his selection as Vienna's mayor in four straight elections. Lueger's fifth landslide victory convinced him to warily accept the will of the people. In 1897, Lueger had become mayor of the world's sixth-largest city.

For two decades he modernized and successfully governed the city supported by a powerful voting block that united German Austrians young and old, conservative Catholics, and pro-Habsburg monarchists. Children and adolescents were continually recruited into his movement through songs, slogans, recreational activities, and handsome uniforms. Hitler was mesmerized by the mayor's political skill and acumen.

One out of four Viennese claimed Czech ancestry, but the mayor focused his most venomous racial diatribes against Jews. "Down with Jewish terrorism" was the battle cry heard at his massive political rallies. It was a calculated political decision. Cracow, Budapest, and Prague had larger concentrations of Jews than Vienna, but the Habsburg capital was where Jewish immigrants found the greatest educational opportunities, political freedom, and upward mobility. Almost half of the city's secondary school students and one-third of its university students were Jewish. Lueger's words reinforced Hitler's increasingly paranoid conspiracy theories. Twice he had been rejected from his school of choice. Twice his talent and genius had been dismissed by non-Jewish academics, but somehow he held Jews responsible for his failure to thrive. His own work ethic was the opposite of many of its industrious immigrants, but in their success, and his failure, he blamed Jews.

The mayor's speeches provided a healing balm to Hitler's troubled soul. Lueger raged, "Here at home, all the influences on the masses is in the hands of the Jews, the major part of the press is in their hands, by far the largest part of capital and, in particular, of big business is in Jewish hands, and the Jews are practicing a kind of terrorism here which couldn't conceivably be worse."

Lueger's virulent racism threatened violence, but to Hitler's disappointment and frustration, he never acted on such threats. The mayor's followers "wore the effigy of a hanged Jew on their watch chains," but hung no Jews. Eventually Lueger toned down his anti-Semitism. He befriended selected Jews in order to cultivate the friendship of the Habsburg court. That behavior frustrated Hitler, but he never stopped admiring the mayor's political and oratorical skills.

On March 10, 1910, Lueger's death brought the artist, the Emperor, and the Archduke together. Adolf Hitler, Franz Joseph, and

Franz Ferdinand were joined by a quarter of a million grieving Viennese when diabetes took the life of the sixty-six-year-old mayor. For a brief moment, friend and foe united. The Emperor and Archduke led the mourners at St. Stephen's Cathedral.

Franz Joseph never warmed to the popular mayor. The Archduke, however, genuinely admired him. When Franz Ferdinand wed Sophie Chotek, Lueger publicly saluted their nuptials as a "triumph of the heart." The Archduke never forgot such gestures. No other public official in Vienna had the courage to champion his controversial marriage.

Hitler later wrote, "When the mighty funeral procession bore the dead mayor from the city hall toward the Ring, I was among the many hundreds of thousands looking on the tragic spectacle. I was profoundly moved and my feelings told me that the work, even of this man, was bound to be in vain, owing to the fatal destiny which would inevitably lead this state to destruction."

That summer Adolf Hitler had his business partner, Reinhold Hanisch, arrested for defrauding him of profits from his paintings. Hanisch underestimated Hitler. He thought he could manipulate and use him. Others would make the same fatal mistake, with disastrous consequences. Hitler called a Jewish friend from their hostel to act as a witness, and won his court case against Hanisch.

Hitler was, indeed, a man of contradictions. Despite his growing anti-Semitism, he continued to depend on Jewish friends. He never forgot Dr. Bloch, the Jewish doctor who lovingly cared for his dying mother. In a postcard sent to Bloch, he wrote, "From Vienna I send you my greetings. Yours, always faithfully, Adolf Hitler." He also sent the doctor a watercolor sketch, dried in front of a hot fire to preserve it and give it the appearance of an antique print. Its caption read, "Prosit Neujahr—A toast to the New Year." On the back he wrote, "The Hitler family sends you the best wishes for a Happy New Year. In everlasting thankfulness, Adolf Hitler."

Free of Hanisch, a newly confident Hitler began selling his paintings and watercolors directly to Jewish dealers. Hoping to get a better price, he sometimes presented himself as a graduate of the Fine Arts Academy. Other times he told dealers financial problems caused him to drop out of the school, or that he had been forced out because of his political beliefs. He had learned much from Hanisch, including self-promotion, but his skill at self-delusion and his lies were his own.

Hitler bought a new set of clothes, shaved, cut his hair, and had his shoes repaired and polished. Some days were again spent at museums, some nights at the opera. He even considered reapplying to the Art Academy, but the deceit over his art credentials caught up with him. When he was threatened with arrest, he could not understand why luck had turned against him. A favorite verse from Wagner's opera *Die Meistersinger* played over and over in his head. "And still I don't succeed. I feel it and yet cannot understand it; I cannot retain it, nor forget it, and if I grasp it, I cannot understand it."

Time was running out for Adolf Hitler in Vienna. Even as his arrest for fraud seemed imminent, an even more serious threat confronted him. He had avoided military service since 1909. But ever since the conscription of his roommate and the annexation crisis over Bosnia-Herzegovina, he paid close attention to the high number of men being called into the army. A fellow resident remembered Hitler saying, "I can't wait any longer until I can finally rid myself of the dust of this country, especially since I might have to go to the military call-up. But under no circumstances do I want to serve in the Austrian army."

In one of his final rambling discourses, Hitler denounced Austrian bureaucracy for smothering all genius. "Patronage and distinguished background was all that counted.... All talented people and all inventors in Austria only found recognition abroad, that's where they found fame and honor." As his twenty-fourth birthday approached, Hitler fled to Munich, calling it "the most German of all German cities."

Hitler had come to Vienna to receive an education, and he had. Its streets, homeless shelters, and hostels had been his classrooms; George Schönerer and Karl Lueger his professors; and their anti-Semitic rhetoric his curriculum to power. The pomp, ceremonies, and palaces of the Habsburg court, like the sets of the operas he loved, and the Catholic church of his childhood, taught him to appeal to the eyes, as well as the ears, of audiences. Hitler claimed the five years he spent in the city provided him "a world picture and philosophy that became the granite foundation of all my acts." In his book *Mein Kampf* ("My Struggle"), he declared:

> Vienna was and remained for me the hardest, though most thorough school of my life. I had set foot in that town while still a half boy and left it a half man, grown quiet and grave. In it, I obtained the foundations for a philosophy in general and a political view in particular which later I only need to supplement in detail, but never left me.

CHAPTER SIX
THE SPY, THE DRAFT DODGER,
AND THE PEACEMAKER

"External peace for us... that is my profession of faith, for which I will work and struggle as long as I live."

—ARCHDUKE FRANZ FERDINAND

"The Archduke sees things through the eyes of his wife."

—POPE PIUS X

Adolf Hitler did not travel to Munich alone. Once again he found a friend who became his audience of one. Rudolf Häusler was nineteen when he met Hitler at the men's hostel in Vienna. Like his new mentor, he was a down-on-his-luck painter estranged from a civil servant father, but close to a devoted mother. Though Häusler's eyesight was poor, he had excellent listening skills. Hitler introduced him to the operas of Richard Wagner. He quickly fell under the influence of Wagner's music and Hitler's words.

A final inheritance from his father's estate allowed Hitler to make a fresh start in Munich. Dressed in a crisp new suit and polished shoes, he left Vienna on Monday, May 26, 1913. Hitler carried with him one small suitcase, a fully formed racist philosophy that would serve him well in the years ahead, and his newly recruited disciple. He wrote of his new home:

A German city! What a difference from Vienna! I grew sick to my
stomach when I even thought back on that Babylon of races!

One day after Hitler left Vienna, Franz Ferdinand received a short
telegram at Konopiste from the Commanding General of the Second
Army Corps. It read, "Colonel of the General Staff Corps Alfred Redl,
General Staff Chief of the Eighth Corps, has this night killed himself
in Hotel Klomser for reasons up to now unknown. Letters left behind."
Colonel Redl was the head of Austria's Counter Intelligence Service,
the Empire's chief spy master. His responsibilities included personally
briefing the Emperor and Archduke on the army's espionage activities.
Suicide was not unusual in Habsburg Vienna. The city had the highest
suicide rate in Europe, but the suicide of Austria's spy chief was different.

Redl had returned from Prague the day before and showed no
signs he was about to take his life. The Archduke had regularly been
receiving "lengthy and brilliant" reports from him. One newspaper
wrote, "The highly gifted officer, who was on the verge of a great
career, killed himself by a shot in the mouth, an act prompted, it is
believed, by mental overexertion resulting from severe neurasthenia."
The always suspicious Franz Ferdinand doubted the version of events
unfolding in Vienna. His instincts were correct.

The Archduke's investigation discovered Redl was a homosexual
blackmailed into becoming a highly paid Russian spy. To protect the
army's reputation and hide the depth of the security breach, Army
Chief of Staff Conrad von Hötzendorf encouraged Redl's suicide prior
to having him interrogated. His death prevented the army and government from learning the full details of what secrets had been leaked,
over what period of time, and what other nations had been involved.
Franz Ferdinand summoned von Hötzendorf to Konopiste.

The General later recalled the meeting as, "One of the most un-
pleasant audiences during my time as Chief of the General Staff. His

Imperial Highness was indignant over the Redl case.... A flood of reproaches flooded over me." The next day during lunch with the Empire's new Foreign Minister, Leopold Berthold, von Hötzendorf openly admitted he had urged Redl's suicide. He also said the Archduke told him, "You see how fortunate it is that we have not gone to war against Russia with a traitor in our midst." With an uncharacteristic laugh, he assured Berthold, "What Redl betrayed was quite insignificant.... The damage he caused was slight."

The Chief of the Austro-Hungarian army was engaged in wishful thinking, in denial, or lying. Over a ten-year period, Redl had sold his nation's complete war plans to Russia, which then passed them on to their Balkan allies. The enemy the Habsburgs most feared gained detailed possession of Austrian fortifications, the time table for mobilization, and all battle strategies. Redl also purposely underestimated Russia's military strength to his Austrian colleagues. In the great European war to come, Austria would be nearly defenseless.

Franz Ferdinand quickly moved to dismiss the officers involved in the Redl fiasco, including von Hötzendorf. The challenge was to remove them without giving Austria's enemies a hint of the disarray in the army's high command. Hötzendorf presented special problems. He had been the Archduke's own protégé, was instrumental in modernizing the army, and was the popular leader of the government's war party. His reputation for belligerence had been used by the Archduke to mask his own behind-the-scenes peace efforts. Finding his replacement was a delicate task that would take time.

Behind his confident bluster, von Hötzendorf and his staff were nervous that the Redl affair would destroy their careers and undermine their aggressive war policies. They hoped a war, any war, would derail the Redl investigation. Like his close friend, German Army Chief of Staff Hellmuth Moltke, von Hötzendorf believed the coming war would be a racial war "between Germanism and Slavism."

Secretly he had a more personal reason for desiring war. He hoped it might allow his mistress, a married mother of six, to divorce her husband and marry him. Only the distraction of war might convince Franz Ferdinand and Catholic Austria to continence such a scandal.

Adolf Hitler was also nervous that spring. As new residents of Munich, he and Rudolph Häusler had to register their name, address, and occupation with the local police. Hitler identified himself as an "arts painter and writer," but the police in his hometown of Linz labeled him a draft dodger. He had avoided military service for four years. In 1913, Austrian authorities began searching for him. It was only a matter of time until they discovered he was in Germany.

With little money to pay for their rented room and no job prospects, Hitler returned to selling watercolors copied from postcards while Häusler framed the paintings and tried to sell them. They also painted signs for local businesses in exchange for simple meals of bread and milk. Hitler briefly considered attending the Munich Art Academy to study architecture, but never applied. His new life in Germany looked very much like the life he had left in Vienna. He wrote Rudolph Häusler's worried mother that all would be well:

> Opportunities in the German Reich with its almost fifty cities with over one hundred thousand people and its gigantic global trade are surely infinitely better than in Austria. I dare say he shouldn't feel sorry to be here even if he couldn't work his way up, for in that case he'd be even worse off in Austria. But I don't believe that at all.

Optimism did not come as naturally to Franz Ferdinand as it did for Adolf Hitler, but by the spring of 1913, time finally seemed to be on his side. Illnesses undermined Franz Joseph's steadily declining health. During a recent medical crisis, bulletins from the palace urging prayers reminded his subjects that even the Emperor was mortal. A train had been kept around the clock with a full head of steam near Konopiste ready to rush the Archduke to Vienna to claim the Habsburg crown.

The people's prayers worked their magic. Franz Joseph miraculously recovered. One Viennese newspaper openly speculated that the eighty-three-year-old Emperor willed himself to live, "by his keen desire to spite his nephew and delay his accession to the imperial throne as long as possible." Still friends and foes recognized that sooner, rather than later, Franz Ferdinand would be Emperor.

In anticipation of that day, German Emperor Wilhelm II carefully cultivated his friendship with the Archduke, the Archduke's wife, and even the Archduke's children. The two men had grown close. Franz Ferdinand genuinely admired Wilhelm for bringing his country twenty-five years of peace and prosperity, but he feared his blind spot for all things military. Wilhelm enjoyed playing soldier so much that he often changed into different military uniforms throughout the day, uniforms he himself sometimes designed. Germany's Emperor loved the precise drills, the salutes, the stirring music, the reflected glory of being a great nation's commander-in-chief. Military trappings flattered his insatiable but fragile ego. Franz Ferdinand worried in a moment of weakness Wilhelm would surrender his political judgment, and the fate of his Empire, to his generals.

The Archduke had been trained as a soldier his entire life. He shared Franz Joseph's belief that the army was the indispensable hinge uniting the diverse ethnic groups of their multicultural empire together. But Franz Ferdinand did not have the blind level of confidence Wilhelm had in his generals. War was the business of generals, but peace, politics, and the prevention of war the responsibility of emperors, especially Habsburg emperors. The Habsburg commitment to peace was one of the reasons Adolf Hitler hated the dynasty.

Hitler believed the peace lionized by the Emperor and his heir a cynical attempt on their part to protect their privileged position even as the influence and position of German Austrians deteriorated. He convinced himself that the German people would only be able to take their rightful place in the sun when a war tore the Habsburg's multinational Empire asunder. Anything less than war was a surrender to racial annihilation. The thought of serving with non-Germans in the "united forces" of Franz Joseph's army was a major factor in his decision to flee Vienna.

Conrad von Hötzendorf, like Adolf Hitler, was anxious for war. In 1913, he made twenty-five separate proposals urging war on real or imagined enemies, even on the Empire's own allies His final, almost desperate attempt was a telephone call to Konopiste on Christmas day. The Archduke's famous temper exploded. He hung up on the General.

Franz Ferdinand did not believe the "brisk gay" wars of previous centuries possible using twentieth-century weaponry. He bluntly told von Hötzendorf, "External peace for us… that is my profession of faith, for which I will work and struggle as long as I live!" It was clear to the General and his war party that as long as Franz Ferdinand lived, there would be no war.

At the beginning of 1914, Franz Ferdinand's commitment to peace was stronger than ever. It was a lonely, unpopular position, but one shared by his wife, the Duchess of Hohenberg. Despite earning a hard-won reputation even among her critics as a deeply religious woman, loyal wife, and loving mother, the Duchess did not fit the expected profile of a 1914 Austrian woman. She was well read, well-traveled, and multilingual. As the daughter of a lifelong career diplomat and a cousin to Countess Bertha von Suttner, founder of Peace Associations throughout Europe, she had a unique worldview few men or women of her time could match. Her longtime American friend, Maria Longworth Storer, wife of the United States Foreign Minister to Austria-Hungary, wrote, "The Archduke Franz Ferdinand was captivated, not only by his wife's unusual beauty, but by her brilliant mind, and the Christian zeal and integrity of her character."

In the cynical patriarchal atmosphere of the Habsburg court, one of the Archduke's aides ruefully explained, "The very happiness of this marriage, however exemplary in itself, cast a rather dubious light on Franz Ferdinand."

During the Bosnia-Herzegovina annexation crisis, the Archduke had asked his wife to share her opinion with his military aides on the need for its peaceful resolution. His request and her input did not go unnoticed in Vienna, Berlin, or Rome. Pope Pius X, apparently an expert on marriages as well as ecclesiastical matters, was quoted as saying, "The Archduke sees things through the eyes of his wife." It was not meant as a compliment.

Despite his friendship with Wilhelm II, Austria's political isolation and military dependence on Germany worried the Archduke. After traveling to Russia to meet Czar Nicholas II, he instructed diplomats and personal friends to "tell everyone that I am Russia's friend, and a friend of the ruler. Austrian and Russian soldiers have never yet met in a battle, and I'd call myself a knave if this changed while I have a word to say."

Franz Ferdinand's peace overtures did nothing to increase his popularity in Vienna. Hötzendorf publicly and privately lobbied for war, and officers in elaborate military uniforms strutted along the Ringstrasse, bragging in crowded cafés about the war to come. The frustrated Archduke resorted to personal diplomacy to gain political influence for himself, and social acceptance for his wife. In 1912, he and the Duchess had made a private visit to England's Chelsea Flower Show. He hoped his friendship with the Duke of Portland, a fellow huntsman and the show's sponsor, might open the doors of Buckingham Palace to them. The Duke was a cousin of the British royal family and an influential member of the Government's Privy Council. The trip was a public and private triumph. The couple were asked to return to England the next year for a hunt, and a visit with King George V and Queen Mary.

To the discomfort of the Habsburg court, when the Archduke and Duchess returned to London in 1913 they were met by cheering crowds and driven to Windsor Castle in a royal carriage. The King and Queen were charmed by their guests and agreed to visit them in Austria the following year. Queen Mary wrote in her diary, "*Her* influence has been and is good, in every way. All the people with us who had known *him* before said how much he has changed for the better."

When the Archduke and Duchess returned to Konopiste, they received a long-awaited invitation. Emperor Franz Joseph asked to be introduced to their three children. Franz Ferdinand was to represent the Emperor at an early morning religious service in the Imperial Chapel. He and his family would spend the previous night at the Hofburg Palace. Later that day, twelve-year-old Princess Sophie, ten-year-old Prince Maximilian, and nine-year-old Prince Ernst would be presented to their great-uncle for the first time.

The Emperor had stopped attending cabinet meetings, military maneuvers, and even hunting. It seemed to the Archduke that one more barrier between his family and the throne was being removed. But it had not completely disappeared. Much to their disappointment, the children were not invited to any of the formal morning activities.

The Archduke's daughter, Sophie, decided to rectify the lack of an invitation. She convinced her governess to allow her to wake her brothers early and lead them to a high empty balcony overlooking the Chapel. From their invisible perch they could secretly watch their father and the ceremonies unobserved, and then silently return to their rooms to prepare for their audience with the Emperor.

Sophie woke her brothers before sunrise and led them in their pajamas through the palace's dark hallways to the balcony. There they could see, but not be seen by anyone. Loud organ music, Latin prayers, the smell of incense and candles, and the angelic voices of the Vienna Boys Choir masked their whispered squeals of delight as they spied on their father below.

Their bird's-eye view and the clandestine nature of their adventure made for a magical memory. At its conclusion, the children softly tiptoed from their hidden vantage point and gently closed the balcony's heavy wooden door, only to be confronted by the muffled sounds of approaching footsteps. A stooped, ghostly figure raised his bowed head and slowly emerged from the shadows. They recognized the wizened face from a thousand portraits. It was Emperor Franz Joseph himself.

Sophie, Maximilian, and Ernst screamed and ran all the way back to their rooms. They failed to mention the early morning encounter to their parents. As the time approached for their scheduled audience with the Emperor, the young Princess later remembered feeling faint from anticipation and fear.

She, her brothers, her oblivious mother, and stately father slowly climbed the palace's grand staircase and entered the white and gold antechamber room. There they nervously waited under the eyes of brilliantly uniformed guards with ceremonial swords drawn. When Sophie entered the audience room, she found her great-uncle had been transformed. No longer the gray old man she had seen shuffling down the dark hall hours earlier, he had become His Imperial and Royal Apostolic Majesty by God's Grace, Emperor of Austria, King of Hungary, and dozens of other titles she could no longer remember.

Franz Joseph knew how to impress and intimidate. He stood as erect as a young military cadet wearing the imposing uniform of an Austrian Field Marshal. His blue tunic perfectly matched his pale blue eyes. With his steel-straight posture, white hair, trademark handlebar mustache, and starched black trousers with red stripes, he looked like God himself.

The Duchess of Hohenberg curtsied. The Archduke bowed and formally introduced each of his children. The Emperor paused momentarily. In a firm but quizzical voice he said, "But we have already met this morning." Franz Ferdinand's masked composure briefly twisted in confusion, and then froze when the Emperor asked, "Why are your children afraid of me?" The awkward silence was broken when the Archduke's daughter bravely stepped forward. After a deep breath, she carefully explained their earlier meeting in the logical parsed words of a twelve-year-old girl.

The Emperor tilted his head forward. He listened intently to her answer, and then for the briefest of moments, slightly smiled. For an instant, he almost seemed human. In the years to come, Franz Ferdinand's children laughed many times over their scheduled and unscheduled imperial audiences with their great-uncle. A gentle touch from her mother on her lamb broach and their father's sense of humor saved them from punishment. If their father had lived, the Hofburg Palace would have become their home, but they never spent another night in the Imperial Palace.

That January, Adolf Hitler had his own less pleasant encounter with the Habsburg bureaucracy. The Munich police notified Linz authorities that the army deserter they were searching for was in their city. His flight from Vienna failed to protect the Austrian draft dodger. The long arm of Emperor Franz Joseph's "inseparable and indivisible" army had traced him to Germany. A highly agitated Hitler was promptly arrested and charged with "residing outside of Austria with the object of evading military service." He was ordered to return to Austria at once.

CHAPTER SEVEN
FATE

"I know I shall soon be murdered."
— ARCHDUKE FRANZ FERDINAND

"Every step of the archducal pair was playing with fire... a virtual challenge to fate."
— MILITARY AIDE of Franz Ferdinand at Sarajevo

"I still believe that the world lost a great deal by my not being able to go to the academy and learn the craft of painting. Or did fate reserve me to some other purpose?" — ADOLF HITLER

Despite his genuine fear and dread, it did not take long for Adolf Hitler to regain his composure, confidence, and arrogance. Within a day of his arrest, he requested a meeting with the Austrian Consul-General in Munich. He then composed a three-page letter to the Linz Municipal Council boldly pleading his case:

> With regard to my failure to report for military service in the Autumn of 1909, I must say that this was for me an endlessly bitter time. I was then a young man without experience, receiving no financial assistance from others, let alone beg for it. Without support, compelled to depend on my own efforts, I earned only a few crowns and often only a few cents for my labors, and it was often insufficient to pay for a night's lodging. For two long years I had no other mis-

tress than sorrow and need, no other companion than eternally un-
satisfied hunger. I never knew the word *youth*. Even today, five years
later, I have the scars of blisters on my fingers, hands, and feet. And
yet I cannot remember those days without a certain pleasure, now
that these vexations have been surmounted. In spite of great want,
amid often dubious surroundings, I never-the-less kept my name
clean, and a blameless record with the law, and possessed a clear
conscience—except for that one constantly remembered fact that
I failed to register for military service. This is the one thing which
I fell responsible for. It would seem that a moderate fine would be
ample penance, and of course I would pay the fine willingly.

Hitler's chameleon ability to package himself for his audience was
evident not only in his letter, but in an accompanying letter of support he received following the meeting in Munich with the Austrian
Consul-General. The Habsburg civil servant wrote, "Hitler seems very
deserving of considerate treatment… in view of the circumstances
and the man's poverty, you should see fit to allow him to report in
Salzburg."

The Consul-General's successful plea saved Hitler the humiliation
of returning to his hometown in police custody. His meeting on the
5th of February 1914 in the fairy-tale city of music and Mozart ended
happily for him. The physical examination declared Hitler "unfit for
combatant and auxiliary duties, too weak, and unable to bear arms."
He was free to return to his adopted country of Germany where he was
certain destiny waited for him.

When he returned to Munich, he learned that Rudolf Häusler had moved out of the room they shared. Häusler had suffered
enough sleepless nights caused by Hitler's endless speeches and political rants. Alone again, with the study of art and architecture closed
to him, a restless Adolf Hitler searched for another purpose in life,
and a new audience.

Franz Ferdinand's own efforts at self-promotion were rewarded in a human-interest story printed in the *London Times*. England's most influential newspaper portrayed the Archduke and Duchess as untraditional representatives of their social class and royal position. Whenever he was home, the Habsburg heir to the throne began and ended each day in the children's nursery. He seemed happiest playing on the floor with his small sons and daughter. Sophie's custom of personally caring for her children when they were ill, and tucking them in at night, was another peculiarity highlighted in the article. One of their few Habsburg allies, Crown Prince Rudolph's widow, Stephanie, was not surprised such simple gestures merited newspaper coverage. She sadly observed, "It was the fashion at that time to despise the joys of family life."

In March 1914, the Hohenbergs returned to a favorite holiday destination, Miramar Castle on the Adriatic. Even today the castle clings precariously to jagged cliffs that seem to thrust the palace into the sea. It had been built fifty years earlier by Franz Ferdinand's uncle Maximilian Habsburg. In 1864, he and his wife, Charlotte, sailed from its dock to become the Emperor and Empress of Mexico. Three years later, their hopes for a Mexican Empire ended with his death before a firing squad and Charlotte's insanity. Every room of the white-walled castle's heavy gothic interior held some memory of the doomed couple. The Archduke's son Maximilian was named for the dead uncle he never met. Despite its tragic history, to Franz Ferdinand's family, Miramar was a world of delights. The Duchess of Hohenberg celebrated her forty-sixth—and final—birthday there.

Days were spent swimming in the bracing waters and sailing until sunset. At night the children navigated Miramar's large rooms, massive staircases, and dark hallways with pocket electric lights since the castle had no electricity. Time was set aside to motor along the coast to enjoy picnics overlooking the sea. The Archduke's military aide warned him of the security risk, but he only laughed and told him,

"I'm sure you have a point, but we can't live our lives under glass. Our lives are always in danger. We must simply trust God."

German Emperor Wilhelm II visited them at Miramar. He sailed to the castle in a small launch from his sleek royal yacht *Meteor*. Two German battle cruisers, much of the Austrian navy, and the city of Trieste served as his backdrop. Ship cannons fired, bells loudly rung, and whistles shrilly piped as he swaggered onto the castle's dock. The Emperor's entourage included German and Austrian admirals, numerous attendants, and his pet dachshunds, Wadl and Hexl. He confided to the shocked Hohenberg children that he preferred traveling with his dogs rather than his family. Despite his unusual choice of traveling companions, his fixation for changing military uniforms throughout the day, and his loud personality, he treated the Archduke's wife and children very well. Franz Ferdinand's daughter, Sophie, remembered that as far as emperors went, he seemed very nice. Wilhelm promised to visit them again at Konopiste that June.

Summer was family time for the Archduke and his family. Only military maneuvers in Bosnia following Wilhelm's June visit clouded their plans. The previous August, Emperor Franz Joseph appointed Franz Ferdinand Inspector of the Army, a post that had been vacant for eighteen years. Among his new responsibilities was the trip to Bosnia, a notoriously warm Balkan province he never wanted as part of the Empire.

Like the weather, Bosnia-Herzegovina's heated political situation may have also been on his mind. The provinces shared a long border with Serbia, a hotbed of state-sponsored terrorism and terrorists. The Serbs, oppressed by centuries of foreign domination, did little to hide their hatred of the Habsburgs or their resentment of their expansion into the Balkans. That spring during a visit to Vienna, Franz Ferdinand invited his nephew Archduke Karl and Zita to dinner. Archduchess Zita never forgot the evening, which she described years later:

At the beginning of May 1914, my husband and I were in Vienna and Uncle Franz rang up one evening asking us to come over to Belvedere Palace for supper. It was just a small family affair with us as the only guests. Everything passed off normally—indeed quite gaily—until after supper, when Aunt Sophie took the children off to bed. Once she left the room, the Archduke suddenly turned to my husband and said, "I have something to tell you but I must say it quickly as I don't want your Aunt to hear any of this. I know I shall soon be murdered. In this desk are papers that concern you. When it happens, take them, they are for you."

Zita's husband protested that surely this must be some kind of a terrible joke, but the Archduke reminded them. "The crypt at Artstetten is finished now. That is where I am to be buried." At that point the Duchess returned, and the conversation abruptly ended. Karl and Zita were never alone again with Franz Ferdinand to ask him further questions.

That June, the most beautiful in many people's memory, five hundred acres of Konopiste's roses bloomed in time for the German Emperor's visit. In addition to his dachshunds, Wilhelm brought with him Admiral Alfred von Tirpitz, founder of Germany's navy. Ever since Franz Ferdinand's cruise around the world as a young man, he loved the sea, and the Admiral loved roses. The Archduke personally escorted Emperor and Admiral to the castle's largest bathroom. It was from that room's high window that he proudly showed them his favorite view of his rose garden.

The Hohenberg children always shared meals with their mother and father, unless their parents hosted a formal dinner. On those occasions they would meet their parents' guests, and then disappear to dine with their tutor. On the special occasion of Wilhelm II's visit, following a day enjoying the heavily scented roses, gentle breezes, and glorious weather, the Archduke's nearly thirteen-year-old daughter, Sophie, received a special invitation. She was allowed to join the adults at the Emperor's farewell dinner. Wilhelm took the Duchess of Hohenberg's arm and the Archduke extended his own arm to his proud daughter. They walked into the dining room followed by the Admiral and two dozen guests. The only other family member present was the Duchess's sister Henrietta Chotek, the favorite relative of all the Hohenbergs.

Everyone was dressed in the finest suits, gowns, and uniforms. A nine-course meal furnished from Konopiste's own gardens and hunting preserves; the German Emperor's raucous voice; the Archduke's basso profundo laugh; the hum, flow, and rhythm of the music; and the murmured conversations of friends and neighbors made it a dreamlike evening.

Princess Sophie Hohenberg later remembered every exquisite detail of the night. Even in its midst she wished she could stop time, but she couldn't. Wilhelm II, Admiral Tirpitz, and the Emperor's two dachshunds were soon on their way back to Berlin. The first grown-up dinner party she shared with her parents would also be her last. The Archduke and Duchess would leave for Bosnia in a few days.

———

That spring Serbian nationalists, terrorists, and anarchists as far away as Chicago were informed of the Archduke's trip to Sarajevo, the capital city of Bosnia. How they learned of his journey before it was publicly announced in Vienna has never been determined. One Serbian newspaper wrote, "If the heir to the throne goes to Bosnia we will make sure he pays for it.... Serbs, make use of every available weapon; daggers, guns, bombs, and dynamite. Revenge is sacred; death to the Habsburg dynasty."

Anti-Austrian propaganda in the Balkans never seemed more violent than in the weeks prior to the Archduke's visit. Pamphlets passed out at Christian Orthodox churches denounced the Catholic Duchess of Hohenberg in words and cartoons as "a monstrous Bohemian whore." Bold headlines read, "Down with the Este' dog and the filthy Bohemian sow!" Assassination rumors became a favorite topic of conversation in Balkan coffeehouses. Austrian counterintelligence agents sat cheek-by-jowl with known and unknown terrorists; yet they reported no unusual activities or need for special security during the Archduke's trip.

On the day Franz Ferdinand left Konopiste, he seemed unusually quiet, even depressed. That morning he handed the keys of his Belvedere Palace desk to Franz Janacek, his onetime valet who now managed the estate. He instructed him to give the keys to his nephew Karl if he did not return.

Janacek had been in service to the Archduke for many years, but he was much more than a servant or Konopiste's overseer. He was the Archduke's shadow, a trusted confidant; the first person to hold Princess Sophie in his arms following her 1901 birth. Franz Ferdinand surprised Janacek that day with a gold watch for his years of loyalty and discretion. He then surprised him with a personal request asking him to stay with his wife and children if anything happened to him. Janacek quickly agreed.

Chlumetz, the Archduke's other estate in Bohemia, was where the Hohenberg family spent their final days before Sarajevo. His son Maximilian was taking school exams in nearby Vienna. The family's last morning together was like a thousand others. They attended early Mass and shared a light breakfast together. Franz Ferdinand took eleven-year-old Max for a long drive through the grounds. Princess Sophie and Prince Ernst spent a quiet morning with their mother. Nothing was remarkable about the day, except there would never be another like it.

At the noontime meal, no one mentioned the trip to Bosnia until suddenly the Archduke blurted out, "I am the Inspector General of the Austro-Hungarian armed forces! I must go to Sarajevo. The soldiers would never understand my absence." He seemed to be arguing with himself. Uncomfortable silence followed. After an awkward moment, his dark mood lifted and the meal continued.

Only later did the children learn their parents had been reluctant to undertake the journey. Franz Ferdinand told a friend, "This thing is no particular secret. I wouldn't be surprised if there are some Serbian bullets waiting for me." Privately he did not fear for his own life, but worried about leaving his children fatherless. The Duchess confided her own fears to her chaplain, concluding with the words, "If there is any danger, my place is at my husband's side." A Konopiste neighbor later wrote, "I think in her mind the poor woman foresaw the catastrophe a hundred times."

More than once the Archduke threatened to cancel the trip. His military aide Baron Albert von Margutti later wrote. "The whole trip appalled him from beginning to end." Maneuvers were traditionally scheduled to prepare the army for deployment in a time of war. But the troops in Bosnia had already successfully mobilized twice and performed well during recent crises in the region.

Following his marriage, Franz Ferdinand had been in excellent health, but recently had been diagnosed with asthma. His doctor feared Bosnia's weather would aggravate his condition. Archduchess Zita later remembered:

> The Archduke used the excuse of the great heat of Bosnia for getting out of attending the maneuvers. Normally he always prevailed with the old Emperor when deciding his travels.... But on this occasion, and over such a relatively routine trip he failed. While leaving the final decision to him, the Emperor made it clear he desired the Archduke to go. Such a wish, especially on a military matter, amounted to an order. Looking back, it is amazing that this Sarajevo trip should have been the one occasion when he did not get his way.

As an incentive for undertaking the trip, Franz Joseph did the unthinkable. He reversed his long-standing policy of excluding the Duchess of Hohenberg from joining her husband when he performed official duties. Earlier visits to Rumania, Germany, and England were considered private affairs between the royal families, but this trip would be different. The Emperor's decision shocked everyone. His suspension of a rule he had rigidly enforced for fourteen years finally persuaded his reluctant nephew to travel to the region that had been a war zone for a thousand years. It was the first and only exception Franz Joseph ever made regarding a joint public appearance by the couple.

Accompanying her husband to Bosnia-Herzegovina allowed the Duchess, whom the Archduke considered his best nurse, to monitor his health. It also permitted her to visit charities in Sarajevo that she had sponsored for several years. He believed Sophie his good luck charm and always felt better with his wife by his side.

The trip gave Franz Ferdinand an opportunity to bring closure to the Redl scandal by finding a replacement for the Army Chief of Staff. He ordered the command structure of the maneuvers divided between three generals. Hötzendorf correctly guessed Franz Ferdinand was using his time there to search for his replacement. The General and Archduke had recently bitterly quarreled again over von Hötzendorf's hectoring for a war against Serbia. They only spoke to each other when absolutely necessary.

All of the minutiae of the trip had been carefully planned except the security. Sarajevo's fifty thousand residents were provided ample opportunities to see the royal visitors. Franz Joseph's Chief of Protocol, Prince Alfred Montenuevo, published the scheduled events the Archduke and Duchess would attend separately and together. It was the first time the Hofburg Palace provided advance publicity for any trip by Franz Ferdinand. Placards were posted throughout the city announcing the route of the motorcade and urging crowds to welcome him:

Citizens! His Imperial and Royal Highness our Most Gracious Successor Archduke Franz Ferdinand will honor our city with his illustrious visit. Our deep rooted feelings of filial gratitude, devotion, fidelity, and loyalty...allow us to show our great joy at this most august visit particularly in the streets which His Highness will pass. These are: Railroad Street, Mastajbeg Street, Appel Quay, Franz Joseph street, Prince Rudolf Street.

Franz Ferdinand's military aide Baron Margutti was incensed. He felt that publicizing "every step of the archducal pair was playing with fire... a virtual challenge to fate." Although twenty thousand troops were available from the nearby maneuvers, none would be used to protect the couple. Bosnia's Military Governor, Oskar Potiorek, insisted the 120-man Sarajevo police force could manage security, even though he did not have direct control over them. That responsibility rested with his longtime political rival Dr. Leon Bilanski, a Habsburg bureaucrat and friend of the Emperor whose office in Vienna was nearly eight hundred miles away from Sarajevo.

The day after the Archduke's travel itinerary was made public, Jovan Jovanovic—Serbia's Minister in Vienna—met with Bilanski. He bluntly warned him the Archduke's visit to Sarajevo on the 28th of June endangered his life. It was not only St. Vitas Day, a Serbian national holiday honoring the Slavic deity of war, but the 525th anniversary of the Battle of Kosovo. The anniversary, the darkest day in Serbian history, marked the loss of the Serbs' independence for five centuries to the Ottoman Turks. The solitary hero to emerge from that debacle was a Serbian assassin who killed the Turkish leader of the conquering Islamic army.

Only recently had the Christian Orthodox Serbs gained independence from their Moslem rivals to the south. Now they felt increasingly threatened by their encroaching Catholic rivals to the north. Jovan Jovanovic warned the trip on the anniversary of the Battle of Kosovo would be seen as a direct provocation to Serbia.

Bilanski was a busy, impatient man. He had no time to remind anyone to do their duty, including the police force responsible for guarding Franz Ferdinand. Before cavalierly dismissing the Serbian Minister and returning to his paperwork, he brusquely thanked him with the haunting words, "Let's hope nothing happens."

CHAPTER EIGHT
INSCRUTABLE DESTINY

"On the 28th of June 1914, a shot was fired in Sarajevo, the shot that in a single second was to shatter the world of security and creative reason in which we had been reared, where we had grown up and were at home, as if it were a hollow pot breaking into a thousand pieces."   —STEFAN ZWEIG

"A stone had been set rolling whose course could no longer be arrested."   —ADOLF HITLER

No one heard the bishop's screams; not his sleeping servants, the gardeners, the cooks, nor his houseguests and mother who were visiting to celebrate his birthday. Outside his bedroom, the 119 rooms of the bishop's palace in the Austro-Hungarian city of Grosswardien were silent and dark in the early morning hours of June 28, 1914.

Today the palace is found in Oradea, Rumania, but that night—as it had for a century and a half—it stood within the borders of central Europe's Habsburg Empire. The screams echoed off the bedroom walls and hung in the air. Outside and across the palace's grounds, all remained quiet. No one stirred in the nearby baroque and art nouveau houses painted pale shades of pink, green, and blue. The city's ornate churches and synagogues, sluggish river, and Transylvania's nearby Carpathian Mountains were silent. The tower clock in the city's tallest building showed half past three in the morning, but only the bishop noticed the time. For those who still clung to the region's old legends and folklore, the Devil's hour had just passed; the hour when the thin curtain between this world and the next lifted, and mischief, or worse, was let loose in the world.

A June rain had caused all 365 palace windows—one for each day of the year—to be closed. The great house was a smaller version of the Belvedere Palace in Vienna—home of the bishop's friend and former student Archduke Franz Ferdinand. The nightmare that caused Bishop Joseph Lanyi to wake up screaming was about the Archduke and his wife. He dreamt they were to be assassinated that morning.

Bishop Lanyi was not a superstitious man. It was 1914. Telephones, electricity, automobiles, and airplanes were continually making life better and safer. The next day he would turn forty-six years old, yet Lanyi had already been a bishop for nearly eight years. His rise in the Catholic Church, not known for youthful leadership or quick advancement, had been meteoritic. Most people, including Lanyi, could not imagine the world they had known was about to end. The supremely confident cleric was a conservative, yet thoroughly modern man, unafraid of the dark, the terrors of the night, or the future. Lanyi could not remember the last time he woke from a bad dream or cried, but the nightmare that awakened him left him shaking and in tears.

Archduke Franz Ferdinand, his wife, Sophie, and their young children remained close to the bishop. For many years he had been a member of their household, lived in their home, and served as their chaplain. He had baptized two of their children, celebrated the safe birth of a third, and buried their stillborn son. He had never known a happier, more loving family, or a more essential man. Bishop Lanyi believed the future of Europe depended on this prince of peace becoming Austria's Emperor.

To him the Archduke was the indispensable man, the catalyst for

European peace and unity. Now he feared for the Archduke, his family, and for all of Europe. Lanyi paced the floor, stared from his window into the darkness. He could not stop shaking. Finally, to clear his head, he sat down at his small writing desk and carefully wrote out the details of his dream:

> I walked to my desk to look at the mail. A black bordered letter lay on top, sealed in black with the crest of the Archduke. I recognized the handwriting at once. I opened it and saw on the letterhead a picture in sky blue, as on a picture postcard, showing a street, a narrow alley, with Their Highnesses sitting in an automobile, a general facing them, an officer next to the driver. Crowds on both sides of the street, then two young fellows stepped out and shot Their Highnesses...

The letter in the black bordered envelope read:

Dear Dr. Lanyi,

This will inform you that today, with my wife, I fall victim to an assassination. We commend ourselves to your pious prayers and holy sacrifice, and beg you in the future to remain as lovingly and faithfully devoted to our poor children as heretofore.

> Cordial greetings from your Archduke Franz—
> Sarajevo—28 June 1914. Half past 3 a.m.

Lanyi had never had such a dream, not as a small boy, or as a young seminarian, and certainly not as a man. Two hours later, his servant entered the room to wake him and found the bishop on his knees silently praying the rosary. Lanyi asked to have his mother and his other houseguests join him in the chapel. He was going to offer a Mass for Archduke Franz Ferdinand and the Duchess. Afterward he told them of his dream and drew a sketch of the assassination scene, of the car entering a narrow street, of the location of the assassins, and other details. Lanyi could not stop thinking about the nightmare. He returned to his room and wrote his brother Edward, a Jesuit priest, a letter detailing the dream and attaching a drawing of what he had seen.

———

Nine hours after Bishop Lanyi's scream, three hundred miles to the south, six terrorists waited for Franz Ferdinand and his wife's open touring car. Four of them froze and silently watched as it passed. The fifth threw a bomb the Archduke deflected with his hand. It exploded behind his car, wounding twenty people. In the chaos of the assassination attempt, no one was calmer than he and his wife. After checking on the injured, Franz Ferdinand said, "I thought something like this might happen." He then joked that the captured bomb thrower would probably be given a medal in Vienna and a government job. No one laughed.

The Sarajevo trip had been haunted by dark omens even before he and the Duchess left Konopiste. Shortly after the train carrying Wilhelm II pulled out of the station to carry him back to Berlin, the Archduke and Duchess noticed a large flock of ravens flying overhead. Ravens were an unusual sight that time of the year. A startled Franz Ferdinand rose from his seat, muttering, "Ravens are ill omens for our House!" Crown Prince Rudolph had seen them on the road to Mayerling shortly before his tragic death.

Once they bid farewell to their children at Chlumetz, the axle on the railroad car taking them to Vienna unexpectedly burned out. The Archduke responded with typical sardonic humor, "This is the way it starts. First the carriage runs hot, next an assassination attempt in Sarajevo and it probably ends with boilers exploding on the ship!" Then the electricity on the night train to Trieste burned out, forcing him to travel there by candlelight. Gloomy shadows danced throughout the darkened car, causing him to quip, "What do you say to this illumination? Like a tomb isn't it? First my own railcar catches fire, and now the replacement doesn't like me either."

Following the failed assassination attempt, the bomb thrower was arrested, the injured taken to the hospital, and Franz Ferdinand's motorcade proceeded to Sarajevo's Moorish-style red-, yellow-, and orange-brick City Hall. The Archduke's wife took his arm and they slowly climbed the steps to meet the welcome committee. The Duchess's face was completely drained of color, but the Archduke's complexion was as red as the scarlet stripe on his black pants leg. No one had apparently informed the Sarajevo officials about the bomb, the injuries, or the near assassination.

The outdoor ceremony had not been cancelled. In the warmth of the brilliant sun a waiting crowd stood within inches of the royal couple. The mayor began his speech, "Your Imperial Highness, our hearts are transported with happiness by your gracious visit…"

Franz Ferdinand's voice exploded. "Mr. Mayor, what good are your speeches? I come to visit Sarajevo, and they throw bombs at me. It is an outrage!"

The Duchess of Hohenberg gently touched the sleeve of her husband's jacket. After she whispered a few words to him, he took a long deep breath, then said, "All right, you can go on."

The confused mayor did. "Our hearts are filled with joy.… All the citizens of Sarajevo are overwhelmed with happiness.… We greet your Highnesses' most illustrious visit with utmost enthusiasm."

When the Archduke was handed his own prepared remarks, they were splattered with the blood of his wounded aide. He calmly read the bloodstained words. At the end of his speech, he added that the friendly reception at City Hall gave proof of the loyalty of the people and their joy "over the failure of the attack."

A sixth and final assassin waited. After leaving the City Hall reception and traveling two short blocks, the Archduke's car turned into a narrow street named for his uncle Franz Joseph. Two shots shattered the quiet. The Duchess threw herself in front of her husband. A bullet pierced her abdomen, a second severed an artery in the Archduke's neck. The shots would be fatal. As they bled to death, Franz Ferdinand pleaded with his wife, "Sophie, Sophie, don't die. Live for the children."

The doomed couple died within minutes of each other.

It was the fourteenth anniversary to the hour the heir to the Austrian throne signed the Oath of Renunciation allowing his marriage. When word of the assassination spread, bells from the city's Catholic and Eastern Orthodox churches rang mournfully as muezzins called the Islamic faithful to prayer. A jubilant accomplice of the assassins sent a five-word telegram to Serbia confirming the success of the mission. It simply read, "Excellent sale of both horses."

Reactions to the news from Sarajevo revealed as much about the people who learned of the assassination as the deed itself. When a military aide informed Emperor Franz Joseph of the violent death of his nephew and wife, he stood in silence for several moments. Then he exclaimed, "Awful! The Almighty will not be challenged.... A higher power has restored the order which I myself could not maintain."

Adolf Hitler recorded his own reaction to the assassination in *Mein Kampf*:

> When news of the murder of Archduke Franz Ferdinand arrived in Munich, I was at first seized with worry that the bullets may have been shot from the pistols of German students, who out of indignation at the heir apparent continuous work of Slavization, wanted to free the German people from this internal enemy. What the consequences of this would have been are easy to imagine: a new wave of persecutions which would now have been "justified" and "explained" in the eyes of the whole world. But when, soon afterward, I heard the names of the supposed assassins, and moreover read that they had been identified as Serbs, a light shudder began to run through me at this vengeance of inscrutable destiny.

The greatest friend of the Slavs had fallen beneath the bullets of Slavic fanatics.

Austria's highest-ranking soldier, Army Chief of Staff Conrad von Hötzendorf, immediately wrote his mistress. He told Virginia von Reininghaus that the assassination might mean a disastrous war. Hopefully, he added, it would distract Catholic Austria long enough to allow her to divorce her husband and marry him. His obsessive passion for his mistress and the war had become one. Hötzendorf's happily concluded, "Thank God! I had to wait for this for eight years! Now you will not say 'No.' Now will you consent to my marriage proposal?"

Nearly the entire world learned about the events in Sarajevo before the three newly orphaned children. Baron Andreas von Morsey, the Archduke's military aide, telephoned Dr. Otto Stanowsky, the Hohenberg children's tutor, at Chlumetz. The Czech priest was having lunch with the children when he was called to the phone and Morsey told him, "Please tell our dear children as gently as possible that the exalted personages have fallen victim to the brutal hands of a murderer." Morsey also telephoned Henrietta Chotek, the children's aunt in Prague, who left at once for Chlumetz.

Dr. Stanowsky's mother had been ill. When he did not immediately return to the waiting children, they whispered that perhaps he had received bad news about her. Their chatter died down as he returned to the dining room, his face drained of color. For several long minutes he did not look at them or speak. The children knew something terrible must have happened, but Dr. Stanowsky could not find the words to tell them what he had learned. The tense meal finished in an awkward silence. Seventy years later, Princess Sophie Hohenberg told her grandson, "We went to lunch that day as children, but left the table as adults. Our childhoods were over."

Even after the arrival of their tearful Aunt Henrietta Chotek, neither tutor nor aunt could bring themselves to tell the children the truth. They were first told their parents had been taken ill; then that they had been in an accident and needed prayers. As the hours ticked away, confusion, foreboding, and fear permeated Chlumetz. Finally, twelve-year-old Sophie burst into tears crying she knew her parents were dead. A deep rumbling moan emerged from ten-year-old Maximilian. Nine-year-old Ernst began to shake uncontrollably. The children clung to each other, but the adults could not bring themselves to tell them of their parents' deaths.

Following a sleepless night of tears and prayers, they were finally told the next morning by Archduchess Maria-Theresa, Franz Ferdinand's beloved stepmother, who arrived from Vienna. Later, Princess Sophie confided to her, "It is a good thing Mama died with Papa. If Papa had died and Mama lived, Mama would have lost her mind." Germany's Emperor Wilhelm II, who was genuinely fond of Franz Ferdinand's children, sent them a telegram that read:

> We can hardly find words to tell you children how our hearts bleed thinking of you and your indescribable misery. Only two weeks ago we spent such lovely hours with your parents, and now we hear of this terrible sadness that you must suffer. May God protect you and give you strength to bear this blow. The blessings of the parents reach beyond the grave.

Queen Mary of England wrote in her diary:

> The horrible tragedy to the poor Archduke and his wife came as a great shock to us... we were really quite attached to them both....
> I think it is a great blessing that husband and wife died together, making the future less complicated with regard to the position of the children.

Her son Edward, the twenty-year-old Prince of Wales, stationed at an isolated Officer's Training Camp, wrote, "I am completely ignorant of all the happenings in the outer World, except that the Austrian

Archduke and his wife have been assassinated. I expect it has caused quite a stir in Germany." His assessment was correct. In Vienna, other feelings stirred in the heart and mind of Emperor Franz Joseph. His favorite daughter, Archduchess Marie Valerie, wrote in her diary:

> I found Papa amazingly fresh. Moved to be sure and speaking of the poor children with tears in his eyes; but as I knew beforehand, not personally stricken. In fact, in the course of a sixty-minute conversation which today was never halting, his only reference to it came as I remarked that Karl (the new heir to the throne) would surely do a good job, and he replied very seriously and firmly, "For me, it's a great deal less worry."

Despite tears over his dead nephew's orphaned children, he sent no telegram, condolence letter, or reached out to them in any way. He did order his nephew's offices at Belvedere Palace closed at once. All the Archduke's official papers and military documents were seized and ordered sealed for fifty years. Archduke Karl tried to unlock Franz Ferdinand's private desk to access the papers meant for him, but those, too, had disappeared. What Franz Joseph and his efficient bureaucracy failed to do was order an investigation into the security lapses at Sarajevo.

Traditionalists in the Habsburg Empire felt a sense of relief over Franz Ferdinand's death. The United States Ambassador wrote Secretary of State William Jennings Bryan, "The news of the death of the Crown Prince was received quietly.... While expressing abhorrence of the assassination, as a whole people seemed to feel that the event has solved a very difficult problem." He may have been speaking for the Emperor and his court, but not for everyone. Count Alphonse Clary spoke for many when he wrote British princess and social reformer Daisy, Princess of Pless:

> I am writing to you with my most aching heart and tears in my eyes, tears of sorrow, of terrible rage. Oh, the misery of it, he our future,

our leader, who was to be a strong man, he to whom we all looked to in the future, our savior after all the years of ineptitude; he is not there anymore. They have slaughtered him and her too, his wife, whose life was only love, who followed him whenever danger was near, and she died trying to protect him with her body. They lived a life, a noble life of love, and to think of those three little children waiting, waiting for their parents to come home again, they who had known every happiness of family life; now they are quite alone, no one to care for them, no one to love and protect them, against the hardness of life, that they must feel so soon.... We are all in such utter misery.

Vienna was seized by suspicions that Austrian or German secret agents engineered the assassination or stepped back and allowed it to happen. Speculation regarding whether sins of commission or sins of omission killed the Archduke vanished once the Habsburg government placed the blame for the murders on the Serbian government. Rumors of war smothered any questions about Sarajevo's faulty security.

Archduchess Maria-Theresa and Chotek relatives brought the Hohenberg children to Vienna for their parents' funeral. No Habsburg relative met them there, but thousands of schoolchildren did. A Viennese newspaper suggested the city's youngest citizens show their sympathy and support by lining the streets where the royal orphans would pass. As they rode to the Belvedere Palace for the last time, the children of Vienna silently paid their respects.

A large wreath of white roses from the children was placed between their parents' coffins in the Hofburg Palace's Imperial Chapel. White was the traditional floral arrangement representing peace. Germany's Wilhelm II, King George V and Queen Mary of England, President Woodrow Wilson, and other heads of state sent flowers. Franz Joseph and his daughters did not. The only Habsburg represented by floral arrangements were Archduke Karl and Zita, and Crown Prince Rudolph's widow, Stephanie. To the day she died, Stephanie believed Rudolph's mysterious death twenty-five years earlier and the Sarajevo assassinations were the work of subterranean elements in Franz Joseph's government.

Many of the Empire's oppressed minorities saw Franz Ferdinand as their only political defender and champion. The ribbon on a bouquet from Hungary's large minority Rumanian population spoke for many. It read, "To Our Last Best Hope, In Loyal Devotion."

Fifty thousand people waited patiently during the night to pay tribute to the slain couple as their bodies rested in the Imperial Chapel. Most were turned away the next morning to allow a fifteen-minute memorial service for the Imperial Family late that afternoon. The Hohenberg children were not invited to attend. Those who did enter the chapel found two identical coffins surrounded by dozens of burning candles. But the Archduke's coffin stood twenty inches taller than his dead wife's since she was not recognized as a Habsburg by the court.

Late that night the coffins were taken to the same train station that had once brought Adolf Hitler to Vienna. They were placed in a hired freight car to transport them to Artstetten Castle for burial. The Habsburgs and the Hohenberg children and their Chotek relatives rode in separate coaches. Court protocol decreed Franz Ferdinand's children be physically segregated from the Imperial family. At Artstetten, the Catholic Mass for the Dead was co-officiated by Bishop Joseph Lanyi whose premonition of the assassination haunted him for the rest of his life.

Following the Artstetten burial, Colonel Carl Bardolff, who had been with the Archduke and Duchess at Sarajevo, was asked to come to Schönbrunn Palace to provide the Emperor an eyewitness account of the assassination. Franz Joseph specifically asked about the moment his nephew was shot, "And how did the Archduke bear himself?" The

Colonel reported, "Like a soldier, Your Majesty." The Emperor replied, "That was to be expected of his Imperial Highness." He paused and then asked, "And how were the maneuvers?" He did not ask about the Duchess of Hohenberg who had been killed trying to shield her husband from his assassin.

Austrian aristocrat Prince Ludwig Windisch-Grätz wrote:

> I was indignant that every ass should now give the dead lion a kick.... Hardly was he in his coffin before all his protégés, all his creatures, friends and officials were swept out of posts and office. The court cliques and military war lords who had been continually harassed by the Heir to the Throne saw to this being a clean sweep. It could be fairly assumed that henceforth the old system would be firmly and immovably established until Franz Joseph's death.

Count Otto Czernin, the Austrian Empire's last Foreign Minister and a friend and neighbor of the Archduke and Duchess, saw the approaching Armageddon and wrote:

> Many there were who breathed more freely on hearing the news of Franz Ferdinand's death. At court in Vienna and in Budapest society there was more joy than sorrow.... None of them could guess that the fall of this strong man would carry them all with it and engulf them in world catastrophe.

A joyful Adolf Hitler celebrated the assassination, and the war he was certain would follow. He wrote in *Mein Kampf,* "Anyone with constant occasion in the last years to observe the relations of Austria to Serbia could not for a moment doubt that a stone had been set rolling whose course could no longer be arrested." He was supremely confident that war would elevate Germany above all other nations, make the German people the dominant race on earth, and sweep away the mongrel Habsburg Empire. "Austria was then like an old mosaic," he wrote, "the cement, binding the various little stones together had grown old and begun to crumble; as long as the work of art was not touched, it could continue to give a show of existence, but as soon as it received a blow, it would break into a thousand fragments."

CHAPTER NINE
A KIND OF DULL CATALEPTIC TRANCE

"I never loved our old world *more* than in those last years before
the First World War; I never hoped more for a united Europe.
I never believed more in its future than at that time, when
we thought there was a new dawn in sight. But its red hue was
really the firelight of the approaching conflagration."

—STEFAN ZWEIG

"A war between Austria and Russia would be very useful to
the Revolution in Western Europe, but it is hard to imagine
Franz Joseph and Nicholas doing us that favor."

—VLADIMIR LENIN TO MAXIM GORKY

The death of Archduke Franz Ferdinand crushed the peace party he
led, and boldly empowered the war party he opposed. Austria's political and military war hawks wasted no time in using his assassination
as an excuse to fight the war he had desperately wanted to prevent.
Even many of his strongest supporters were swept along by the emo-
tions unleashed by his murder.

On July 23, 1914, Count Alphonse Clary wrote to Daisy, Princess
of Pless:

> We are spending horrid days waiting, and nobody knows for what.
> I hope it will be for *war*, because we cannot go on living with an
> abscess on our side, stinging and poisoning us day by day; it is bet-

ter to cut it open right away and see if we can possibly get over the operation.... To talk of the future seems rash just now, when the peace of our country, perhaps of Europe, is hanging on the edge of a hair.... We have lost our great leader who was a man of peace. The next man will have to be a man of war.

The day Clary wrote his letter, Austria's Ambassador presented an ultimatum to Serbia—the home country of Franz Ferdinand's accused assassins. It was designed to provoke a military, rather than a diplomatic, response. Among its demands were the closing of Serbian newspapers unfriendly to the Habsburg monarchy, the dismissal and arrest of political and military leaders hostile to Austria, a virtual surrender of the country's independent judiciary in investigating the assassination, and the suppression of all groups, organizations, and clubs Vienna labeled as "terrorists."

After reading its contents, a young British politician described it to his wife as "the most insolent document of its kind ever devised... I wonder whether these stupid kings and emperors could not assemble together and revivify kingship by saving nations from hell, but we all drift on in a kind of dull cataleptic trance." The politician's name was Winston Churchill.

Franz Ferdinand's daughter, Princess Sophie Hohenberg, turned thirteen one day after the ultimatum was delivered. For the rest of her life, she had no recollection of her thirteenth birthday. Four days later, one month to the hour of the Sarajevo assassinations, Franz Joseph declared war on Serbia. He did not want armed conflict, but he was loath to lose face. Without Franz Ferdinand to strengthen his resolve, he supported a man he despised and a war he feared. General Conrad von Hötzendorf and his war party won the day.

Kaiser Wilhelm II of Germany confidently predicted, "The Czar will not place himself on the side of regicides." He was wrong. As Franz Ferdinand had feared, Russia immediately came to Serbia's defense. Leon Trotsky, at that time a resident of Vienna, wrote about what he saw that day in the capital of the Habsburg Empire.

> I walked along the main streets of the familiar city and observed the crowds which gathered in unusual density on the magnificent Ringstrasse.... They were fired by hope.... Something new, something extraordinary appeared on the scene. The future promised change. Change for the better, or change for the worse?

The Habsburg Empire and Germany were now at war with Serbia and Russia. Privately, Czar Nicholas II of Russia seemed in genuine anguish when he ordered mobilization, telling his government ministers, "Just think of the responsibility you're advising me to assume! Remember it's a question of sending thousands and thousands of men to their deaths." Germany's Wilhelm II said of his cousin the Czar, "The Czar is not treacherous, but he is weak. Weakness is not treachery, but it fulfills all its functions." He might have been describing himself.

Austria-Hungary's declaration of war was issued in fifteen languages, reflecting the multinational character of its army. Russia's ally France quickly declared war on Germany. England followed, and so, too, did their colonies around the globe. The First World War had begun. In Munich, Adolf Hitler described himself as engulfed in "stormy enthusiasm... I fell on my knees and thanked heaven from an overpowering heart for granting me the good fortune of being permitted to live at this time." After carefully avoiding Austrian military service for five years, he immediately enlisted in the Bavarian army, writing:

> My joy and gratitude knew no bounds.... For me, as for every German there now began the greatest and most unforgettable time of earthly existence. Compared to the events of this gigantic struggle, everything else receded to shallow nothingness.

———

War of another kind was being waged within the Habsburg family over the future of Franz Ferdinand's orphans. Henrietta Chotek, their unmarried aunt, had moved to Konopiste to live with them. Count Jaroslav Thun, husband of their Aunt Marie Chotek, assumed management of their legal and financial affairs. Their father's estate manager, Franz Janacek, continued running Konopiste. But creditors wasted no time in demanding full payment of the Archduke's debts. Money quickly became a problem.

The Oath of Renunciation the Archduke had signed in 1900 permitted his marriage, but made his wife and children solely his financial responsibility. The Archduke's will would take years to settle, but his sons and daughter could inherit no money from Habsburg or Este' family funds. Despite his wealth on paper, Franz Ferdinand was, in fact, land poor. His orphaned children could inherit their father's homes and the land around them, but received no funds to support them. The Emperor believed that the assassination of a nephew he did not love, and his nephew's wife, a woman he did not like, did not change his financial obligations to the orphans he barely knew.

Following Sarajevo, Franz Joseph's government even refused to pay for the autopsies and embalming of the Archduke and Duchess. Events there, officials stated, ended any financial responsibilities on their part to the dead heir, his morganatic wife, or their family. Count Thun insisted Franz Ferdinand had died fulfilling his official duties. The embalmer was "carrying out his duties incumbent on him as an Austrian state medical official.... There can be no question of payment." The Habsburg court never paid the $400 bill. Mounting debts forced Count Thun to quickly sell the Archduke's hunting lodge in the Alps, and even the Duchess of Hohenberg's jewels. The Emperor remained unmoved by financial appeals from their guardians. If he refused to pay for the autopsy of his assassinated heir, why would he be obligated to assist his children?

Maria-Theresa, their Habsburg grandmother, was determined to force the issue. She threatened to make a public announcement that she was selling everything she owned to provide for the financial security of her orphaned grandchildren. Few things were as important to the Habsburg court as the carefully constructed façade of the Emperor as benevolent father to his subjects. Many believed that image, not his army, was the only thing holding his fracturing realm together. Her blackmail worked. Franz Joseph reluctantly offered to provide the orphans a yearly stipend. Archduke Karl made a counter offer: "Wouldn't it be better to give them property?" He knew Franz Ferdinand would not want his children dependent on the Habsburg court. The Emperor agreed to Karl's request. He quietly transferred fifty thousand acres of heavily wooded mineral-rich Styrian-mountain land to the Hohenberg children. Ordinarily the old monarch would have stubbornly resisted Maria-Theresa's threats, and the plea from his fifth and newest heir. But during the summer of 1914, he needed all the sympathy he could wring from Franz Ferdinand's assassination as he led his country into war.

General Conrad von Hötzendorf's "brisk gay war" began poorly for the Habsburg forces. Two weeks and fifty thousand casualties after invading Serbia, the incompetent Governor General Oskar Potiorek's badly defeated army was driven back into Bosnia. Following Russia's invasion in the north, Austria's Minister of War declared the war against Serbia had become "a matter of secondary interest." On the Russian front near the city of Lemberg, today the Ukrainian city of Lviv, Hötzendorf's armies suffered 400,000 casualties. The disastrous war Franz Ferdinand feared had become a reality on two fronts.

Hötzendorf wrote at the time, "If Franz Ferdinand had been commander-in-chief he would have had me shot after Lemberg." The city of Lviv was the home of Colonel Alfred Redl, the spy whose selling of military secrets to Russia left the Empire militarily crippled. Austria's last Foreign Minister wrote in his memoirs, "We were at liberty to choose the manner of our own death, and we chose the most terrible." The chaos and carnage of Europe's eastern front was matched by stalemate and slaughter in the west. German Army Chief of Staff Helmuth von Moltke, eager for war like his friend Conrad von Hötzendorf, had a complete nervous breakdown six weeks into the fighting. Germany's Crown Prince publicly declared to an American newspaper, "Undoubtedly this is the most stupid, senseless, and unnecessary war in modern times." Kaiser Wilhelm II reprimanded his son for telling the truth.

Soldiers, officers, and civilians found much to hate about the war. Adolf Hitler found much to like. He was quickly promoted to corporal, volunteered for the highly dangerous position of dispatch runner, and by December 1914 had earned the Iron Cross second class for his bravery. He wrote his Munich landlady about the decoration:

> It was the happiest day of my life. True, most of my comrades who had earned it just as much were dead.... For four days we were engaged in the fiercest battle, and I can proudly say that our regiment fought like heroes. On the very first day we lost nearly all our officers.... For all that, we beat the English.... Our company was reduced to a mere 42 men.... Ever since, I have, so to speak, been risking my life, every day, looking death straight in the eye.

The only gunfire heard at Konopiste were Max and Ernst's hunting volleys. No battles were fought near the Hohenberg's home, but the war was never far from their thoughts. Casualty lists contained the names of many officers who had served their father. Gardens on the estate and plentiful game supplied them with food, but meals were kept spartanly simple in solidarity with the sacrifices being made on distant battlefields.

In response to the many condolence letters and telegrams she and her brothers received, Princess Sophie composed a short statement published worldwide. It read, "We are very touched by the sympathy and prayers of the public. I ask you to continue to pray for our parents and for us." One letter sent to them stood out from all the rest. It was from the fifty-five-year-old Jesuit priest who had administered the last rites of the Catholic faith to their parents. Father Anton Puntigam had been in charge of the Sarajevo charities the Duchess of Hohenberg supported. After touring the priest's youth programs the day before she was assassinated, the Duchess donated an additional $5,000 in gold to continue his work. It had been her final gift to the children of Bosnia.

Archduchess Maria-Theresa invited the priest to Vienna where he preached a well-publicized sermon portraying the Archduke and Duchess as Catholic martyrs. Puntigam had one other unique connection to the Hohenberg orphans. He knew Nedjo Cabrinovic, the nineteen-year-old terrorist who had attempted to kill their parents with a bomb. The small but loquacious Cabrinovic once visited Puntigam's Youth Center, engaging him in a conversation the priest never forgot. During Cabrinovic's Sarajevo trial, he admitted he never imagined the assassination would start a world war, even as gunfire between the opposing armies could be heard in the courtroom. He ended his emotional remarks by declaring:

> There is something else I would like to say.... Although all of us play the hero, never-the-less we are very sorry, because we did not know in the first place that the late Franz Ferdinand was the father of a family. We are deeply touched by the words which he said to his late wife, "Sophie, don't die. Live for our children." Think what you will of us but we are not criminals. For myself and in the name of my comrades, I beg the children of the late Heir Apparent to forgive us. Render whatever verdict you like. We are not evildoers. We are honest people, honorable, idealistic. We wanted to do something good. We loved our people. We will die for our ideals.

Father Puntigam believed Cabrinovic. He wrote the Hohenberg children and asked them to follow Christ's example by writing a letter of forgiveness to the Serb terrorist. Princess Sophie read and reread the priest's letter many times. She spoke with her Aunt Henrietta, Uncle Thun, and her Habsburg grandmother. At one point Jesuit lawyers were consulted because Thun feared any response from the children might be used by Cabrinovic to launch a legal appeal for mercy. Her guardians allowed Sophie to decide for herself whether or not to respond. She wrote the letter and asked her brothers to also sign it. Maximilian did. Ernst refused.

Years later the memory of the letter continued to bring a spark of lightness to that dark time in her life. She never regretted her decision, believing it was the first time she felt alive following the assassination. Puntigam's Jesuit superiors ordered him not to deliver the letter, but he did. He wrote Sophie that he talked his way past the prison guards, entered Cabrinovic's cell, and read the letter aloud to him. Cabrinovic sobbed when he heard its contents and confessed he was ready to face any punishment because the letter had saved his soul.

Despite writing lengthy letters to people Adolf Hitler considered friends in Linz, Vienna, and Munich, he never received a single response during four years of war. A soldier who served with him wrote, "Every man had gotten letters or parcels from home. Everyone, that is, except Hitler. Somehow Hitler never got even a letter!" That winter Hitler wrote to a Munich acquaintance and revealed his thoughts, feelings, and desires that Germany would be cleansed by the war. "Those of us who are lucky enough to see their homeland again will find it a pure place, less riddled with foreign influences, so that the daily sacrifices and sufferings of hundreds of thousands of us and the torrent of blood that keeps flowing here day after day against an international world of enemies, will not only smash Germany's foes outside but that our inner internationalism, too, will collapse. This would be worth much more than any territorial gains." As the war stretched into its second summer, even Hitler found himself worn down by the blood, mud, and fighting as he wrote to his Munich landlady, "The enthusiasm gradually cooled and the exuberant joy was stifled by mortal fear. The time came when every man had to struggle between the instinct for self-preservation and the admonitions of duty."

On July 7, 1916, an article in the *New York Times* that was carried by other American newspapers reported, BOYS IN AUSTRIA PRAYING FOR PEACE. SON OF MURDERED ARCHDUKE FORMS A LEAGUE WHICH DRAWS 14,000 MEMBERS. The story read:

> A Vienna dispatch says that Prince Maximilian Hohenberg, son of the murdered Archduke Franz Ferdinand heir to the Austrian throne had founded the "Youth Association of Prayer for a Speedy and Favorable Peace." The Association already has 14,000 members.... As Prince Maximilian is only 14-year-old; he must have had a good deal of help, presumably from high official circles, in the accomplishment of a task so large. The organization, or the announcement of its existence, has therefore considerable significance of Austrian sentiment.... The significance, however, is confirmatory of what has already been known, rather than a revelation that the Austrians are tired of the conflict in which they have suffered so much.

With the exception of formal birthday greetings to the Emperor, the Hohenberg children had no contact with "high official circles" at the Habsburg court. The *un*official circle behind the league seemed to have been Archduchess Maria-Theresa, Archduke Karl, and Archduchess Zita. Maria-Theresa's supervision of nurses and caring for the wounded in Vienna's hospitals turned her against the war. Karl and Zita were equally horrified and sickened by the casualties and carnage caused by Army Chief of Staff Hötzendorf's battlefield blunders.

The future Emperor, Empress, and Habsburg grandmother they shared with the Hohenberg orphans wanted Austria's desire for peace known. Maria-Theresa decided newspapers in a large neutral country like the United States could best convey that message. It was her decision Franz Ferdinand's oldest son was the perfect messenger. Like

Emperor Franz Joseph's four previous heirs, Karl was frustratingly excluded from government and military decisions inside of Austria. On November 16, 1916, that abruptly changed.

After sixty-seven years on the throne, his Imperial and Royal Majesty Franz Joseph died at Schönbrunn Palace, the same palace where he had been born eighty-seven years earlier. In many ways, he had never left its suffocating walls.

Karl Habsburg then wasted no time in earning the title the "Peace Emperor." His first proclamation read, "I shall do everything in my power to end the horrors and sacrifices of war at the earliest possible moment, and to restore the blessings of peace as soon as honor, the interests of our allies, and the cooperation of our enemies permit." To the Hohenberg children and millions of others, peace suddenly seemed possible. The twenty-nine-year-old Emperor recalled many of Franz Ferdinand's scattered advisors back to Vienna. The new Prime Minister and new Foreign Secretary had both been members of the late Archduke's inner circle at Belvedere.

Much to the disgust of Austria's war party and to Adolf Hitler, Field Marshal Conrad von Hötzendorf was relieved of his command. Despite his repeated military blunders and the resultant slaughter, Hitler later claimed Hötzendorf "the most intelligent commander of the first World War." Karl sent his new Foreign Secretary to meet the Kaiser with a pledge and a question: "We shall hold out to the last until the collapse of the monarchy, but tell me, what is the advantage in that?" In Berlin, Adolf Hitler had been taken to a Red Cross Hospital to recover from a wound in his thigh. He was stunned by what he found there. "Dire misery everywhere" and "a few wretched scoundrels agitating for peace." To Hitler, Karl was one such scoundrel.

Austria's Peace Emperor did not forget Franz Ferdinand's children. He granted Maximilian the hereditary title Duke of Hohenberg. It was the title Franz Ferdinand had wanted and hoped for his son. He and Zita also became the royal sponsors of Father Puntigam's plans to build a Church of Atonement in Sarajevo dedicated to Franz Ferdinand and his wife, and co-sponsored a youth home to be built in the city named for the Duchess of Hohenberg. Directly across from the assassination site, crews were building an impressive monument as a memorial to the slain couple in time for the third anniversary of their deaths. Puntigam invited the three Hohenberg children to the dedication on June 28, 1917. Sophie thanked him, but declined for herself and her brothers.

Archduchess Maria-Theresa continued to work to ensure the future of her stepson's royal orphans. She wrote the German Emperor reminding him of an offer he once made to Franz Ferdinand. Wilhelm suggested the Archduke's oldest son, Maximilian, might be the ideal candidate to become Duke of the long-disputed territory of Lorraine. Franz Ferdinand had rejected the offer, but his stepmother thought an independent Lorraine ruled by Maximilian might bring a peaceful solution to a region fought over for centuries by both France and Germany. Wilhelm wrote Maria-Theresa that he agreed but felt the time not right for peace negotiations. In fact, relations between Austria and its German ally were about to get much worse.

In 1917, the United States entered the war due in part to Germany's unrestricted submarine warfare, a policy Emperor Karl and Zita had vehemently opposed. But the German Emperor was no longer listening to his Austrian allies. As Franz Ferdinand had feared, the Kaiser became a hostage to his generals. Karl personally appealed to Wilhelm II to seek peace. "We are fighting against a new enemy... international revolution, which finds its strongest ally in general starvation. I beseech you to not overlook this portentous aspect of the matter and to reflect that a quick finish to the war, even at the cost of heavy sacrifice, gives us a chance of confronting upheaval with success." Convinced by his generals that victory was just one battle away, Wilhelm rejected Karl's plea.

Another of Franz Ferdinand's predictions turned prophetic. The war he feared brought revolutions. Czar Nicholas II abdicated the Russian throne in 1917, but the abdication saved neither him nor his family. His Imperial Majesty, Emperor and Autocrat of all the Russians, his wife, and five children were brutally assassinated by the revolutionary government. The deaths personally touched and frightened the Hohenberg children. Their father had known and personally liked the Czar and Czarina. Nicholas's youngest daughter, Anastasia, was Sophie's age. His murdered son Alexis was the same age as Maximilian.

Political unrest and revolutions did not stop in Russia. On October 28, 1918, thirty miles from Konopiste, the Czech national assembly declared independence from the Austro-Hungarian Empire. Thousands of Czechs marched in Prague to celebrate the event in Wenceslaus Square. Habsburg portraits, flags, banners, and insignias were torn down, smashed, or burned. Three days later, Red Guard soldiers in Budapest broke into the home of the Hungarian Prime Minister. He was assassinated in front of his family. The Habsburgs' multinational empire imploded.

Otto von Bismarck, Germany's greatest statesman, had once declared, "The continued stability of Austria-Hungary is indispensable for Europe's equilibrium." In the light of two world wars, the racism and ethnic cleansing unleashed by Hitler, and the subsequent subjugation of central and eastern Europe by communism for half a century, Winston Churchill concluded that Bismarck had been right.

In the closing days of the war, Serbian troops finally captured Sarajevo. After four years of fighting, a self-appointed local spokesman welcomed the warriors to the embattled city in the names of the assassins of Franz Ferdinand. The soldiers found a huge pile of bricks and construction materials for Father Puntigam's planned Church of Atonement and nearby Youth Home. Nine hundred and forty thousand Kronen (eight million dollars in today's money) had been raised to build the monuments. No construction had begun. The elaborate granite monument in Sarajevo recently dedicated to the assassinated Archduke and Duchess was promptly torn down. The lives of the Hohenberg children, not bricks and mortar, would be their memorials to their parents in the difficult years ahead.

Five days after Sarajevo fell, Germany surrendered. On November 11, 1918, an armistice was signed. It was the birthday of former Army Chief of Staff Conrad von Hötzendorf. He lost two sons in the war and saw the Empire he served destroyed; but he retired to the Austrian resort town of Klagenfurt with his former mistress as his bride. As he had hoped, the war had allowed him to marry Gina von Reininghaus. Her ex-husband kept custody of their six children.

Striking workers and disillusioned soldiers filled the streets of Berlin and Vienna. Kaiser Wilhelm II and his Crown Prince abdicated and fled to neutral Holland. Emperor Karl refused to abdicate but signed a document reading, "I renounce all participation in the affairs of state." For the first time in two thousand years, no emperor sat on a European throne. The Hohenberg orphans and their guardians found themselves isolated and alone. In his final public proclamation, the last Habsburg emperor ended his statement with the words, "Only an inner peace can heal the wounds of this war." There was no "inner peace" at Konopiste, or for Adolf Hitler, temporally blinded by a poison gas attack. Shortly before his injury, Hitler had been awarded the Iron Cross First Class by Hugo Guttmann, his Jewish battalion commander. The citation certifying him as a genuine war hero read, "For personal cold-blooded bravery and continuous readiness to sacrifice himself." He proudly wore the decoration the rest of his life. Hitler learned of Germany's unconditional surrender while recovering from the gas attack in a military hospital. He was so stunned by the news that his temporary blindness returned. As he struggled to regain his sight and comprehend the German defeat, he conjured up Jews and Marxists as interchangeable villains responsible for "the greatest villainy of the century." He wrote:

> Miserable and degenerate criminals! Kaiser Wilhelm II was the first German emperor to hold out a hand to the leaders of Marxism without suspecting that scoundrels have no honor. While they still held his imperial hand in theirs, their other hand was reaching for the dagger. There is no making pacts with Jews.

Years later, Hitler wrote this was the epiphany that convinced him to enter politics. His admiration for the Kaiser vanished, his revulsion toward Marxism was reinforced, and his hatred for Jews solidified. Hitler declared, "The example of William II shows how one bad monarch can destroy a dynasty. In the same way, those who wish to play their parts in history must understand that one single bad generation can cause the ruin of a whole people."

Like Archduke Franz Ferdinand, Adolf Hitler had a gift for prophecy.

CHAPTER TEN
EXILES

"In life, things turn out differently, quite differently, from what one wishes." —ARCHDUKE FRANZ FERDINAND

"I was born... in a great and mighty empire, in the monarchy of the Habsburgs. But do not look for it on a map; it has been swept away without a trace." —STEFAN ZWEIG

Newspapers in Prague and across the newly created nation of Czechoslovakia looked for villains and scapegoats to blame for the deaths, destruction, and defeat of the war. The assassinated "Austrian" Archduke and his Czech-born wife became popular targets. Headlines and articles, cartoons, and editorials denounced the dead couple for their wealth, their aristocratic background, and their friendship with the exiled German Emperor. No one came to their defense.

Czechoslovakia's new leaders moved quickly to assess the future role of the nation's large estates and the aristocrats who owned them. Konopiste was put under the "protective care" of the government. Bureaucrats soon arrived to inventory its assets. Every farm animal and piece of agricultural equipment, every piece of furniture, oil painting, work of art, and family pets were counted and catalogued. State police and detectives were sent to Konopiste to search for the secret soundproof room where Franz Ferdinand and the German Emperor had planned the war. No such room was ever found.

For the three adolescent Hohenbergs, the uncertainty in their lives since the death of their parents continued. Four years after their father's death, the Archduke's will was finally probated, making sixteen-year-old Maximilian Konopiste's legal owner. Thirteen-year-old Ernst inherited Chlumetz. Seventeen-year-old Sophie was to receive an annual income from both estates. Since she was expected to marry and live in the home of her future husband, she received no property. Local courts and international treaties brought them no peace.

There were days and nights when telephone lines no longer worked, cutting them off from neighbors, friends, and relatives. Game wardens reported that trespassers were becoming bolder with each passing day. Count Thun and the owners of all the large estates were struggling with gangs of pillaging locals and returning soldiers armed with weapons and revolutionary propaganda against landlords and aristocrats.

That March of 1919, death threats drove Emperor Karl and his family into Swiss exile. Aunt Henrietta assured her three wards all would be well. But rumors of revolution and disorder, homes being looted, and lives threatened seemed everywhere. No one knew if marauders were coming to drive the owners off the large estates or kill them. Many estate managers reported that their field workers and house servants had fled. At Konopiste, Franz Janaczek and nearly the entire Konopiste staff remained in loyal service to the orphans.

In mid-April a distant cousin whose father had been a hunting partner of Franz Ferdinand visited Konopiste. Count Friedrich von Nostitz-Rieneck was a handsome twenty-six-year-old war hero. Family and friends called him Fritz. He told Sophie, Maximilian, and Ernst that since his return from the front he could not stop thinking about them. He wanted to be sure they were safe. They appreciated his thoughtfulness, especially Sophie. The visit provided her, her brothers, and their aunt comfort and companionship.

Sophie had kept a diary since she was a young girl, but the only page she ever read and reread from those unhappy days was the page on which she wrote about the Count's welcome arrival. She had him sign the guest book her parents kept at the castle for distinguished guests. None of them knew it at the time, but Fritz von Nostitz-Rieneck would be the last guest they would ever host at Konopiste.

During his visit, Czech police arrived at the castle informing everyone within it they were no longer safe. The country's newly elected president, Tomas Masaryk, ordered them to leave at once until their safety could be guaranteed. Despite all that was happening around them, the order to leave Konopiste came as a shock. Assurances were given that they would be able to return as soon as the countryside could be cleared of armed looters.

Sophie never told her younger brothers at the time, but the fate of the Czar and his family in the Russian revolution rushed through her mind. Horror stories of Russian aristocrats being hunted down and murdered continued to be reported in the newspapers. She was careful to show no emotion or display any fear in front of their Czech "protectors."

Each of the Hohenberg orphans was allowed to pack one small suitcase with a change of clothes and their school books. No mementos, personal possessions, family photographs, or photo albums could be taken. The children and Aunt Henrietta carefully packed under the watchful gaze of their evictors. When one of the police officers briefly looked away, Sophie slipped her diary into her bag. Maximilian tried to return to his room to get a photo of their parents but was turned back.

They were assured everything at Konopiste and Chlumetz would be guarded by the Czech government so that nothing could be stolen, damaged, or destroyed by looters. As they left the castle, it became clear this was no ordinary evacuation. The police searched their bags. Sophie's diary was found, but she was allowed to keep it.

Fritz Nostitz-Rieneck traveled with them until they safely reached the home of their Uncle Thun. Konopiste, the castle their father had saved and lovingly restored, had become government property. Each of the children would live in many places during their lives, but in their minds, Konopiste remained their true home. Following a brief stay with Thun relatives, they traveled to Vienna to visit their Habsburg grandmother, Archduchess Maria-Theresa. They then made their way to Artstetten where they waited for the call to return to Konopiste that never came.

Franz Ferdinand had renovated and modernized Artstetten, capping its seven distinctive towers with onion domes he had seen on Eastern Orthodox cathedrals. The castle's most famous neighbor to the east was the thousand-year-old Melk Benedictine Abbey. To the west was their parents' favorite place of worship, the pilgrimage shrine of Maria Taferl. Artstetten's own large chapel served as the local village church. Underneath its sanctuary rested the tombs of their mother and father.

In the nearby village square stood a memorial to local soldiers killed in World War I. Like thousands of other stone and wooden monuments in Austria, and around the world, the names of the fallen were preserved there. The first two names on Artstetten's monument were Archduke Franz Ferdinand and the Duchess of Hohenberg. The castle was large and comfortable, but it contained none of the happy memories of Konopiste.

The year and a half following the armistice was a time of disillusionment across Europe. Adolf Hitler remained in what was left of the German army. He had no other home, no other place to develop his political skills. After guarding Russian prisoners of war and the Munich rail station, he was selected for training in political agitation and public speaking. He excelled in both. Hitler was then ordered to spy on revolutionary activities in and out of the army.

Hitler was sent to a beer hall in Munich to attend a meeting of the tiny German Workers' Party. He was told to be as inconspicuous as possible, dress as a civilian, take note of any revolutionary propaganda, and quietly disappear. He disobeyed orders. A speaker advocating the union of German Bavaria with Austria enraged him. Hitler verbally attacked, mocked, screamed at, and belittled the speaker, a highly educated professor, until he silenced him. He attended other party meetings including one at Munich's much larger Hofbräuhaus. There he made an impassioned speech to an attentive audience of more than one hundred listeners. A secret police report on the event took special notice of "his extraordinary talent as an orator."

The public response to his speech was a revelation to Hitler. He wrote, "I could speak! After thirty minutes the people in the small room were electrified and the enthusiasm was first expressed by the fact that my appeal to the self-sacrifice of those present led to the donation of three hundred Marks." Three days later, he officially joined the small party. Hitler had found a political outlet for his anger, racism, and rhetorical skills. He later wrote, "From 1919 to 1923, I thought of nothing else but revolution."

Adolf Hitler believed the party could be used to revitalize and unite Germany against its political and military enemies. It soon changed its name to the National Socialist German Workers Party with Hitler himself as its principal spokesman. On February 24, 1920, Hitler publicly presented its new platform at Munich's Hofbräuhaus. Two thousand enthusiastic listeners cheered his performance. Anyone from his Vienna years would have recognized his themes. But he seemed transformed when speaking about a united Germany and channeling his audience's hidden fears, prejudices, and aspirations. Hitler appealed to his listeners to join him in "a greater Germany… only people of German blood may be citizens of the state… no Jews belong to the nation… foreign nationals (non-citizens) must be deported from the Reich…. All non-German immigration must be prevented."

Hitler made no attempt to hide his anti-Semitism. Despite his having Jewish friends at Vienna's Men's Hostel, a commanding officer who awarded him the Iron Cross, and a Jewish doctor who cared for his mother, he labeled Jews "a racial tuberculosis among nations." His rabid anti-Semitism found an appreciative audience. In March, he resigned from the army to work full-time for what popularly became known as the Nazi Party. At that time, almost no one in Germany, and certainly no one in England, had heard of Adolf Hitler.

But they did know about Franz Ferdinand's royal orphans.

When word of their expulsion from Konopiste reached England's Duke of Portland, he took up their cause. The Duke initially believed the eviction to be a bureaucratic mistake, but also feared it might be an act of blind revenge against the Habsburgs. Portland wrote a letter to President Masaryk of Czechoslovakia that read, "The definite sequestration of the house and estate of Konopiste was illegal, in view of the Archduke's marriage being morganatic." The president personally responded, "The property in question has been seized in order to prevent damage being done by people residing in the neighborhood… as soon as this danger has subsided, the children of the Archduke will be able to remain in possession of the house and its contents… the remainder of the estate will be purchased by the government for the benefit of the children."

Masaryk's letter offered the orphans uncertain hope, but something positive emerged from the Hohenberg's final days at Konopiste. Sophie and Fritz Nostitz-Rieneck began corresponding. Through their letter writing, they fell in love.

A year and a half after their expulsion, Sophie, Max, and Ernst returned to Czechoslovakia, but not to their home. In 1920, they traveled to their Uncle Thun's estate at Kwassitz for Sophie's wedding to Fritz. She and her husband would have a large home in Prague, and country homes and estates. Seventeen-year-old Maximilian and sixteen-year-old Ernst were allowed to attend the ceremony, but ordered to immediately leave the country following the reception. The nineteen-year-old bride would remain in Czechoslovakia to begin her new married life.

Prior to her wedding, Sophie and her Aunt Henrietta were permitted to visit Konopiste hoping she might find something of her mother's to wear on her wedding day. The return was painful. Former servants who continued to care for the estate greeted them warmly, but surly guards followed them everywhere. Sophie was not permitted to touch anything that had belonged to her parents. Family treasures were no longer where they had been left. Some had vanished. Despite being carefully watched, scribbled notes and whispers from the family's former cook told Sophie that President Masaryk's family had used the house as a department store. His American-born wife walked out wearing the Duchess of Hohenberg's winter fur coat. His daughter took Sophie's saddle and riding equipment. They had been the last gifts given to her by her parents. Franz Ferdinand's only daughter left her childhood home with a pair of her own shoes and some underwear, but nothing that had been her mother's.

The three Hohenbergs had never been apart since their births. Sophie's marriage meant that now miles, national boundaries, and government bureaucrats separated them. She could visit her brothers at Artstetten, but a hostile Czech government made visits by them to Czechoslovakia difficult. Her wedding day was touched by sadness.

Sophie never liked her wedding photos. The only person smiling in them was Count Thun. Pictures from that day reveal Ernst had inherited the wavy blond hair of his Habsburg cousins and had grown tall and handsome. He was a wiry young man but looked angry and unhappy. Maximilian, with dark hair and features favoring their mother, looked dazed. Sophie, now shorter than her younger brothers, had blossomed into a stately dark-haired beauty, but her face showed no joy.

Weeks before Sophie Hohenberg's wedding, Prince Joachim of Prussia—the youngest son of the exiled German Emperor—committed suicide. It was whispered that he was unable to face the uncertainty of the future. The despondent Prince was not alone. No one in Europe knew what the future held. Economic uncertainty and political chaos seemed everywhere.

Of Archduke Franz Ferdinand's three children, only his daughter had dreams that seemed briefly to come true. She married a man she loved who shared her deep religious faith, values, and interests. They settled down in the land, if not the country, of their births. Her husband's large estates northwest of Prague provided them the leisurely life of country squires. Fritz could hunt on lands his aristocratic family had owned for centuries and he and his bride happily embraced nature and the athletic life they enjoyed.

Their large baroque mansion in the heart of Prague held 15,000 rare books, including original manuscripts by Nicholas Copernicus. Its location in the shadow of Prague Castle on Maltese Square gave them ready access to the city's culture, theatres, and music. Fritz's family had been the musical patrons of Chopin and Mozart. They had built the city's opera house where the famous opera *Don Giovanni* premiered. In time, three sons and a daughter completed their family circle.

If Sophie Hohenberg's life had been orchestrated as one of the symphonies she loved, her childhood might have played to an allegro tranquillo tempo: quick, bright, lively, but peaceful. The second movement, the sleepwalking years after Sarajevo, might have been a slow, almost lethargic, adagio. Her years as a young wife and mother, the main allegro or scherzo movement, would have been swift paced and joyful but it would have had an unexpected coda, an unforeseen, abrupt end.

In 1921, the Czech government passed a law seizing the country's large estates, redistributing the land, and striping aristocrats of their titles. Nearly everyone continued calling the nobility by their ancient titles, but the government strictly enforced their land confiscation policy. Sophie and Fritz kept their country homes at Falkenau and Heinrichgrun, but the estates around them vanished with the stroke of a pen.

Maximilian and Ernst Hohenberg were not as fortunate. Konopiste and Chlumetz, and all the buildings and land surrounding them, were confiscated. Nothing was left for them in Czechoslovakia but their memories. Despite earlier pledges and written assurances to the Duke of Portland, President Masaryk kept none of his promises.

Masaryk cited a clause in the Treaty of St. Germain permitting the seizure of "all property of the crown, and the private property of members of the former royal family of Austria-Hungary." Count Thun immediately filed a lawsuit to fight the seizures of the Hohenberg properties. He argued the Archduke's children had never legally been recognized as members of the royal family by their Habsburg relatives or the state.

The Renunciation Oath signed in 1900 separated Franz Ferdinand's unborn children from the Imperial House. Following the Archduke's 1914 assassination, his sons became the owners of Konopiste and Chlumetz, properties he had bought with his own funds, or had inherited from his Este cousins. That inheritance was confirmed by Prague courts in 1916 two years prior to the signing of the Treaty of St. Germain, three years before Sophie and her brothers were expelled from their home, and four years before the treaty was legally enforceable.

When the Czechoslovakian government seized the "Habsburg" properties of his Hohenberg children, Franz Ferdinand was dead eight years. After losing his initial suit in Czech courts, Count Thun took his case to the Allied Reparations Committee in The Hague. The Committee declared it had no authority to interpret the treaty that ended the war. Thun continued filing lawsuits on Max and Ernst's behalf, but neither property nor the estates surrounding them were returned. They were never compensated for their seizure. Sophie's brothers retained their land holdings in Austria. But the loss of Konopiste and Chlumetz stole the future they had always imagined they would have managing their estates and raising families in the Bohemian countryside of their youth.

Franz Ferdinand's sons did not lack for options, opportunities, or temptations. They were young, handsome, famous, unmarried princes with a storied history, and few responsibilities. Current and former royalty filled newspaper headlines with scandalous escapades, romances, marriages, divorces, illegitimate children, and political misadventures. Maximilian and Ernst Hohenberg refused to join their ranks.

Ernst, the youngest Hohenberg, struggled to complete his studies. Only when he took a course in forestry and agriculture did he finally find himself. Following his graduation, he settled in the Austrian countryside north of Graz. There in the isolated beauty of Styria, as the steward of the land given his family through the intervention of Emperor Karl, he finally began to heal from the wounds of Sarajevo.

Maximilian took a different path. As he approached his twentieth birthday, he held his first political meeting at a small Austrian inn. In carefully measured words he announced plans to lead a campaign to restore his nation's constitutional monarchy and recall his cousin Emperor Karl to the vacant Habsburg throne. The task would not be easy. The punitive Austrian constitution written after the war seized all Habsburg assets, and outlawed Emperor Karl and his descendants from returning to their homeland. Claims to the throne, political involvement, and all former palaces, farms, and estates had to be renounced. The meeting called by Maximilian Hohenberg was a quiet, low-key affair, very different from the bombastic political meetings Adolf Hitler was holding at Munich's Hofbräuhaus. Only twenty-six people attended. Ernst was one of them, but it put the Hohenbergs on a collision course with Adolf Hitler.

CHAPTER ELEVEN
THE MOST GOLDEN TONGUED
OF DEMAGOGUES

"All that is not Race is dross!"   —ADOLF HITLER

"Dictators are very popular these days, and we may want one in
England before long."   —EDWARD, PRINCE OF WALES

"One must judge a public speech not by the sense it makes to
scientists who read it the next day, but by the effect that it has
on the masses."   —ADOLF HITLER

Threats of violence and civil war, and a march on Rome by thousands
of his Fascist supporters, resulted in thirty-nine-year-old Benito Mussolini being appointed prime minister of Italy in 1922. One year later,
Adolf Hitler and two thousand of his followers attempted a similar
march in Munich. It failed and he was arrested for treason.

Hitler brilliantly used his trial to promote himself as a patriot,
not a traitor. His putsch was portrayed as an attempt to rescue Germany from communists and the country's real traitors who stabbed
the country in the back, losing the war so they could seize power. He
famously exclaimed, "There is no such thing as high treason against
those who betrayed the country in 1918." His defense was dazzlingly
bold and deceptive. In effect, he put Germany's postwar government
on trial.

After serving 264 days of a five-year sentence, Hitler left prison more famous, and with more support, than when he entered. On the day of his release, Munich's Chamber of Commerce, looking for an ally to protect their profit margins, gifted him with a new Mercedes automobile. Hitler would spend the next decade establishing the Nazi Party as the major political force to be reckoned with in Germany. He envisioned a German Reich that was racially pure and homogenous, the exact opposite of the tolerant, inclusive, multinational Habsburg Empire he loathed. Hitler was not the only political activist seeking change. Dissidents in Czechoslovakia campaigned to return the ancient kingdom of Bohemia to its monarchial roots. One name suggested as a possible future king was Prince Maximilian Hohenberg. His handsome features and charming manner reflected his princely heritage, but he refused to flaunt his position, wealth, or intelligence. Like his mother, he was a soft-spoken, meticulous dresser, never a hair out of place. He stood erect, always on time, always the perfect gentleman. The oldest son of Archduke Franz Ferdinand and the Duchess of Hohenberg had all the natural instincts of a gifted diplomat, a successful lawyer, and a master chess player. His warm brown eyes were friendly, but his strong face revealed neither his thoughts nor his true feelings, qualities that would serve him well in the tumultuous days ahead. Max quickly and diplomatically disavowed any connections or ambitions with Czech politics; but suspicions of political ambitions made it even more difficult for the Hohenberg brothers to visit their sister in Prague.

Sophie Nostitz-Rieneck remained close with her brothers through letter writing, phone calls, and visits to Austria. The happiness of Sophie's marriage may have motivated Archduchess Maria-Theresa, their Habsburg grandmother, to actively assume the role of family matchmaker. Ernst gently refused her overtures. It had taken years of living in the rugged solitude of Styria's mountains, forests, and lakes to bring peace to his restless soul. Once he emerged from his Styrian cocoon, his shy personality and boyish good looks attracted the company of strong, beautiful women who wanted to take care of him. Ernst thoroughly enjoyed their attention but was in no hurry to exchange the joys of bachelorhood for domestic bliss.

Maria-Theresa redoubled her efforts to find a suitable marriage partner for Maximilian. She found a willing ally in her childhood friend Princess Marie Lobkowicz Waldburg-Wolfegg. Two years of orchestrated meetings between the Archduchess's grandson and the Princess's granddaughter brought the desired result. Weeks after he earned a law degree at the University of Graz, a Viennese newspaper reported on July 2, 1926, "Dr. Maximilian von Hohenberg, the eldest son of Archduke Franz Ferdinand of Austria, who was assassinated at Sarajevo in June of 1914, became engaged today to Countess Elisabeth Waldburg-Wolfegg."

There was no escaping Sarajevo. Even in Maximilian's wedding announcement, the assassination of his father was prominently featured.

And although Elisabeth Waldburg-Wolfegg descended from her own ancient, princely family, her ancestral home in southern Germany, a twelfth-century medieval castle fortress, could not protect them from the violence of the twentieth century. Two of her brothers had been killed in the First World War. Following their marriage, Dr. Hohenberg and his wife would be addressed in Austria as the Duke and Duchess of Hohenberg, but mention of Sarajevo usually quickly followed.

On November 16, 1926, Max and Elisabeth's wedding provided the Hohenbergs the opportunity for a family reunion. Sophie and Fritz Nostitz-Rieneck traveled to Germany for the ceremony. Ernst served as his twenty-four-year-old brother's best man. Maximilian's marriage to his twenty-two-year-old bride supplied his sister with wonderful memories, a sister-in-law she loved, and wedding photographs she could finally enjoy.

Maximilian chose Lequieto, a small fishing village on the northeastern coast of Spain, for their honeymoon. It was the home of the exiled, penniless, widowed thirty-year-old former Empress Zita.

Twice in 1921, Emperor Karl had tried to restore the monarchy in Hungary. Twice his efforts failed. He and Zita were exiled two thousand miles from their homeland off the coast of Africa on the rocky Atlantic island of Madeira. Within months, pneumonia, exhaustion, and a broken heart claimed the Emperor's life. He was thirty-eight years old. His tragic life and death seemed to encapsulate the uncertainty of life and death in the twentieth century. It also abruptly ended any attempt by Max to restore Karl to the throne.

But Karl and Zita had eight children, five of them boys. There was more than a whiff of curiosity during the visit to Lequieto about the possibility of one of Max's male cousins as a future monarch. In the final months of Karl's reign, Austria's last Habsburg Emperor had proposed federalizing the multinational Austro-Hungarian Empire along the lines that Max's father had proposed, but it was too late. Millions of lost lives, ethnic rivalries, and the rising tide of nationalism ended any hopes of uniting the peoples of central Europe. Prior to his premature death, Karl worried that Austria and central Europe would be caught in a power vacuum Germany and Russia would fill by force. He drafted a proposal for a neutral Danubian Federation to unite, protect, and safeguard its people.

In the year of his marriage, Maximilian wanted to connect with someone who shared the vision of his father. His visit with the Emperor's widow and her oldest son, Otto, fulfilled that need. It also gave his life a new sense of purpose.

———

In 1929, the New York stock market crashed, followed by the collapse in Vienna of the Rothschild's Creditanstalt Bank. The depression that followed destabilized Europe's political and economic landscape. Everyone was impacted. Artstetten's Austrian neighbor, the Benedictine Melk Abbey, sold its Gutenberg Bible from the year 1455 to Yale University. In Vienna, apartments in Franz Joseph's vacant Schönbrunn

Palace were rented to pay for its upkeep. A suite of rooms for a family of five was advertised for seven dollars a month. There were few takers.

Members of the former royal houses were not immune to the financial disaster. Archduchess Maria-Theresa quietly attempted to sell her family jewels. The most famous was Napoleon's 263-carat diamond necklace given to his second wife, Empress Marie Louise Habsburg, on the birth of their son. The appraised value was $450,000. It was offered for sale in New York for $100,000 and sold for $60,000. Maria-Theresa's destitute grandnephew, Leopold Habsburg, and two partners negotiated the deal—claiming $53,730 in expenses. The Hohenberg's grandmother demanded the necklace be returned, and had her grandnephew, a Habsburg Archduke, arrested and jailed for fraud.

Desperate times clouded the judgment of many people. Countries across Europe searched for a leader, a savior, a dictator to rescue them from their economic and political woes. Hitler believed he was that man. He spoke only German, but nevertheless was an extraordinary linguist, a chameleon able to articulate the unspoken emotional language of his listeners. His oratorical talent allowed him to forge a political coalition that Vienna's mayor Karl Lueger might have envied.

Wealthy industrialists secretly financed Hitler's rise to power after 1924. In return he quietly promised to destroy the country's burgeoning Communist Party, smash the nation's labor unions, and provide his benefactors unparalleled profits. The unemployed were assured full employment, and the forgotten man—respect. Hitler promised the military recruits, rearmament, and a restoration of power and prestige. Aristocrats heard in his siren call the possibility of themselves and the German Imperial Court becoming masters of European society. Veterans of the lost war saw him as one of their own.

But no single group rallied to Hitler more than the young. To them, his dazzling speeches promised a new generation of youthful, vigorous, charismatic leadership. Two-thirds of Hitler's followers were under the age of forty.

Adolf Hitler had financial support and hundreds of thousands of followers, but he craved legitimacy and political power to make his vision a reality. It was handed to him by the country's respected president, Paul von Hindenburg, the popular former Chief of the German General Staff in the war. In 1933, in an effort to recognize Hitler's growing popularity, the eighty-six-year-old appointed him Reich Chancellor. Only Hindenburg held more power in the government. Germany's new forty-three-year-old Chancellor promised to pursue a policy of peace, "despite our love of the army." Many doubted his words.

General Erich Ludendorff, Hitler's ally a decade earlier in his failed putsch attempt, denounced Hindenburg for delivering "our holy Fatherland to one of the greatest demagogues of all times. I solemnly prophesize this accursed man will bring our Reich into the abyss and cause our nation unimaginable suffering." He ended his prophetic warning with the words, "For this act you will be cursed in your grave by future generations." Hitler's own first message as Reich Chancellor sent "best wishes" to the "brotherly German people of Austria." His mind, heart, and plans were never far from Austria.

In order "to overcome economic catastrophe" and root out "high treason and treachery," Hitler quickly persuaded the Reichstag to pass the Enabling Bill, granting him dictatorial powers. Labor unions were banned and books by Jewish authors and other "enemies of the state" were publicly burned. Munich's law and order police chief, Heinrich Himmler, opened the country's first "concentration camp" dedicated exclusively to housing political prisoners. It was named Dachau for a nearby picturesque village, and quickly filled with labor, trade, and union leaders. Hitler wasted no time in turning his gaze to Austria. A tariff of one thousand Reichsmarks was placed on any German citizen traveling there. The tariff was designed to destroy Austria's thriving tourist industry. In a cynical nod of rendering to Caesar the things that were Caesars, Hitler wasted no time neutralizing Germany's politically powerful churches. On the anniversary of the Sarajevo assassination, June 28, 1933, independent Lutheran Churches across Germany were united into the newly christened "Protestant Reich Church." An ardent Nazi, Ludwig Müller became its presiding bishop. He carefully vetted Lutheran clergy to ensure they were "politically reliable," meaning they accepted the principle of "the superiority of the Aryan Race."

One month later, Vatican Secretary of State Eugenio Pacelli signed a concordant with Germany's Vice Chancellor, Franz von Papen. The Faustian bargain removed the Catholic Church from involvement in the country's politics or from speaking out on social justice issues. In return for the strict separation of church and state, spiritual, non-political matters were conceded to the Vatican. Within a year, von Papen, a charming German Catholic aristocrat unburdened by a moral compass, became Germany's Ambassador in Austria. His mission was to encourage Austrian Nazis to undermine the government there. Eugenio Pacelli's diplomatic skills earned him his own earthly reward. Five years later, he was elected Pope Pius XII.

Adolf Hitler understood the disappointments, fears, and dreams of the underclass. The impoverished had been his constant companions on Vienna's streets, in soup kitchens, and homeless shelters. They had dogged his footsteps in the trenches of World War I and during the bitter defeat that followed. He recognized their anxiety and dread, the unsaid prejudices of the marginalized. Once he entered politics, he boldly said aloud what many hid in their hearts. They rewarded Hitler by making him the most powerful man in perhaps the most cultured, literate, educated country on earth.

American journalist Dorothy Thompson interviewed Hitler and described him as "an agitator of genius. "She reported, "Hitler is the most golden tongued of demagogues. Don't bother about the fact that what he says, read the next day in cold news print is usually plain nonsense."

She warned her readers. "You must imagine the crowds he addresses: Little people. Weighted with a feeling of inferiority.... Patriotism is the cheapest form of self-exaltation. If one is in debt, if one has not made a success of life—still, says Hitler, one belongs to RACE.... 'All that is not Race is dross!' is one of his exclamations. He tells audiences, 'The Germans are a superior race and it is ordained that this superior race shall conquer the earth.'" Hitler portrayed himself as the powerful voice of the voiceless. His followers loved him for validating their hidden feelings. They loved him because he seemed to love, respect, and champion them.

Hitler also had a nearly mystical appeal to many aristocrats. Exiled German Emperor Wilhelm II and three of his sons all saw Hitler as their ally in reclaiming the vacant throne for themselves. Crown Prince Wilhelm hosted Hitler in his home, and in 1930 his younger brothers Prince August Wilhelm and Prince Oskar openly joined the Nazi Party. Prince August introduced Hitler to enthusiastic crowds, and behind closed doors to wealthy monarchists. One-third of Germany's ancient nobility openly joined the Nazi Party. Others supported him through their silence.

Yet to Hitler's great frustration and annoyance, Otto Habsburg in exile and Maximilian and Ernst Hohenberg in Austria loudly spoke out against him, condemning his Nazi Party, exposing and denouncing the abhorrent racism he sought to legitimize.

Archduke Franz Ferdinand had waited a quarter of a century to become Emperor, and died without achieving his goal. Hitler waited 599 days. When President Paul von Hindenburg died in August 1934, Germany fell into Hitler's waiting arms.

Economic turmoil and the rising fear of communist revolutions saw Portugal, Spain, Poland, Greece, and Rumania, like Italy and Germany, embrace dictatorships. Britain's Edward, Prince of Wales, told a German prince, "Dictators are very popular these days and we may want one in England before long." Joseph P. Kennedy, America's Ambassador to Great Britain, confided to President Roosevelt that the United States might need to assume, "under other names, the basic features of the Fascist state." To fight and defeat totalitarianism, Kennedy believed America might "have to adopt totalitarian methods." Roosevelt demurred.

George Messersmith, an American diplomat and former Pennsylvania schoolteacher stationed in Berlin, recognized what the Habsburgs, the Hohenbergs, and few others did. He wrote:

> I wish it were really possible to make our people at home understand how definitely the martial spirit is being developed in Germany. If this government remains in power for another year, and it carries on in the measure of this direction, it will go far toward making Germany a danger to world peace for years to come. With few exceptions, the men who are running the government are of a mentality that you and I cannot understand. Some of them are psychopathic cases and would definitely be receiving treatment elsewhere.

Messersmith soon became the United States Ambassador in Vienna. He had no illusions about Hitler's anti-Semitism or his designs on Austria. In 1925, Hitler had written in *Mein Kampf,* "In my earliest youth I came to the basic insight which has never left me, but only became more profound: that Germanism could be safeguarded only by the destruction of Austria."

Maximilian Hohenberg refused to dismiss Hitler's words as mere rhetoric, fantasy, or fiction. He believed Hitler had to be stopped and Otto Habsburg, the oldest son of Emperor Karl, was the only person able to stop him. With Otto's approval and himself as president, Maximilian helped organize and then lead a political alliance of Christian socialists, young idealists, conservative Catholics, clergy, former aristocrats, and Jews known as the "Iron Ring." Their goal was to offer Otto Habsburg to Austria as an alternative to Adolf Hitler. Ernst and Sophie quietly supported their brother's efforts.

When Otto reached the age of eighteen, the Austrian town council of Ampass voted to make the former Crown Prince an honorary citizen. Eighteen was the age Franz Joseph had become Austrian Emperor, Victoria became Queen of England, and Wilhelmina, perhaps contemporary Europe's most popular monarch, Queen of the Netherlands. Over the next three years, fifteen hundred Austrian towns declared themselves "Emperor Communities." As Hitler's shadow grew, the monarchist restorationist movement also grew. On September 28, 1933, one Austrian newspaper reported:

> Through Duke Max [von Hohenberg], son of the Crown Prince
> Franz Ferdinand who was assassinated at Sarajevo in 1914, the
> Archduke Otto [Habsburg pretender to the Austrian throne] has
> accepted honorary citizenship in the towns of Hain, Mamau and
> Ragelsdorf and have pledged allegiance to the Pretender, hoping
> that he will soon be sovereign.... Duke von Hohenberg presented
> the Mayors of the three towns with letters signed, "Otto in Exile"
> stating that the exile was doubly hard when the fatherland was heroically fighting for existence against malicious and unscrupulous
> attacks. Archduke Otto condemned the Nazi movement and added
> that he trusted the present regime would remove the remaining
> unjust laws of the revolutionary period against the Habsburgs. He
> trusted the day was not far distant when relying on God's help,
> and with a strong hand, he would lead the Homeland to a happy,
> certain, and great future.

Adolf Hitler had no intention of allowing Otto, or any other Habsburg, to claim the Austrian throne. In a candid conversation with the Yugoslavian minister, he revealed his outsized hatred of the Habsburgs. He told him his beloved mother was buried in Austrian soil. If he allowed Austria to again be ruled by that "degenerate dynasty," it would feel as if he was spitting on her grave.

He was determined to unite Germany and Austria under *his* leadership. *Mein Kampf* bluntly made that clear. The book was begun in a German prison cell following his failed putsch attempt, but he finished it in a small cabin in the Bavarian mountains surrounded on three sides by the Austrian Alps. Salzburg, only twelve miles away, could be seen in the distance. Profits from *Mein Kampf* later allowed Hitler to buy his own house there, but he quickly redesigned it to face Austria.

Over the years it was expanded, rebuilt, and remodeled many times, making it the most famous, and infamous, political retreat in the world. The house was officially called the Berghof, but journalists christened it Eagle's Nest because of its location above the clouds. The retreat's most celebrated feature were its floor-to-ceiling windows offering spectacular views of the surrounding forests, lakes, and mountains. Hitler, the frustrated artist and architect, positioned them toward his homeland. Leni Riefenstahl, Germany's best-known female film director, a personal favorite of Hitler, visited the Berghof twice. She was awestruck by its location and scenery. During her final visit before the war, Hitler told her:

> Look, that's Austria over there. Every day that I come up here, I gaze across and beg the Almighty to allow me to live until the day when Austria and Germany will be united in a single German Reich. That is the only reason I bought this house, because from here I can look at Germany *and* Austria.

CHAPTER TWELVE
IMPENDING HORRORS

"Restoration of Habsburgs within Year is Predicted"
— *NEW YORK TIMES* HEADLINE, October 28, 1934

"What will happen to Austria, will also happen to you.... You
too will be the victim. You too will be destroyed by the Nazis."
—MAXIMILIAN HOHENBERG TO BENITO MUSSOLINI

A David and Goliath struggle was about to take place in Europe. American ambassador George Messersmith could see it during his introduction to the small country of Austria and its even smaller Chancellor. They met at the conclusion of a cabinet meeting when he saw a tiny man "scurrying about emptying ashtrays." Dollfuss, four feet eleven inches tall, smiled shyly and said, "Well, you've caught the Chancellor cleaning up." The American and Austrian quickly became friends.

Engelbert Dollfuss was a confirmed monarchist determined to keep his country free from internal or external intimidation. When Austria's Nazi Party and local communists provoked violence, he declared martial law banning both from political activities. Along with most of his cabinet, Dollfuss believed the young Otto Habsburg might be Austria's best defense against the Nazis. In large and small ways, Dollfuss attempted to create nostalgia for a Habsburg restoration. The Habsburg hymn again became the national anthem, the Austrian army was outfitted in the old Imperial Guard uniforms. Veterans were encouraged to wear their war medals bearing images of Franz Joseph and Emperor Karl. Postcards of Otto Habsburg went on sale throughout the country and became immediate best sellers. *Time* magazine reported that Otto could end the divisions in Austrian politics by offering "a common figure to rally around... a more glamorous figure to draw impressionable youth from Adolf Hitler."

Austria, like its neighbor Germany and most of the industrialized world in 1930, found itself in desperate financial straits. One out of every three workers had lost their jobs. One in five family farms had been auctioned off to pay debts. Only the country's tourism industry provided a fragile lifeline, but Hitler's placement of a punitive tariff on German travelers to Austria threatened economic collapse there. Engelbert Dollfuss, Maximilian Hohenberg, and thousands of others hoped Otto Habsburg might rescue the country.

But more immediate help came from another prince.

Edward, His Royal Highness Prince of Wales, the handsome son of King George V and Queen Mary of England, was heir to the most respected, powerful monarchy on earth. In the 1930s, he was unquestionably the most popular royal of his generation, celebrated across Europe and around the world as a genuine Prince Charming. Edward's love of Austria's spectacular mountains, crystal-clear lakes, and fairy-tale cities made it his favorite holiday destination, bringing with him wealthy tourists from as far away as America. In the mid-1930s, he may have single-handedly saved Austria's tourist industry. When his American-born mistress Bessie Wallis Warfield Simpson and her cuckolded, compliant husband joined him there, the American press followed.

Gossips in Viennese coffeehouses and newspapers across the United States breathlessly reported the unholy trinity's every move. Only the British press provided a news blackout, explaining Edward's visit was "unofficial and devoted to pleasure." The irony was not lost on pundits. The activities of the world's most eligible royal bachelor

provided a pleasant diversion from troubling economic and political news, but headaches for MI-6, the British Intelligence Service.

The British Prince was enamored with Adolf Hitler despite the Führer's book burnings, political persecutions, and spreading of anti-Semitism across Germany. As heir to the throne of a constitutional monarchy, he was forbidden from discussing politics, yet was heard to exclaim, "It was no business of ours to interfere with Germany's internal affairs (regarding) Jews or anything else."

Mrs. Simpson presented additional problems. British Intelligence Services feared she might be an agent of Nazi Germany. Ambassador Messersmith quickly entered Edward's inner circle and described Mrs. Simpson as "charming and intelligent." He was not naïve. The way to Edward's heart was through his mistress.

On July 25, 1934, the day following Sophie Nostitz-Rieneck's thirty-third birthday, Engelbert Dollfuss was assassinated in a failed Nazi coup attempt. As he lay paralyzed in his chancellery office with two bullets in his neck, he slowly bled to death in the shadow of the Hofburg Palace. His Nazi assassins ignored his pleas for a doctor and a priest. Three quarters of a century later, Maximilian's son Georg, who later became an Austrian diplomat, recalled his feelings at the time:

> It was my first political remembrance, a total horrible shock that this good man was killed. He was a loyal Austrian who tried to save the country. We admired him greatly because he took the country into his strong hands. He was not afraid—so we were not afraid. Until his death, we felt safe.

One day before his assassination, Dollfuss confided to Karl Winter, Vienna's deputy mayor, that the only hope for Austria's survival was a quick restoration of the constitutional monarchy headed by Otto Habsburg. Dollfuss's successor, Kurt Schuschnigg, was also a monarchist, an admirer of Franz Ferdinand and his son Max. In his memoir, Schuschnigg wrote of his recollections of Sarajevo as a sixteen-year-old

schoolboy. His feelings of "impending disaster" might have also described how many Austrians felt following the Dollfuss assassination: "We Austrian boys had been accustomed to look on Archduke Franz Ferdinand as the living embodiment of our patriotic hopes... no one could picture what would come afterwards. National reorganization and consolidation, the conception of a stronger Austria... hope was associated with his name."

The assassination of Austria's Chancellor brought the nightmare of Sarajevo back to the Hohenbergs. Half a million Austrians attended Dollfuss's funeral. The Nazi perpetrators were caught, tried, and quickly executed. Feelings ran so high that one of the wounded assassins was carried to the gallows on a stretcher. The country teetered on the brink of chaos.

Schuschnigg did not inspire the confidence of his predecessor. Yet he did his best to find allies in the fight against the rising Nazi tide. Baron Gabriel Apor, a member of Hungary's Foreign Service, reached the same conclusion, but with a Habsburg twist. He wrote, "It was becoming clearer that Austria and Hungary would have to begin sleeping with each other again... and they might have to take a Habsburg into bed with them." Many in Czechoslovakia agreed, but their Foreign Minister did not. Eduard Beneš, who hated all things Habsburg, would have rather seen Austria disappear into Germany than a Habsburg restoration. His pronouncement had a chilling effect throughout the region. Czechoslovakia and Hungary stepped away from Austria.

At the time of the Dollfuss assassination, only one foreign leader offered Austria help. Minutes after learning of the attempted Nazi coup, Benito Mussolini mobilized the Italian army. He dispatched troops to the Austro-Italian border and threatened to repel any German advance into Austria. Hitler quickly backed down. Messersmith wrote that Mussolini was the only "head of state in Europe with no illusions about Hitler." In the early years of the 1930s, Benito Mussolini seemed the most human of dictators, declaring Mark Twain his favor-

ite author and dismissing *Mein Kampf* as a "boring tome." Dollfuss's wife and children were his guests in his Adriatic villa at the time of the assassination. Mussolini personally informed them of the tragedy with tears in his eyes. He took the timing of the attempted coup as a personal and political affront. For a time, Mussolini was Europe's most powerful dictator, respected, even admired by many. He was the lone voice on the public stage loudly condemning Hitler's anti-Semitism. In a well-publicized interview with American publisher Cornelius Vanderbilt Jr., Mussolini was widely quoted as saying, "Peace! That is my motto! Eternal peace…. Another world war? Nonsense! There will be no war in Europe as long as Mussolini is alive." Many believed him. Compared to Nazi dictator Adolf Hitler in Germany and the communist dictator Joseph Stalin who had assumed power in Soviet Russia, the Italian dictator seemed Austria's best and only hope for a supportive ally.

Schuschnigg could have sent any diplomat as his personal representative to Rome, but he selected Maximilian Hohenberg—the man Adolf Hitler, Otto Habsburg, and many Austrians considered the leader of the Habsburg restoration movement. He wanted assurances the country could count on Mussolini's loyalty, but also wanted to uncover the dictator's position on the Habsburg restoration. Schuschnigg may have hoped sending Otto's cousin to Rome could positively influence the answer. Mussolini and Italy's own monarchy continued to coexist side by side. The Fascist leader privately confided, "You seize power with one set of people, but govern with another."

Mussolini not only pledged strong support for Austrian independence, but to Max's relief, offered no objections to a Habsburg restoration. The dictator told him Otto would make an excellent constitutional monarch. He even offered to play matchmaker between the unmarried Habsburg prince and the daughter of the King and Queen of Italy.

With the support of Chancellor Schuschnigg and Benito Mussolini, Maximilian redoubled his efforts to return his cousin to the throne of Austria, and perhaps Hungary. A headline in the October 28, 1934, edition of the *New York Times* read, RESTORATION OF HABSBURGS WITHIN YEAR IS PREDICTED. Count Anton Sigray, the monarchist leader in Hungary, confidently declared, "The restoration of the Habsburgs has ceased to be an academic question and has become a burning question of practical politics.... Only a great State in which various races live in equality offers a possibility of peace; and only the institution of monarchy can guarantee its permanence."

A November *New York Times* headline and following article documented escalating events, VIENNA CELEBRATES BIRTHDAY OF OTTO—MONARCHISTS HAIL 'EMPEROR' AT SERVICES—MUSSOLINI'S APPROVAL OF RESTORATION SEEN.

> Celebrations of Archduke Otto's twenty-second birthday were conducted by monarchists in Vienna today on a scale never previously attempted.... The main demonstration... (with) over 2000 included the wife of Chancellor Kurt Schuschnigg. Duke Max of Hohenberg presided.... The Duke said... "The time was near when Archduke Otto would return to his country...." Baron Wiesner declared "one of the greatest triumphs for legitimism was securing Premier Mussolini's approval of restoration as indicated by a declaration in the newspaper he founded, Popolo d'Italia."

Maximilian was interviewed by the Anglo-American Press Association following a second address to seven thousand monarchists. Thousands more had been turned away due to a lack of space. Two hundred thousand Austrians sent birthday greetings to the young Habsburg heir. That same afternoon, a former Field Marshal wearing his Imperial Army uniform addressed Jewish war veterans honoring Otto at a Viennese synagogue. News from Germany added a fresh incentive to the festivities. Jewish names from the country's war memorials were being removed from monuments there.

The following summer, the Austrian parliament passed a law partially restoring Habsburg properties that had been seized in 1919. Maximilian Hohenberg represented his cousins during the negotiations. The Hofburg and Schönbrunn Palaces would remain the property of the state, but other homes and estates would be returned to them. Adolf Hitler and others kept a close watch over Max's activities, certain they were the first legal step toward Otto's return. Austria's Foreign Minister responded to critics of the move, "The law restoring Habsburg property was a simple act of justice and had no connection with the question of restoration of the monarchy." Few people in Berlin or Vienna believed him. That November, a plebiscite in Greece recalled the deposed monarchy there by an overwhelming vote of 1,491,992 to 43,454.

Legislation that Max himself negotiated permitted "the Habsburgs to return to Austria as private citizens." Many did, but Otto and former Empress Zita were not among them. They waited for a more specific invitation. Twice Schuschnigg met secretly in France with Otto promising unequivocally "to carry out the restoration as soon as possible in the coming year... even if this should eventually lead to a serious European conflagration." He further promised any attempt by Germany to annex Austria would be met by force.

Otto later wrote of his cousin's role during this time:

Max Hohenberg was a key person. He was very active, held a great deal of meetings, and often came to see us. He was one of our most important links with the government, especially in discussions over my possible return to Austria. He was unconditionally loyal, was an excellent orator, and had the gift of bringing people together who were at odds with one another.

That winter the country's tourist and skiing industry was hurt by light snowfall and the absence of the Prince of Wales. As 1936 began, King George V of England was dying, which forced Edward to cancel his scheduled Austrian holiday. Many expected the popular prince to soon become an even more popular monarch. King George, on his deathbed, had his doubts. He sadly predicted, "After I am dead the boy will ruin himself in twelve months."

The King certainly knew his son, but few people could have imagined a royal scandal in England involving an heir to the throne, his mistress, and her cuckolded husband would have such a dramatic impact on monarchists in Austria. In Vienna, their confidence had never been higher. The government sponsored a series of winter balls in the Hofburg Palace prominently featuring members of the Habsburg family. Archduke Eugene made a flamboyant entrance upstaging the republic's president. Princess Ileana of Rumania, married to a Habsburg Archduke, attended wearing a diamond and sapphire tiara that once belonged to the Empress of Russia. Many of the couples happily dancing to Viennese waltzes expected the next winter's Carnival season to be hosted by Emperor Otto Habsburg. In the midst of the turbulent decade Ernst, the Hohenberg's own bachelor prince, provided his family a happy respite from politics. Newspapers across Europe made the announcement. Under the headline PRINCE ERNST VON HOHENBERG, SON OF THE LATE ARCHDUKE FRANZ FERDINAND, WITH HIS ENGLISH FIANCÉE, MISS MAISIE WOOD the *Illustrated London News* reported the engagement of the Austrian prince to the daughter of a British diplomat posted in Vienna and her Hungarian Countess mother.

Ernst was thirty-two, the same age as his mother when she had married. Like Max he had grown a Franz Ferdinand mustache. With his heavier physical build, he resembled a younger version of their father. Ernst's future bride, the radiant twenty-four-year-old Maria Theresa Wood, had been named for the Habsburg's most famous Empress. Despite her regal name, nearly everyone called the down-to-earth countess Maisie. She was fluent in the language of her aristocratic Hungarian mother, and in the high-pitched clipped British accent of her diplomat father, but she spoke very little German. Due to a severe hearing loss, she was also a masterful lip reader.

The wedding would take place a short distance from Belvedere Palace at Vienna's beautiful Karlskirche on the city's Karlsplatz. Years earlier, Adolf Hitler's first postcard sent from Vienna had featured an image of the famous landmark. The day provided the Hohenberg family a last treasured memory before years of war and imprisonment separated them. And like everything else in 1936 Austria, the wedding was filtered through a political lens.

Karlskirche had a long association with the Habsburgs. Members of the Austro-Hungarian Empire's ancient aristocracy, diplomats, and political leaders from across the country were guests. Their attendance was seen by many as a way of showing public support to the Hohenbergs for their loyalty to the Habsburgs and their efforts to restore the monarchy.

Despite the joy of the wedding, the political situation was deteriorating. Chancellor Schuschnigg sent Max back to Italy. Mussolini had offered repeated assurances that he would continue to stand with Austria, but military entanglements in east Africa reordered his priorities. The lure of nationalism, colonies, and racism seduced him. A headline in the *New York Times* read: ETHIOPIA NOW SEEMS HEADED FOR DOOM… ITALY TAKES UP WHITE MAN'S BURDEN IN AFRICA'S LAST NATIVE-RULED LAND.

Following his invasion of Ethiopia, Mussolini wrote of Max's father, "Franz Ferdinand did not weigh the power of race consciousness. He cherished a dream of melding three races together. Races, I know, are difficult to meld." Mussolini also rethought his relationship with Austria and Germany. Adolf Hitler's recent call for "the perpetual domination of the world by the white race" had suddenly become more alluring to him. During a private meeting in Rome, Mussolini signaled his surprising change of heart to Hitler favorite Leni Riefenstahl, "Tell your Führer that I believe in him and his mission."

Surprised by a statement refuting his public support of Austria, she asked, "Won't you have problems with Hitler because of Austria?"

He scowled, telling her, "You can tell the Führer that whatever happens with Austria, I will not interfere in Austria's internal affairs." Riefenstahl returned to Berlin, and shared Mussolini's conversion with Hitler.

Maximilian Hohenberg's last meeting with Benito Mussolini took place in the Palazzo Venezia, a fifteenth-century Renaissance palace that had once been the Austrian embassy. The bombastic Mussolini often spoke to cheering supporters from its balcony. Nearby were the ruins of the Roman Forum where Julius Caesar had been assassinated by former friends and allies, and the city's two-thousand-year-old Jewish ghetto. Like their Austrian neighbors, Rome's Jews were about to be betrayed. Mussolini had made the palace's longest corridor into his private office. Visitors were forced to walk the entire length of the room as the sounds of their footsteps loudly echoed off the marble floor and walls. His heavy wooden desk was the largest Max had ever seen. The rapport from earlier meetings between the Italian dictator and the Austrian Duke was absent. The atmosphere was considerably cooler, the discussion shorter, and the ending more abrupt. With the sounds of the busy Roman traffic as a backdrop, Maximilian concluded the meeting with a prophecy. He warned Mussolini:

> We are a small country, all that is left of a great Empire, but what will happen to Austria, will also happen to you. Here in the heart of Rome where you work the German army will march. Here German banners will be unfurled and wave above the very palace where we are meeting. Just as there is no one to help us today, there will be no one to help you tomorrow. You too will be the victim. You too will be destroyed by the Nazis.

CHAPTER THIRTEEN
ONE BLOOD DEMANDS ONE REICH

"Goethe tells us in his greatest poem that Faust lost the liberty
of his soul when he said to the passing moment, 'Stay, thou
are so fair.'"
—JOHN F. KENNEDY

"Now that the king has been dethroned, there is certainly no
other person in England who is ready to play with us."
—ADOLF HITLER

The major news story occupying the hearts and minds of most people
in 1936 was not the Berlin-Rome axis Hitler and Mussolini announced
that autumn. It was the royal scandal shaking England. American journalist H. L. Mencken called it "the greatest news story since the resurrection." Three hundred twenty-seven days after the Prince of Wales
became the British King he abdicated his throne to marry his mistress.
His determination to marry Mrs. Simpson, an American divorcée with
two living ex-husbands, created a constitutional crisis, a romantic fantasy for believers in fairy tales, and a nightmare for monarchists. Diplomat Harold Nicolson and other members of the British establishment
worried that belief in royalty itself was being undermined. For Austrian
monarchists, the timing was their worst nightmare. At the very time
they were feverishly promoting their own royal prince as their nation's
savior, the indiscreet romantic entanglement of England's young king
cast a dark shadow over the institution of monarchy.

Stanley Baldwin, his country's Prime Minister, bluntly told Edward, "There is an obligation on the king as head of the British Empire to choose a queen who definitely meets the obligations of her position. The king and queen are symbols of the Empire—not just the king. If the king wants to sleep with a whore, that's his private business, but the Empire is concerned that he doesn't make her the queen."

Edward did not appreciate the Prime Minister's frankness.

Much to the embarrassment of the Hohenbergs, Winston Churchill and other supporters of Edward cited the morganatic marriage of Franz Ferdinand and Sophie Chotek as a possible solution to the crisis. Edward would be king. His wife would be his consort, but never queen. The British government and the Church of England vetoed the proposal, pointing out Mrs. Simpson was no Duchess of Hohenberg.

In addition to her tangled marital history, British Intelligence had become convinced that even if Mrs. Simpson was not a spy, she was certainly a dupe of the Nazis. They may have identified the wrong dupe. A disappointed Adolf Hitler wrote his Ambassador in London, "Now that the king has been dethroned, there is certainly no other person in England who is ready to play with us."

Following his abdication on December 10, 1936, the former King could have flown anywhere, but he chose to fly to Austria until Mrs. Simpson's divorce became final. He took up residence in the remote country home of Baron Eugène Rothschild, a visit that dragged on for four headline-grabbing months. The Baron's wife, Kitty, also an American-born divorcée, was a friend of Mrs. Simpson. To the surprise of his host and hostess, Edward passed some of his time watching old films of Emperor Franz Joseph's Diamond Jubilee celebrations. The movies seemed to distract and relax him. Privately he confided to friends that the only thing he was bitter about was the uncensored American press that initially reported his liaison with Mrs. Simpson. The former King naïvely complained, "It is because of the American newspapers, I am here today."

Baroness Rothschild soon visited American Ambassador Messersmith to complain about hordes of newsmen who "crawled over the walls, roamed through the garden, and even peeped into windows." The Ambassador spoke to the regular American correspondents. But they were only a small part of the deluge of frenzied journalists besieging Edward, who following his abdication, was retitled the Duke of Windsor.

Once Mrs. Simpson's divorce became final, the Duke immediately left Austria on the Orient Express. The couple married in France in a beautiful chalet borrowed from Charles Bedaux, a Franco-American businessman who would later be arrested as a Nazi collaborator and die in prison. The marriage allowed Wallis to become a Duchess. To the dismay and frustration of Max Hohenberg and his fellow monarchists, the world's most famous newlyweds returned to Austria to honeymoon. First, however, they took a well-publicized romantic detour to Venice, where Benito Mussolini treated them royally.

The Windsors brought with them dozens of journalists, 266 pieces of luggage, Dudley Foxwood (the only British servant to remain loyal to Edward), two cairn terriers, and Scotland Yard detectives assigned to protect and spy on them. Their every move filled newspaper headlines. A short time after they returned to Austria, Ambassador Messersmith had dinner with the forty-two-year-old Duke whom he characterized as "a stubborn, underdeveloped boy, but in others he is a man of keen intelligence and wide interests."

In the fall of 1937, the former boy-king of England and his bride journeyed to Hitler's Germany. The onetime Prince Charming who had almost single-handedly saved Austria's tourist economy embraced the dictator who tried to destroy it. Nazi luminaries Herman Goering, Heinrich Himmler, Rudolf Hess, and Joseph Goebbels entertained the couple from one end of the country to the other. The most infamous stop for the British exiles was a well-publicized visit with Adolf Hitler at his Eagle's Nest retreat in Bavaria. There the dictator and the Duke of Windsor met one-on-one for nearly an hour. The Duchess had tea with Deputy Führer Rudolf Hess. Widespread coverage of their tour helped legitimize the Nazi regime. But Ralph Wigram, a British Foreign Service officer, wrote that Edward's behavior threatened to pound "a firm nail in the coffin of monarchy." Austrian monarchists were beside themselves. The Duke and Duchess told friends they hoped to settle in Austria before returning permanently to England; but history intervened.

That autumn, Czechoslovakia's first president, Tomas Masaryk, died. To most Czechs, he was the beloved father of their country, their nation's greatest patriot. But not so for Sophie Nostitz-Rieneck, Maximilian and Ernst Hohenberg's sister. She loved Czechoslovakia, the ancient Bohemian land of her birth. Its ethnic patchwork of nationalities made it a smaller version of the once mighty Austro-Hungarian Empire. She had no love for President Masaryk. During the worst winters of the depression, she and Fritz had worked with his government to sponsor soup kitchens in Prague; but she always associated him with the day he expelled her and her orphaned brothers from Konopiste.

Outside his small country, Masaryk's death merited few headlines. But to Adolf Hitler, Masaryk's passing was significant. It removed the one man who might have saved Czechoslovakia from Nazi Germany. Two months following the Czech leader's death, Hitler convened a secret meeting in Berlin, informing military and government officials, "Our first objective must be to overthrow Czechoslovakia and Austria simultaneously in order to remove the threat to our flank in any operation against the west.... Everything will depend on the degree of surprise and swiftness of our action." To Hitler, Czechoslovakia was no less a racial abomination than the Habsburg Empire of his youth.

Masaryk's overflowing library contained thousands of books, but the former professor kept only two volumes on his desk. One of them was Goethe's *Faust*—the story of an intellectual who sold his soul to the devil. Many considered it Germany's greatest contribution to literature. His other book was Adolf Hitler's *Mein Kampf.* Masaryk was a realist who had no illusions about Hitler or the Germany he had transformed into his own image.

Each book in its own way reflected the tragedy of twentieth-century Europe. In the war to come, the Frankfort home of Goethe, his birthplace, his museum, the quaint streets where he walked, his entire prosperous neighborhood, and most of the city where he wrote were destroyed. Much of Europe would suffer the same fate.

In *Mein Kampf,* Hitler bluntly detailed his hopes for wars, conquests, and the enslavement of those he considered racially inferior. No villain in history and no other mass murderer ever so boldly publicized his plans for all the world to see. Hitler declared that all of Europe would be ruled by Germany's "master race," and everyone else would become German allies or their slaves. On page one he stated that Austria would be his first conquest:

> German Austria must return to the great German mother country, and not because of any political considerations. No and again no; not even if such a union was unimportant from an economic point of view. Yes, even if it were harmful. It must never-the-less take place. One blood demands one Reich... from tears of war, the daily blood of future generations will grow.

By the mid-1930s, Hitler was no longer a racist author of a popular book many bought but never read. He was a dangerously empowered dictator of one of the largest nations in Europe positioned to put his racist rants into action. Hitler's fantasies had metastasized into a genuine threat to millions of innocent people.

In response, Maximilian Hohenberg did something no one else in Austria had the courage, audacity, or position to do. On the twentieth anniversary of Sarajevo, June 28, 1937, he publicly spoke out about his parents' assassination. Like Hitler, Max believed words mattered. He chose as his forum not an Austrian or Czech publication, but a French magazine with two and a half million readers, the largest mass circulation journal in Europe. Max was seeking the most substantial possible audience to discredit Germany. He wrote:

> [Franz Ferdinand] envisioned forming a federal entente of all national groups comprising the Austro-Hungarian Empire, and of settling in the best interest of each people the troubling Danubian problem.... But this union of national groups, simply administered from Vienna, threatened the interests of certain powers which harbored projects of annexation and conquests. My father's plans embarrassed them, and it was in order to stop his fulfilling them that they armed in Sarajevo the wretches whose crime was to unleash on the world the most frightful of all slaughters.

It was what he wrote next that caused a firestorm of controversy across Europe, especially in Austria and Germany. "This project worried Berlin very much and it was established that the German secret police worked hand in hand with the conspirators in the preparation of the Sarajevo assassination."

Whether the Duke of Hohenberg was referring to rogue elements within the German and Serbian secret police or was claiming higher-ups in one or both governments planned his father's assassination was not clear, but his words unleashed an anti-German backlash across Austria. He wrote his article at the very time Hitler was appealing for Anschluss, the annexation of Austria to Germany.

Max's words enraged Hitler, the Nazi leadership, and growing numbers of Nazis in Austria. Soon even sporting events took on a political hue. A riot broke out in Vienna Stadium between the Austrian and Italian football teams after an Austrian player "thumbed his nose at his opponents, and was knocked down by one of the Italian players.... Four Italians were severely hurt." Benito Mussolini responded by expelling Austria's football team from the Central European cup tournament being held in Italy.

Tensions were running high and Hitler's calls for racial purity and German nationalism penetrated into the tiny mountain town of Radmer where Ernst was quietly living with his wife and newborn son. American Ambassador Messersmith reported Nazi activities on the rise in Styria, Upper Austria, and Carinthia where the Duke and Duchess of Windsor honeymooned. Salutes of "Heil Hitler" and public support for the Nazis caused Chancellor Schuschnigg to demand that local authorities suppress Nazi activities there. The pro-Nazi sympathies of some of Ernst's closest neighbors persuaded him to become the leader of the region's anti-Nazi Home Guard. Sophie Nostitz-Rieneck, who lived in the heart of Czechoslovakia's ethnic quilt of Czechs, Slovaks, Hungarians, Poles, and Germans, also recognized the danger behind Hitler's rhetoric.

Others did not. In October 1937, British Prime Minister Neville Chamberlain encouraged Edward Halifax, his Foreign Secretary, to begin "relaxed and informal face to face meetings with the Nazi leadership."

While Maximilian wrote Sophie of his concerns about the Nazi menace, that fall Chamberlain wrote his own sister regarding "the far reaching plans I have for the appeasement of Europe and Asia and for the ultimate check to the mad armaments race." When Lord Halifax returned to London from Berlin, he wrote, "Nationalism and Racialism is a powerful force, but I can't feel that either is unnatural or immoral."

Sophie's recollections of the years before World War II were memories of praying for a miracle. Prague is a city of churches, and she visited many of them. The Carmelite church of Our Lady of Victories, a short walk from her Maltese Square home, became her prayer sanctuary. Within its walls was the legendary statue of the Infant of Prague. Many Catholics prayed there for miracles. Sophie was one of them.

The famous statue had special ties to her family. Pope Leo XIII had been instrumental in persuading Franz Joseph to approve her parents' marriage. He designated it and the church a Catholic pilgrimage site. Three centuries earlier, the small wooden statue of the Christ child was donated to the church by the Lobkowitz family, friends of the Hohenbergs, and the onetime owners of Konopiste.

Sophie prayed for all her family there, but especially for Ernst. The youngest Hohenberg inherited their father's short fuse, not their mother's diplomatic skills. She worried that the increasing boldness of the Austrian Nazis would trigger an explosion. The outburst she feared happened on a rare visit he made to Vienna in January 1938.

The tariff on German citizens vacationing in Austria continued crippling tourism there. A large illuminated swastika in the showcase window of the German Tourism Office caught Ernst's attention. Within seconds his umbrella shattered the window. In the confrontation that followed, the swastika and pictures of Hitler in the showcase were destroyed. Police were called. To avoid arrest for vandalism and disorderly conduct, the Hohenberg Prince was required to offer a personal apology to German Ambassador Franz von Papen. The incident was promptly reported to Berlin.

The following month, February 1938, Hitler invited Chancellor Schuschnigg to his Bavarian Eagle's Nest retreat overlooking Austria. The Chancellor was promised "whatever the course of the negotiations in no case would they alter Austro-German relations to the disadvantage of Austria, nor lead to any aggravation of the Austrian situation." A histrionic ten-hour verbal assault on Schuschnigg and his country followed. Hitler's insults, screaming, and bullying were calculated to shock and demoralize the soft-spoken, gentlemanly Austrian Chancellor. Hitler ranted:

> I, an Austrian by birth, have been sent by Providence to create the Greater German State! And you stand in the way! I will crush you! The whole history of Austria is just one uninterrupted act of high treason... I am absolutely determined to make an end of all this.

The German Reich is one of the great powers and nobody will raise his voice if it settles its border problems… I have achieved everything I have set out to do, and thus become perhaps the greatest German in history.

He demanded Schuschnigg allow the Nazi Party to operate legally and openly, grant amnesty to imprisoned Nazi terrorists, appoint a leading Nazi to his cabinet, and establish closer economic and political ties with Germany. If his demands were not immediately accepted, he shouted that Austria would forcibly be incorporated into the German Reich. Britain's Ambassador in Vienna reported that during the meeting Hitler "raved like a madman."

Schuschnigg, shaken to his core, returned to Vienna determined to resign, but was unable to find anyone willing and able to stand up to the Nazi leader. He approached the monarchist mayor of Vienna, the city's former police chief, the country's secretary of state for public safety, and other outspoken opponents of Hitler. They all refused. He then offered the chancellorship to Maximilian Hohenberg, the Habsburg who was not a Habsburg. Family loyalty dictated his answer.

The Duke of Hohenberg told Schuschnigg that the man to lead Austria was Otto, then living in Belgium exile. His cousin was only twenty-five years old, but by that age Franz Joseph had sat on the throne for seven years. The Chancellor believed in the restoration of the monarchy but seemed paralyzed by the rush of events. Otto sent Schuschnigg a letter urging him to make no further concessions. He also made him a remarkable offer:

In this critical hour of acute danger should you feel unable to withstand further pressure… I ask you then, whatever the situation may be, to hand over to me the office of Chancellor. I am not demanding a restoration of the monarchy… I call on you to only give me the Chancellorship so that we could gain the same advantages achievable through a formal restoration of the monarchy, but without any change in the constitution or any new recognition… I am acting as I do because I see it as my duty that, when Austria is in peril, I… should stand or fall with my country.

His offer stood in dramatic contrast to the damning silence emanating from the Duke of Windsor living in French exile. The Duke's complete lack of response as Austrian friends feared for their lives did nothing to restore his tattered reputation.

The bold proposal by the Hohenberg's cousin seemed to give Schuschnigg the voice and courage he never had before and would never have again. Even as Nazi terrorists created chaos with bombs and bomb threats, he rejected Otto's offer. Instead he called for a national election to allow Austrians to decide for themselves if their country would remain free and independent or be absorbed into Nazi Germany. The date for the plebiscite was scheduled for March 13, 1938, the eve of the Ides of March.

Adolf Hitler was determined the vote would never take place. Two corps of Germany's Eighth Army mobilized on Austria's northern borders waiting for orders to advance. The secret code name Hitler gave for his Austrian invasion was Operation Otto, named for the man he feared might thwart his lifelong ambition.

Many in Czechoslovakia fantasized that the death watch taking place at their doorstep would stop at their border. Sophie and Fritz Nostitz-Rieneck were not among them. As the date for the plebiscite approached, she and her brothers spoke daily over the telephone. If Chancellor Schuschnigg's government surrendered and Hitler's army entered Austria, no Hohenberg would be safe.

Two days before the election, Schuschnigg announced he would make a radio address to the nation. America's Ambassador in London, Joseph P. Kennedy, cabled President Franklin Roosevelt, "In talking with the various Government officials of foreign countries… they regard the situation as acute in Central Europe, but in the words of the French Ambassador this morning, nothing is likely to happen except to have Schuschnigg eventually give in." Kennedy's assessment proved correct. Schuschnigg secretly decided at 2:45 that afternoon to give in to Hitler's demands even as loudspeakers throughout Vienna played the national anthem throughout the city.

The address, just forty-eight hours before the scheduled election, caused many Austrians to suspect the worst. Panicked throngs made their way to the Viennese rail station to take the 11:15 train to Prague. A second train had to be added to keep the crowds from rioting. The Hohenbergs made their own plans. If Hitler moved against Austria, Ernst and his family would seek asylum in Vienna's British Embassy. Maisie's diplomat father offered them sanctuary there. Max arranged for an unmarked taxi to drive his family to Czechoslovakia. Bags were packed and the children sent to bed early.

The Chancellor began his broadcast from the same office where Engelbert Dollfuss had been assassinated. "Men and women of Austria, today we face a difficult and fateful situation." Within minutes he yielded to all of Hitler's demands, cancelled the election, and resigned his office. Austrians were urged to peacefully accept German annexation. "We are yielding to force, because we are resolved on no account to spill blood. We have ordered our armed forces, in the event of an invasion by the German Army, to offer no resistance." Schuschnigg ended not with the traditional, "God Bless Austria," but with the words, "God Protect Austria." A recording of Schubert's *Unfinished Symphony* concluded the broadcast. Almost simultaneously swastikas and German flags appeared throughout Vienna, and in villages and towns across the country. For Austrian Nazis and their supporters, it was a time to celebrate. For anti-Nazi Austrians like the Hohenbergs, the speech seemed like a death sentence.

CHAPTER FOURTEEN
WITCHES SABBATH

"The very thing we loved most, our common optimism,
betrayed us, for everyone thought that everyone else would
back down at the last minute."   —STEFAN ZWEIG

"Tell Mussolini that I shall never, never, never forget this!"
                                         —ADOLF HITLER

Sophie and her husband, Fritz, listened to Chancellor Schuschnigg's
address over Radio Prague. When it finished, the Czech newsreader
urged calm. He denied that the Czechoslovakian army was mobilizing
and appealed for national unity. As Schubert's *Unfinished Symphony*
played in the background, their telephone rang. It was Max calling
from Austria. The conversation was brief. He told Sophie they were
leaving for Prague at once hoping to reach the border before it closed.
For most Europeans, the Second World War would begin a year and
a half after the Austrian Anschluss. For the Hohenbergs and other
opponents of Hitler, the war began that evening.

Time was running out for them and Austria. Maximilian and his
family drove over winding, deserted roads in a car packed floor to roof
with suitcases, a driver unfamiliar with the route, two anxious parents, and five sleepy children. They avoided familiar towns and villages
where local Nazis celebrated, but each detour cost more time. As they
raced to the border, a telephone call at 10:25 p.m. from Rome to Berlin

promised Mussolini's full support for the Anschluss. Hitler sent a return message. "Tell Mussolini I shall never, never, never forget this! If he should ever need any help or be in any danger, he can be convinced that I shall stick to him, whatever may happen, even if the whole world were against him." Both scenarios came true, but the telephone call between the dictators sealed the fate of Austria, and of Benito Mussolini.

Shortly before dawn, Maximilian Hohenberg and his family arrived at the Czech border. It was open; but the regular border guards had been replaced with Nazi partisans drunk with power and beer. When he stepped out of the car, Max tried to appear as if he were taking his family, and over packed car, on a regularly scheduled holiday. He was certain he was about to be arrested. To his surprise, the Nazis drunkenly motioned their car through the checkpoint without asking to see their passports. He could barely believe their luck.

The Czech guards were less compliant. Taunting began immediately. "You wanted Hitler, now you have him! Go back to Austria. Go back to Hitler where you belong." Freedom was inches away, but Max's quiet pleas were loudly rejected. Max's wife, Elisabeth, later remembered being unable to breathe as her husband confronted the Czech border patrol. They had escaped Austria, but Czechoslovakia had sealed its borders. They were not allowed to enter the country that had been their childhood home. When the insults grew louder, Elisabeth whispered to Max, "There is no possible escape. We must return to Artstetten." It was a long, silent ride home.

At three minutes past midnight on March 12, 1938, the Germans entered Austria. When Max returned home with his exhausted family, he telephoned Sophie and whispered three simple French words. "Il est ici." *He is here.* Then the phone went dead. It was their prearranged code. They had not escaped.

Hitler had flown from Berlin to Munich before being driven to Braunau am Inn, his Austrian birthplace. Church bells and cheering crowds greeted him. His next stop was to his childhood home of

Linz. There he signed the "Bill of Reunification of Austria with the German Reich" and granted an exclusive interview to the *London Daily Mail,* telling the reporter, "Wait a little and see what I will do for Austria… you will see how much better off and happier the people of Austria will be."

Hitler also addressed thousands of enthusiastic supporters: "If Providence once called me forth from this town to be the Führer of the German Reich, in so doing it must have charged me with a mission, and that mission could be only to restore my dear homeland to the German Reich." Even those who could not hear his words, or those who knew him as a sullen youth, cheered.

Early on the morning of the German invasion of Austria, Ernst and his family arrived at Artstetten. Minutes after Schuschnigg's address, an angry mob had surrounded their Radmer home. Neighbors whom Ernst had known for years, including men and women who worked for him, yelled Nazi salutes and fired guns in the air. Stones, threats, and oaths were thrown at the house. One of the leaders of the mob, the foreman of Ernst's own estate, shouted, "We are the masters now! Today we are *your* boss!"

The scene was being repeated in towns, farms, and cities across Austria. Maids and field hands, waiters and waitresses, butlers and chauffeurs, even janitors who for years silently listened to their employers' private conversations, had been gifted with unimaginable power. A few words to the country's ascendant Nazi overseers could destroy a family overnight.

When the heckling outside the home failed to provoke a confrontation, the mob disappeared into the darkness to celebrate the new Austria. Ernst, fearful of what he might find in Vienna, decided to take backroads to Artstetten. There he and Max decided with their wives to travel together with their children to Vienna to seek the advice of Maisie's British diplomat father. Hopefully he could help all of them safely escape the country.

The fifty-mile trip from Artstetten to Vienna was their second nightmarish journey in twenty-four hours. By the time they reached the city, they no longer recognized it. The day before, red and white flags of the Austrian Republic had hung from every flagpole and public building. Now every streetlight, tree, window, and balcony seemed covered by Nazi swastikas. Even police officers directing traffic wore swastikas armbands. American radio journalist William L. Shirer provided an eyewitness account of Vienna's transformation:

> When I emerged from the subway at Karlsplatz... I was amazed to find an abrupt change. A mob of several thousand shouting hysterical Nazi slogans was milling around the vast square... I found myself being swept by the riotous, yelling throng... past the Ring, past the Opera... to the offices of the German Tourism Office with its immense flower draped portrait of Adolf Hitler in the window... I had seen those faces at party rallies in Nuremberg: the fanatical popping eyes, the gaping mouths, the contorted expressions of hysteria and paranoia... screaming: Sieg Heil! Sieg Heil! Heil Hitler! Hang Schuschnigg! Hang Schuschnigg! Ein Volk, Ein Reich, Ein Führer! [One people! One country! One leader!] The brown shirts at Nuremberg had never bellowed the Nazi slogans with such mania.

The Hohenbergs silently drove past Franz Joseph's empty palace of Schönbrunn and the huge Hofburg palace in the city center. Some streets seemed deserted. Others were filled with jeering mobs driving Jews from their homes, shops, and businesses. Individuals and small groups of people were taunted as they were forced to scrub sidewalks clean of the pro-Schuschnigg graffiti written just days earlier. Edward R. Murrow, recently arrived from Berlin, reported the scene for CBS radio:

> Young storm troopers are riding around in trucks and vehicles of all sorts singing and tossing oranges out to the crowd. Nearly every building has its armed guards.... There are still huge crowds along

the Ringstrasse and people still stand outside the principle hotels…
there is a certain air of expectancy about the city, everyone waiting
and wondering where and at what time Herr Hitler will arrive.

Austrian writer Stefan Zweig described with disgust the horror
of Vienna that day, "All the sickly, unclean fantasies of hate that had
been conceived in many orgiastic nights found raging expression in
broad daylight." Carl Zuckmayer, the exiled German screenwriter of
the Marlene Dietrich film *The Blue Angel*, called the euphoria and unleashed hatred of the Viennese "an indescribable witches Sabbath."

Cars bearing German license plates prompted cheers, Austrian
plates indifference. The horrors taking place throughout the city focused the revelers' attention away from the Hohenbergs, who silently
drove past the Karlskirche where Ernst and Maisie were married and
Belvedere Palace where Max had been born.

Once they reached the British Embassy, Ernst and his family
quickly disappeared inside. Maximilian, Elisabeth, and their five sons,
aged one to ten, crossed the street and climbed the steep stairs to the
apartment of Ernst's in-laws. Heavy curtains were drawn over the windows. Seventy years later, Georg Hohenberg, who was nine years old
in 1938, could still remember silently staring at the closed curtains for
hours waiting for some word from the Embassy.

———

In Prague, Sophie prayed for news about her brothers. Cascading
bulletins reported events in Vienna, but she heard nothing from Max
or Ernst. The reports only increased her anxiety. Kurt Schuschnigg
had been placed under house arrest at Belvedere Palace. Austria's
new Chancellor, Arthur Seyss-Inquart, pledged allegiance to the
Nazi Party. He served as puppet chancellor for only forty-eight
hours, but that allowed him enough time to quickly move against
the Hohenbergs.

The Belgian, French, and Hungarian embassies were granting political asylum to hundreds of refugees, helping spirit them out of the country. In the first chaotic hours of the German occupation, Seyss-Inquart journeyed to only one foreign embassy and spoke with only one Ambassador: Britain's Michael Palairet. Telephone calls and telegrams were exchanged between Vienna and London. Prime Minister Chamberlain ordered no exit visa be issued for Prince Ernst Hohenberg and instructed the staff to immediately expel him and his family from the Embassy. Austria's new government had labeled Ernst and Maximilian Hohenberg enemies of the state. The date was March 14, 1938. It was the first birthday of Ernst's infant son who had been baptized Franz Ferdinand Maximilian Hohenberg.

Maisie's stunned father silently watched Ernst and Maisie, with their toddler son, grimly cross the street to his apartment. They had nowhere else to go. The decision was a gamble. Their only hope was that the Gestapo might not arrest Ernst in the home of a British diplomat. Maximilian and Elisabeth had a bolder plan. They moved seven blocks away to the Ringstrasse's most famous five-star luxury hotel. Max believed no one would dare arrest him in such a well-known landmark in the heart of Vienna. The building had once been the city palace of the Württemberg royal family, the Hohenbergs' own cousins. The manager was a family friend. Max had no way to know the Hotel Imperial he selected was also Adolf Hitler's Vienna destination. He and his family had barely unpacked when they learned Hitler would also be staying there. As the Nazi leader's triumphant motorcade slowly approached Vienna, Max and his family fled to a less public location.

Hitler followed the same road to the city that the Hohenbergs had taken forty-eight hours earlier. Prague radio reported hundreds, then thousands, of Austrians greeting him with the Nazi salute. Leni Riefenstahl described the "delirious" scene. "They stretched their arms and hands towards Hitler in almost religious ecstasy. Elderly men and women were crying. The universal jubilation was simply beyond belief."

Sophie and Fritz could not believe what they were hearing. With no news about her brothers, Sophie nervously retraced her steps back and forth between her home and the Lady of Victories church. At some point during those anxious hours as Franz Ferdinand's sons hid in Vienna and his daughter prayed in Prague, Adolf Hitler passed Artstetten Castle where their assassinated parents were buried. Nicholas Horthy, Hungary's dictator and infamous Nazi collaborator, later connected the dots in his memoirs: "Those two shots at Sarajevo were the first two shots of the First World War, from which sprang the yet more murderous Second World War." Echoes of those Sarajevo bullets would soon be heard around the world. Millions would die, including many Austrians joyfully cheering the man they would have ignored or scorned if years earlier they had met on the same Viennese streets.

Hitler's caravan finally reached the outskirts of Vienna and the Schönbrunn Palace. He knew the palace gardens well. It was on a Schönbrunn park bench that the young Hitler dreamed of the day the "racially superior" German people would destroy all remnants of the "mongrel" multicultural Habsburg Empire. A quarter of a century later, pealing church bells and thousands of cheering Viennese told him that day was near. Vienna's Cardinal Archbishop Innitzer enthusiastically welcomed Hitler. In a published letter to his flock he wrote, "Catholics in the Vienna diocese are asked on Sunday to offer thanks to the Lord God for the bloodless course of the great political change." He signed his letter "Heil Hitler" and soon traveled to the Hotel Imperial to pay his respects.

Shortly before Franz Ferdinand's birth, Emperor Franz Joseph had removed the stone walls that for nearly six hundred years had protected Vienna from foreign invaders. The medieval fortifications were replaced by wide streets, green walkways, and miles of riding and hiking trails. Sun and winds swept through the old city bringing with them green parks, flowering gardens, and breathing space for its citizens. The city's most famous boulevard, the tree-lined Ringstrasse, stood where ramparts once guarded the capital of the Habsburg Empire.

Hitler slowly rode along the Ringstrasse beneath a double row of tall Linden trees planted as saplings during the early days of Franz Joseph's reign. Banners of red, white, and black swastikas transformed the exterior of the Hotel Imperial into a Nazi cathedral. After a few hours of sleep in the hotel, Hitler was driven the following morning to the city's Heroes' Square. There three quarters of a million Viennese waited impatiently to hear him speak from the Nazi-bannered balcony of the Hofburg Palace.

A few blocks to the south, a knock at the door interrupted the quiet meal Ernst was having with his wife and son. The Gestapo had come to arrest him. He was informed if he resisted or tried to escape, his brother would be hunted down and killed. Ernst left quietly. When Maximilian learned of the arrest, he immediately left the safety of his own refuge to surrender to the Gestapo. He knew Ernst would die rather than reveal their location. Elisabeth could barely hear his parting words as the sounds of hundreds of thousands of cheering Austrians shook the walls and windows where they hid. The Nazi leader was speaking from the Hofburg Palace's balcony, built in 1913 for Franz Ferdinand but never used by him. Austria's new Nazi Chancellor, Arthur Seyss-Inquart, spoke first, proudly surrendering himself and his country to Hitler:

> As the last highest agent of the federal state of Austria I report to my Führer and Reich Chancellor the completion of the lawful degree according to the will of the German people and of its Führer. Austria is a province of the German Reich.... My Führer! Wherever the road leads we will follow! Heil my Führer!

Shortly before Hitler spoke to his fellow Austrians, he was presented with flowers by two small Czech boys holding a banner that read, "The Sudeten Germans of Czechoslovakia greet the Führer." The gift generated one of the few smiles Hitler produced on that remarkable day.

The Prague Radio newsreader failed to mention the banner or its implications when reporting the events, but few in or out of Czechoslovakia doubted that the country was Hitler's next target. Three and a half million Czechs of German ancestry lived in its Sudetenland region; and Hitler had pledged to return all European Germans to his Reich.

Herman Goering, Hitler's closest deputy, offered reassurances Czechoslovakia was in no danger. Within days of the Austrian Anschluss, a German plane entered Czech air space dropping leaflets that read, "Tell Everyone in Prague Hitler Says Hello." That September Goering thundered in a public speech in Nuremberg:

> A petty segment of Europe is harassing human beings.... This miserable pygmy race (the Czechs) without culture—no one knows where it came from—is oppressing a cultured people (the Sudeten Germans) and behind it is Moscow and the eternal mask of the Jew devil.

In the immediate aftermath of the Austrian Anschluss, American Ambassador Joseph Kennedy in England, a leading Roosevelt Democrat, wrote about the future position of Czechoslovakia: "Jan Masaryk, the Czech Foreign Minister here and son of the old President, gave me to understand that his country will make a deal with Germany, unpalatable as it may be... it does not consider... putting up resistance against Berlin." Following a trip to Germany, the former American president Herbert Hoover, a Republican, received a rousing ovation at the Foreign Policy Association in New York. He declared to his enthusiastic audience, "The form of government which other people pass through in working out their destinies is not our business." American politicians from both political parties were not interested in events in faraway Europe.

Following the Anschluss, Hitler was in a rare good mood. He took a victory lap across Austria to visit Graz, Klagenfurt, Innsbruck, and Salzburg before returning to Linz. In Klagenfurt he visited his retired schoolteacher; the Habsburg-hating Dr. Leopold Pötsch. His admiration for "this old gentleman" had not diminished. He wrote of Pötsch, "Who could have studied German history under such a teacher without becoming an enemy of the state which, through its ruling house, exerted so disastrous an influence on the destinies of the nation?"

August Kubizek, Hitler's former Vienna roommate, was now a minor civil servant living with a wife and three sons in Upper Austria. He wrote Hitler in 1933 after learning of his appointment as German Chancellor. Kubizek received a quick response from his Linz childhood friend:

I would very much like—when the time of my hardest struggles is over—to revive personally the memory of those wonderful years of my life. Perhaps it would be possible for you to visit me? Wishing yourself and your mother all the best, I remain in the memory of our old friendship.

It was not until 1938, shortly after the Anschluss, that the two old friends finally met again in Linz. Hitler warmly greeted Kubizek and spontaneously volunteered to "sponsor the education of your three sons," telling him:

I don't like it when young, gifted people are forced to go along the same track we did. You know how it was for us in Vienna. After that, for me, came the worst time of all, after our paths separated. That young talent goes under because of need, must not be allowed to happen.

Dr. Eduard Bloch, the Jewish doctor who had cared for his dying mother, also wrote Hitler in 1938. He asked for help in immigrating to the United States. Hitler ordered the Gestapo to help the man he referred to as a "Noble Jew" resettle in New York City. Bloch died there in 1945 at the age of seventy-three.

Two Jewish officers who had served with Hitler on the western front, Hugo Guttmann and Ernst Hess, were also offered his protection. With the Gestapo's help, Guttmann immigrated to America and settled in St. Louis, Missouri, a city with a large German population. Heinrich Himmler personally wrote a letter to Nazi authorities in Dusseldorf, the German city where Hess lived. They were ordered to afford him "relief and protection as per the Führer's wishes." Like his hero Karl Lueger, Hitler's anti-Semitism could be selective.

No such exception was made for Maximilian and Ernst Hohenberg. Hitler and Joseph Goebbels, Nazi Minister of Public Enlightenment and Propaganda, discussed the sons of Franz Ferdinand as they returned to Berlin by train. The Gestapo had not silenced Otto Habsburg, who remained in Belgian exile, but they had successfully arrested the public leaders of the Habsburg restoration movement in Austria. As far as Hitler was concerned, a Hohenberg was a Habsburg. The only thing that made the Hohenbergs worse was that their mother was a Slav. As they enjoyed breakfast in the comfort of their rosewood-paneled dining car, Hitler gleefully denounced Max and Ernst, telling Goebbels, "They are worthless and must never be allowed back. . . . Get rid of the rubbish."

Nazi propaganda photos of
Maximilian and Ernst Hohenberg,
the defiant sons of Franz Ferdinand,
taken at Dachau. The date was June
28, 1938, the 24th anniversary of the
assassination of their parents. *BArch,
Bild 152-21-30 / Friedrich Franz
Bauer…and BArch, Bild 152-21-35 /
Friedrich Franz Bauer*

Ausfahrt Sr. k. u. k. Hoheit Erzherzog Franz Ferdinand und Gemahlin.

A postcard of Franz Ferdinand and his wife, Sophie, leaving Belvedere, their Viennese palace, in 1903. Adolf Hitler later selected Belvedere as his favorite palace for celebrating the Nazi "new intercontinental order." *Author's Collection*

Franz Ferdinand's ten-year-old son, Prince Ernst Hohenberg, was affectionately teased as "the beauty of the family." *Library of Congress*

Prince Maximilian Hohenberg was eleven at the time of his parents' assassination. *Library of Congress*

Princess Sophie Hohenberg was twelve in 1914 when she and her brothers became the world's most famous royal orphans.
Library of Congress

An informal portrait of the archduke with his family. He hated wearing military uniforms and strongly opposed any efforts to involve Austria in a war.
Author's Collection

A formal portrait of Archduke Franz Ferdinand and his wife, the Duchess of Hohenberg, with their three children.
Author's Collection

Minutes before they were assassinated, the archduke and his duchess greeted dignitaries at the City Hall in Sarajevo. They had already survived one assassination attempt earlier in the day. Shortly before leaving for Sarajevo, Franz Ferdinand had confided to his nephew, "I know I will soon be murdered." *Author's Collection*

A propaganda postcard issued after the assassination. Contrary to the romanticized sketched image, the coffin of the archduke's morganatic wife was placed several inches below his in the Imperial Chapel. Despite the fact that the duchess died trying to save her husband's life, the lower position of her coffin left no doubt of her outside status in the class-conscious Habsburg court. *Author's Collection*

A memorial postcard of the assassinated heir to the Austro-Hungarian throne and his wife. His death was the only assassination to trigger a world war. *Author's Collection*

A photo purported to show a youthful Adolf Hitler in Munich celebrating Germany's declaration of war on August 3, 1914. He rejoiced at the news of Franz Ferdinand's assassination, certain it would bring war, destroy the Habsburgs' multicultural Empire, and make a victorious Germany the most powerful nation on Earth. *Glasshouse Images / Alamy Stock Photo*

Franz Ferdinand's sons, Maximilian and Ernst Hohenberg, with their wives, Elisabeth and Maisie, in 1937. For many Austrians, including Adolf Hitler, the Hohenbergs had become the leading opponents of the Nazi takeover of Austria. *Scherl / Sueddeutsche Zeitung Photo*

On March 12, 1938, a triumphant Adolf Hitler returns to conquer the city that once conquered him. The first two Austrians ordered arrested by the Gestapo, deported from the country, and imprisoned at Dachau were the anti-Nazi sons of Franz Ferdinand. Hitler told Joseph Goebbels, "They are worthless and must never be allowed back…away with the rubbish." *BArch, Bild 146-1985-03083-10 / o.Ang*

Hitler speaks to three-quarters of a million cheering Viennese from the balcony of the Habsburg palace. In the distance is Vienna's city hall where his anti-Semitic role model, Mayor Karl Lueger, once mesmerized the city with his hate-filled rhetoric. *BArch, Bild 183-1987-0922-500 / o.Ang*

ERZHERZOGIN MARIA THERESIA

Countess Marie Theresa Wood (known in the family as Maisie) with her husband, Prince Ernst Hohenberg. Her ability to read lips allowed her to navigate through and around the Gestapo during her long fight to free her husband from Nazi imprisonment. *Imagno / Austrian Archives / Sueddeutsche Zeitung Photo*

Franz Ferdinand's stepmother, Archduchess Maria-Theresa Braganza, known as the "melancholy beauty of the Habsburg court." She was a fearless champion of Franz Ferdinand and his royal orphans from the days of Emperor Franz Joseph to the dark nights of Adolf Hitler. The archduchess told her grandson Maximilian Hohenberg, "Trust God, but never try to understand God." *Author's Collection*

Franz Ferdinand's daughter, nineteen-year-old Princess Sophie of Hohenberg, with her brothers—seventeen-year-old Maximilian and sixteen-year-old Ernst—and their guardian Count Thun on Sophie's wedding day, September 8, 1920. Only Count Thun seemed happy. *Photo courtesy of Friedrich Count Nostitz*

Adolf Hitler on his fifty-second birthday accepting the stolen plaque from Sarajevo commemorating Franz Ferdinand's assassination. Hitler's rise to power was made possible by the assassination. Winston Churchill wrote, "This war would have never come unless, under American and modernizing pressure, we had driven the Habsburgs out of Austria and Hungary...by making these vacuums we gave the opening for the Hitlerite monster to crawl out of its sewer onto vacant thrones." *Bayerische Staatsbibliothek München / Bildarchiv*

The Anschluss monument in Klagenfurt, Austria, depicting the crushing of the Austrian people under the heel of the Nazis in 1938. *Author's Collection*

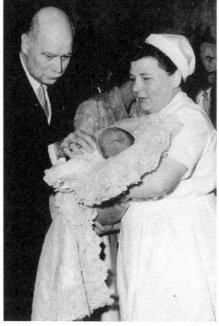

Maximilian, Duke of Hohenberg, with granddaughter Princess Sophie and nurse, at her 1960 christening. "With the next generation, there is always hope." *Photo courtesy of Princess Sophie de Potesta of Hohenberg*

CHAPTER FIFTEEN
DUEL

"Would it be better to draw it out, leave these men in jail for years where they belong, and then kill them, or send them to the gallows immediately?"
—HERMAN GOERING

Eighty-three-year-old Habsburg Archduchess Maria-Theresa was born a Braganza, a direct descendant of an ancient Portuguese family that provided England and Spain queens, Brazil two emperors, and Portugal fifteen generations of royalty. She had never been intimidated by the house of Habsburg, and she refused to be intimidated by Hitler. Her family motto—"Braganza blood does not tremble"—safely navigated her through family feuds, assassinations, revolutions, and wars.

Within hours of Ernst and Max Hohenberg's arrest, their wives made their way to the home of the family matriarch.

Like most women of her time, Maria-Theresa lived her life in the shadows of powerful fathers, brothers, and husbands. Her ancestry condemned her to the royal wedding bed; but it also required that she use her intelligence, strength, charm, and gender to survive in a male dominated world. She mentored generations of Braganza and Habsburg women to do the same. In 1938, it was Elisabeth and Maisie Hohenberg's turn. In the coming duel with Adolf Hitler and his Gestapo, they would need the wisdom, experience, and expertise of Maria-Theresa.

She offered three pieces of advice. "Never give up. Never show fear. Use personal diplomacy with the highest possible authorities." The Archduchess had followed her own advice when she supported Franz Ferdinand's decision to marry Countess Sophie Chotek, enlisting Pope Leo XIII as an ally against her brother-in-law, Emperor Franz Joseph. As the women met at Maria-Theresa's imposing palace on Favoritenstrasse, Max and Ernst reunited in a Viennese prison cell. They were soon joined by the mayor of Vienna and the country's secretary of state for public safety. Like Maximilian, weeks earlier they had each been offered the position of Austrian Chancellor. Now they were prisoners of Adolf Hitler. Just days before the Anschluss, public opinion polls indicated Austrians planned to vote overwhelmingly against annexation. German General Alfred Jodl wrote in his diary the Nazis feared the plebiscite would deliver "a strong majority for the monarchists."

Early the next morning, Elisabeth and Maisie appeared at Vienna's Gestapo headquarters. Each had a role to play. Elisabeth, the Duchess of Hohenberg, was their spokesperson. Maisie used her ability to read lips to learn the location of the office of Dr. Ernst Kaltenbrunner, the Austrian-born Gestapo Chief. Kaltenbrunner looked like a Nazi villain from a Hollywood movie. He was a tall, dark-skinned hulk of a man with a pockmarked, deeply scarred face and deep-set, small eyes he used to great advantage to intimidate opponents. Prior to the Anschluss, he had been arrested by Austrian law enforcement three times for conspiracy and treason. Now the thirty-four-year-old Nazi henchman some referred to as a gorilla was in charge of Austria's state security.

At some point during the tension-filled morning, the conservatively but impeccably dressed women slipped their way past layers of security to suddenly appear in Kaltenbrunner's private office. In the surprise confrontation that followed, they demanded to know why their husbands had been arrested. What charges had been filed? When could they see them? Most importantly, what was the day and time of their release? The flustered Nazi was so startled that he ordered the women escorted out of the building. They may have been the only two Austrians thrown *out* of Vienna's dreaded Gestapo Headquarters.

A story from the *New York Times* on March 23, 1938, reported on the arrests taking place across Austria. "It is a heterogeneous list, including as it does leading monarchists, Catholics, Socialists, Communists and peasant leaders." An accompanying article was headlined, HABSBURG PRINCES ARRESTED BY AUSTRIAN NAZIS. Large photographs of "Prince Ernst of Hohenberg" and "Prince Max of Hohenberg" were prominently featured. A second article provided further details. "The Hitler Elite Guard organ, the Schwarze Korps, announces their imprisonment and expresses contempt for their families and personal character."

The next day a *New York Times* headline read, UNIVERSITY PURGE PUSHED—RESTRICTIONS ON JEWS ARE RAPIDLY INCREASED. Jews as "non-Aryans" lost their jobs, but they were not alone. Catholics, a Nobel Prize winner in Medicine, and a Nobel laureate in Physics were also immediately "retired" from their university posts. Past and present government ministers continued to be arrested.

That same morning, Elisabeth and Maisie Hohenberg again appeared at the Gestapo Headquarters. Despite Kaltenbrunner's refusal to see them, they continued to return on a daily basis. Hundreds of stunned, protesting, beaten, sobbing, terrified prisoners were brought past them to be interrogated. Among them was Anna Freud, Sigmund Freud's daughter. She was eventually released, but her arrest by the Gestapo convinced her legendary eighty-two-year-old father, then under house arrest in Vienna, to leave Austria. For others it was too late. Many of the arrested were never seen again.

On March 26, 1938, when the women arrived at the Gestapo Headquarters they were informed their husbands were no longer in the city. No further information was provided. They immediately made their way to the Favoritenstrasse residence of Archduchess Maria-Theresa. She counseled them to aim higher. Within hours, Maisie's father, Captain George Jervis Wood, took her advice literally. He flew to London hoping the British Foreign Office might help locate the men.

Events taking place in Berlin that afternoon would soon impact the Hohenbergs, Czechoslovakia, and all of Europe. That day Hitler finalized plans to annex the Sudetenland region of Czechoslovakia. The rest of the country, including Prague, would soon follow. On orders from Berlin, "spontaneous" riots broke out throughout the Sudetenland. A banner headline in the *New York Times* read, CZECHS SEE BLOW TO AUTONOMY; ITALY, FRANCE AND BRITAIN ARE READY TO SUPPORT ANY SCHEME TO KEEP PEACE. In smaller print the article reported the country's Sudetenland Party demanded immediate independence and unification with Germany.

In Vienna, the Hohenberg women filled their days and nights writing letters seeking information from Austrian and German officials about their missing husbands. On April 14, 1938, their efforts were rewarded. Maisie received a letter from the thirty-seven-year-old Chief of German Police and Minister of the Interior Heinrich Himmler. Among his many responsibilities was supervision of the Gestapo. He informed her that the arrests were the result of the "terrible behavior" both men had perpetrated against the Nazis since 1934. Himmler wrote, "Your husband, Prince Ernst Hohenberg, and his brother are in the Dachau concentration camp. Like any other protective custody prisoner, they will be treated fairly there, without any danger to their lives." He had recently visited Dachau and told the Austrians, "You know from now on you are in protective custody; that means I shall accord you my most special protection."

Heavily censored letters from Maximilian and Ernst, postmarked from Germany, confirmed their Dachau imprisonment. Thousands of Austrians had been arrested. Hundreds had been released, others had been killed. Few felt safe, but one who did offered help. Baron

Wilhelm von Ketteler, the Austrian secretary to Franz von Papen, contacted Elisabeth and Maisie. He told them he could obtain an exit visa for them and their children to Switzerland. The women refused his offer. They feared that if they left Austria they would never see their husbands again. A short time later, Ketteler's body was found floating in the Danube. Seven thousand suicides had been reported in Austria since the Anschluss, most of them Jews. The Catholic Ketteler was not one of them. His battered, bloated body still smelled strongly of the chloroform used to silence his screams. The message was clear. No one was to help the Hohenbergs.

Countess Rosa von Lonyay Wood, Maisie's mother, spoke directly to Ambassador von Papen, a longtime friend. He assured her the arrest of her son-in-law was an "unfortunate mistake" he would rectify immediately. When he learned Hitler had personally ordered the Hohenberg arrests, he never spoke to Mrs. Wood again.

From her ancestral castle in Württemberg, Elisabeth's mother, Maria Lobkowicz, Princess of Waldburg, took matters into her own hands. She had her chauffeur prepare her large Maybach touring car for a road trip. The black and yellow car, the colors of the Waldburg and Habsburg dynasties, drove the 115 miles to the gates of Dachau. There she demanded the guards grant her permission to visit her son-in-law, Duke Maximilian von Hohenberg, and Prince Ernst his brother. She was politely refused. Only after Dachau's Commandant, Hans Loritz, came to the car and respectfully informed her she was not permitted to enter the camp, and that Max and Ernst were not available to speak, did she reluctantly leave. Ironically the brothers were regularly marched out to the camp's parade ground to be publicly mocked and humiliated by visiting Nazi dignitaries.

Word of their treatment filtered back to the capitals of Europe. A number of influential persons began working on their behalf including the Pope, the Vatican Secretary of State, the King and Queen of Sweden, and the Grand Duke of Luxembourg. Even the wives of Neville

Chamberlain and Edward Halifax, England's Prime Minister and Foreign Secretary, tried to help but were rebuffed.

Otto Habsburg traveled from his Belgium exile to London to ask the General Consul of the British Diplomatic Corps, "How is it possible that the sons of Franz Ferdinand are being detained in a German Concentration Camp and the English government does nothing?" The diplomat had no answer Otto then contacted England's Queen Mary, widow of King George V, the mother of the Duke of Windsor. The Dowager Queen asked that British diplomats in Berlin speak directly to Herman Goering. The British Ambassador asked Goering, "Who ordered Maximilian and Ernst Hohenberg to be delivered to Dachau?" His question was rebuffed, but Goering told him, "The Princes need to stay there as long as possible. They are sadists like their father. If you had the knowledge we do, you would know there is nothing we can do for these people." To Queen Mary, who knew and personally liked Franz Ferdinand, it seemed as if the world had gone mad.

The Hohenberg homes at Artstetten and Radmer were looted by the Nazis. Neighbors were encouraged to join in the pillaging, and they did. Their extensive landholdings and properties were confiscated, and their bank accounts and financial assets seized. Sophie tried to convince her sisters-in-law to come to Prague; but Czechoslovakia itself was no longer safe. Thousands of Jews were fleeing the country. Martial law had been declared. Pro-Nazi demonstrations and anti-Semitism rocked nearly every village, town, and city.

Lifelong friends of the Hohenberg family joined the Nazi Party or became silent collaborators. Most people were too frightened to speak out; but Elisabeth and Maisie continued campaigning for the release of their husbands. Finally, Elisabeth was informed that a Nazi official from Berlin would meet with her at the Hotel Imperial on his next trip to Vienna. The man Hitler selected to discuss the Hohenberg case with Max's wife was Herman Goering.

Only the Führer himself had more power, prestige, and influence in Nazi Germany. Shortly after the arrests of the Hohenberg brothers, the elderly Archduke, Joseph Ferdinand, a Habsburg, was also arrested by the Gestapo, and sent to Dachau. Goering's brother and sister, living in Austria, asked him to release the retired non-political World War I veteran as a favor to them. He was promptly released, but the shock and trauma of the experience shattered his health. Joseph Ferdinand's story brought both hope, and fear, to Elisabeth Hohenberg.

As she did for all appointments, she arrived early for her morning meeting with Goering. He kept her waiting. As the hours ticked away, she sat alone in the bustling lobby beneath brilliantly lit crystal chandeliers, carved marble statues, and the hotel's imposing grand staircase. In the midafternoon, a very polite, very respectful Luftwaffe officer invited her to wait upstairs. She followed him to a private elevator, up two floors, down a long corridor, and then sat on a chair outside Goering's suite for the rest of the afternoon. She'd had nothing to eat or drink since she arrived hours earlier. Finally, she was invited to enter the salon where the meeting would take place.

The large ornate room was dominated by an oversized desk that sat empty. Goering's assistant walked throughout the apartment opening and closing doors seemingly to search for him, but he was not found. Then, as if on cue, the forty-five-year-old Goering stepped gingerly into the room from an outside balcony. He was not wearing his usual military uniform, but was flamboyantly dressed head to toe in a dazzling white business suit. Even his hat, shoes, and socks were white.

Perhaps to present the appearance of distinction, he wore a monocle and a signet ring, props she had never seen him wear in any of his newsreel or newspaper photographs. He looked to her like a supernumerary from a Viennese operetta. If he was known for having a sense of humor, she might have smiled.

Addressing her as the Duchess of Hohenberg, he asked her to be seated. Then he sat at the desk, spun the chair away from her so she found herself facing his back, and quietly played with his monocle. She stared at the back of his chair waiting for him to break the silence. Goering finally said, "I know you have come to ask for two people. I have thought about your request a great deal, but I am undecided. Would it be better to draw it out, leave these men in jail for years where they belong, and then kill them, or send them to the gallows immediately?"

He waited a long time for her response. She said nothing. Goering then swung around, faced her, and began asking questions as if he were a prosecutor, and she a defendant. Later she could barely remember his rapid-fire questions until he asked, "How can you defend Ernst Hohenberg who as a leader of the Home Guard tortured and burned patriotic pro-German Austrians? Your brother-in-law has been roasting good National Socialists in his castle!" Elisabeth Hohenberg told him, "Surely, even you cannot believe such things." Her cool response momentarily silenced him.

At some point during the meeting, she became the interrogator. The Duchess asked Goering how she was to care for five children— all sons, all born to a German mother, their father arrested with no charges filed, and their home and all their assets taken? They argued for over an hour, but neither backed down. When the duel ended, he told her, "Heads up German woman. Write your letters and all will be well."

Elisabeth Hohenberg felt she had stared the devil in the face and not blinked. Her husband and brother-in-law remained at Dachau. But following the meeting, she was notified that she could return to Artstetten Castle. With her father's financial support, the Duchess and her five children took up residence as a renter in a small corner of her own home.

When she determined the teacher at the local school was an ardent Nazi, she sent her two oldest sons, eleven-year-old Franz and ten-year-old Georg, to live with her parents in Württemberg. Elisabeth felt they would be safer in Germany, under less suspicion and surveillance. Nazi racist propaganda was more virulent in Austrian schools than in rural Germany. In the Württemberg village school, Nazi teachers, students, and propaganda were in less evidence. Two fewer mouths to feed in a crowded household with no regular income was also a benefit; but mostly she wanted her sons under the positive influence of her father.

No one in Württemberg was more respected than Elisabeth Hohenberg's father—Prince Maximilian IV of Waldburg, who made no attempt to hide his contempt for Adolf Hitler. From his castle on the town's highest hill he was able to easily receive uncensored news from Radio Switzerland about what was happening in Germany. Since he was hard of hearing, he turned the radio up as loud as possible so everyone in the nearby village could also hear the broadcast. The Prince was so loved in the region that not even the Gestapo dared tell him to turn his radio down.

Elisabeth carefully chose which battles to fight. Once she returned to Artstetten, she was continually harassed to join the local Nazi Women's Auxiliary. She refused, but fund-raisers relentlessly pressured her to buy busts of Hitler and Goering to prove her loyalty to the German Reich. In an attempt to stop future visits, Max's wife finally agreed to purchase two small busts. Prior to placing them out of sight, she noticed the busts of both men were hollow, and Goering's did not include the monocle he had twirled throughout their visit at the Hotel Imperial. When the Nazi solicitors continued their visits, she traveled to Vienna and filed a harassment complaint against them. The Duchess of Hohenberg may have been the lone Austrian man or woman bold enough to file such a complaint, but it worked. They never returned.

Originally she explained to her younger children their father was traveling. Later she told them he and their uncle were staying at a camp in Germany. Dachau's prisoners were allowed to send a postcard home every two weeks. They were so heavily censored that her young sons had no idea they were being written from prison.

Twenty thousand Austrians were taken into custody following the Nazi Anschluss. Only those labeled the most "dangerous" were deported to Dachau. Max and Ernst had the infamous distinction of being the first Austrian "criminals" sent there. Four days later, they were joined by 153 of their countrymen. In May, another 120 detainees arrived. The Austrians were segregated from other prisoners but suffered the same cruel treatment.

A journalist who survived later wrote: "Amongst them were two ambassadors, three ministers, a state secretary, a senior judge, a state prosecutor, the mayor of Vienna, a general, a colonel, three majors, two university professors, some senior police officers, two prominent Viennese lawyers and a number of well-known journalists and authors." Another survivor wrote, "Looking at them, you would almost be ashamed to be free."

It wasn't until years later that Maximilian and Ernst's family came to understand the horror that was Dachau, not from them, but from others. Guards wielding bull whips and wearing skull-and-crossbone insignias on their uniforms mockingly addressed them as "Your Imperial Majesties." The brothers were photographed, stripped of their clothes, marched naked to the barber, their heads and mustaches shaved, given a cold shower, and issued striped uniforms and wooden shoes. They were also required to fill out forms that asked their age, date of birth, religion, occupation, and whether or not their parents were living. Guards delighted in asking details about when, where, and how their parents had died.

Neither was ever officially charged with a crime. But the Duke of Hohenberg, prison number 13742, wore the green triangular badge of a "protective custody prisoner." Prince Ernst, prison number 13741, was designated a "political criminal" for his attack on Vienna's German Tourism office. His "anti-German behavior" earned him the red badge of a terrorist. During the winter, Ernst was also required to remove the snow from the front of the SS headquarters, and scatter sand and ashes on the paths where Gestapo officers walked. The task eerily mocked Hitler's winter memories of shoveling snow in front of the Hotel Imperial for the Royal and Imperial Habsburg family.

The brothers were assigned latrine duty, the endless job of empty-ing and cleaning the camp's overflowing toilets. They were only given a spoon to assist them in their task. A witness later wrote of their treatment, "They were harnessed to the sewage cart like roped ani-mals. Their slave driver, a professional criminal, beat them mercilessly as they were chased from one latrine to another where they had to shovel excrement into buckets and cart them away." Another eyewit-ness remembered:

> Soon word got around that they were the two sons of Archduke Franz Ferdinand, assassinated at Sarajevo. On the cart was a ton of muck. The SS-men stopped them and made fun of them. They took a flat stone, had the two prisoners put their heads close to the pile of muck and then threw the stone into the pile so that the brothers' faces were splattered with excrement.

After the war, Leonard Figl, a fellow "political criminal" at Dachau, wrote of seeing the Hohenberg brothers filling, pulling, and emptying their two-wheeled cart of human waste:

> Stripped of all titles and offices and with death before their eyes every hour of every day, they endured the most excruciating humil-iation, not with the stoic pride of the "master race," but with the unwavering, serene dignity of descendants from an ancient family meant to serve and to rule. … They shared with us their last bite and their last sip, and were the most charming of companions.

One other survivor later wrote:

> They had a calm, cheerful, majestic dignity about them, an un-

shakable sense of humor, and unbreakable solidarity. If the system set group against group by encouraging one to look down on another, the Hohenbergs made it clear they were not looking down on anyone.

The brothers followed all the orders demanded by their Gestapo guards. That is, all but one. They refused to hate any of their fellow inmates, including Jews. On November 10, 1938, Jewish synagogues, homes, and businesses across Germany and Austria were attacked, looted, and burned. The infamous event became known as Kristallnacht, the Night of Broken Glass, but the violence continued throughout the following day. Police officers, firefighters, and neighbors stood by and did nothing as sixty-two Austrian synagogues were burned to the ground, Jewish cemeteries vandalized, and Jewish men, women, and children attacked, beaten, and robbed.

Six thousand Austrian Jews were then deported to Dachau. The guards took special pleasure in tormenting, humiliating, and killing them. Crossing lines drawn in the dirt or not wearing a prison cap were offenses immediately punishable by death. Sometimes guards grabbed the cap of a Jewish inmate and tossed it into a restricted area, a game that meant quick death for the bareheaded man. In an episode that became legendary among the prisoners, a guard grabbed the hat of an elderly Jew, a once famous comedian, and attempted to throw it into a prohibited area. Ernst instantly jumped high in the air, caught it, and returned it to the head of the stunned man. The guard aimed his gun but did not fire.

Maximilian came to respect many of his fellow prisoners, Jews and Jehovah's Witnesses for their sincere faith, foreign Legionnaires for their stoic physical courage, and communists and republicans for the strength of their political beliefs. Each person, including Max, found ways of quietly resisting the Nazi merchants of fear. At the end of a long workday as Max returned tools to a large wooden storage box, he heard heavy footsteps running toward him. A terrified Gypsy boy ran around the corner. They made eye contact. Max opened the box, the boy jumped in, and he closed and latched the heavy lid. The guard came sprinting around the corner like a hunting dog that had just lost its tracer scent. When Maximilian walked past the furious Nazi, he heard him curse that he would find and kill the Gypsy in the morning.

Late that night, Max sneaked out of his barracks, an offense punishable by immediate execution, crossed the camp, and unlatched the bulky lid. The boy jumped from the box and disappeared into the darkness. He wondered if the next day the guard made good on his threat and killed him. Maximilian might have given the young Gypsy only a few more hours of life, but that was enough for him. It was a small victory, but small victories made Dachau bearable.

CHAPTER SIXTEEN
BARGAIN WITH THE DEVIL

"How horrible, fantastic, incredible it is that we should be digging trenches and trying on gas masks here because of a quarrel in a faraway country of whom we know nothing."
—BRITISH PRIME MINISTER NEVILLE CHAMBERLAIN
on Czechoslovakia

"I am now at the very peak of my vitality and vigor, and no other German will possess the strength or authority to complete what I have set out to achieve."
—ADOLF HITLER

Sophie Nostitz-Rieneck did not lack confidence in herself, or her cause. When she learned her brothers had been sent to Dachau, she took it upon herself to negotiate their release with Heinrich Himmler. Like her Habsburg grandmother, she believed in direct personal diplomacy. Czechoslovakian, Austrian, and German friends were horrified. Nearly everyone refused to help her, fearful of the long arms of the Nazis.

The only person offering assistance was her longtime personal maid. Through a friend in service with the Himmler family, she tried to arrange a meeting between the Czech Countess and the German Nazi; but no time or place was ever found. The Countess decided to travel to the Gestapo Headquarters in Berlin. She went alone.

It was a dangerous time for someone from Czechoslovakia to visit the Nazi capital, especially someone whose brothers were imprisoned at Dachau. Hitler was escalating his threats against the Prague government on an almost daily basis and Sophie's destination, No 8 Prinz-Albrecht Strasse, was Berlin's most feared address.

The block-long building housed the Reich's Main Security Office. Torture and executions regularly took place in its basement. On its middle floors were the bureaucratic departments in charge of Dachau and other concentration camps. On the top floor of the former Museum and Art School sat Heinrich Himmler's office, grimly overlooking the city. His henchman Reinhard Heydrich was at his side.

Most people in 1938 Nazi Germany tried to be invisible. The Countess of Nostitz-Rieneck did not. She repeatedly returned to No 8 Prinz-Albrecht Strasse in attempts to meet Himmler, Heydrich, or any of their deputies. The immaculately dressed, always punctual Czech Countess became a familiar fixture in the building's lobby. Secretaries, guards, and even low-ranking Gestapo officers respectfully whispered to her, "Well, perhaps tomorrow," or "Maybe the day after tomorrow." Himmler and his immediate subordinates avoided her.

The days when a citizen of Czechoslovakia could freely travel to Nazi Germany were drawing to an end. In September, Adolf Hitler granted an interview to the *London Daily Mail* bluntly stating his views on race and the Czech Republic:

> This Czech trouble has got to be ended once and for all, and ended now. It is a tumor which is poisoning the whole European organism.... The creation of this heterogeneous Czechoslovakian Republic after the war was lunacy.... To set an intellectually inferior handful of Czechs to rule over minorities belonging to races like the Germans, Poles, Hungarians, with a thousand years of culture behind them, was a work of folly and ignorance.

That autumn, American diplomat George Kennan arrived in Prague and wrote:

Prague could not have been more beautiful than during the September days when its security hung by so slender a thread. Baroque towers—themselves unreal and ethereal—floated peacefully against the skies in which the bright blue Autumn made way for isolated drifting clouds.... Yet rarely, if ever, has the quaint garb of this old city seemed more museum-like, more detached from the realities of the moment, than it did these strange days.

Czechoslovakia's President Eduard Beneš trusted his country's fate to a military alliance with France, childlike faith in England, and a belief that Joseph Stalin's Soviet Union would not desert his nation. He was wrong on all counts. British Prime Minister Neville Chamberlain met with Hitler at Berchtesgaden to decide the future of a country that was not invited to the negotiations. His desire for peace at any price was as naked as the reclining nude woman in the Italian Renaissance painting on the wall behind them. An eyewitness later wrote of the meeting, "There was a somewhat macabre tea party at the round table in a room with the great window looking out over Austria." With the Italian nude painting on one side, and Austria on the other, Czechoslovakia was betrayed. One response to the Berchtesgaden meeting was an editorial cartoon in the *Washington Post*. It showed a skeletal finger turn back the clock from 1938 to 1914.

On the afternoon of September 21, 1938, loudspeakers set up in Prague announced that France and England had agreed to allow the Czech Republic to be partitioned. The Soviet Union remained silent. Much of the country's military installations, most of its industrial base, and one-third of its citizens and land mass would disappear into Hitler's Germany. The announcement ended with the words, "This case is unique in history. Our friends and allies have imposed on us such terms as are dictated to a defeated enemy."

Prague's dazed citizens filled the streets in disbelief. Traffic stopped. Most were silent. Some cried. Others sang patriotic songs, but with a melancholy dirge-like cadence. Czech flags were every-where. The streets and Wenceslas Square remained filled for two days. German newspapers reported, "Red Riot in Prague." There was no riot, just a national funeral attended by half a million mourners. Hit-ler's troops entered Czechoslovakia's Sudetenland region on October 1, 1938. Franklin Roosevelt privately denounced the move as "armed banditry." Publicly he said nothing.

George Kennan reported that once Germany entered the country, "No trains were running. No planes were flying. No frontier stations existed." Falkenau and Heinrichgrun, the Nostitz-Rieneck country homes northwest of Prague, disappeared deep inside Sudetenland ter-ritory. A kind of paralysis settled over the country. German-Czechs loyal to the republic had nowhere to go. One observer lamented:

> Germans who hated Nazism were forced to remain in the area....
> Many of those who fled and sought visas for England had their re-quests denied. The British, though claiming the power to guarantee the truncated state, could offer its threatened inhabitants neither refuge nor security.

Telephone, telegraph, and mail delivery stopped; so, too, did So-phie's visits to Berlin. Contact with her family in Austria became nearly impossible. Everyone believed the rest of Czechoslovakia was doomed. German-Czechs were not alone in being trapped. A Jewish refugee from Vienna wrote that people fled Prague as if the plague itself were approaching; but the unwelcome emigrants had nowhere to go.

In London, American Ambassador Joseph P. Kennedy wrote Secretary of State Cordell Hull, "Lord Halifax reiterated that they are instructing everybody not to make any more speeches on the Czech-German situation... all has been said that should be said. Hal-ifax and Chamberlain feel strongly that silence on their part and hop-ing on our part will get the best results." Ambassador Kennedy, a fierce isolationist opposed to war, agreed. His college-age son John, the future president of the United States, traveled to Prague and interviewed dozens of Czechs. He predicted that what was left of the gutted, traumatized country would fall to the Nazis without a fight.

One month after the Sudetenland's annexation, Hungary demanded a return of its own territories taken by Czechoslovakia following the First World War. Hitler convened a meeting with Mussolini to arbitrate the dispute. The site he chose was Belvedere Palace. The city had hundreds of available palaces, the German Reich and Fascist Italy thousands more, but Belvedere—the former home of Franz Ferdinand and Maximilian's birthplace—held special significance to him. He confided to Henrietta von Schirach that it was the only Habsburg Palace he painted as a young artist in Vienna. Hitler selected it as his palace of choice for signing treaties and military alliances.

As rumors of war again threatened Europe, Franz Ferdinand's old friend the Duke of Portland published his memoirs. Portland looked back on the Sarajevo assassination and wrote:

> It was criminal and tragic in its senselessness. How desperately sad it is that England would never witness the ascension to the throne of this great Habsburg prince. Would it not have been an immense advantage today if there was an entire strong and peaceful power in the Danubian basin? This noble prince was also a true European and what we see now when it is too late—he saw at the time. In justice to his memory—one must admit how much would have been different had he lived.

Five months after seizing the Sudetenland, one year after the Anschluss, Hitler's armies swallowed the rest of Czechoslovakia. The Nazis, a blizzard, and the Ides of March arrived in Prague simultaneously. As John F. Kennedy predicted, the country, government, and military surrendered without firing a shot. Hitler again triumphantly followed his army into a conquered European capital, but Prague was no Vienna. He was greeted with no cheers, no Nazi salutes, only empty streets and cold silence.

After declaring that the state of Czechoslovakia no longer existed, Hitler surveyed the city from the thousand-year-old Prague Castle. He proclaimed the ancient kingdoms of Bohemia and Moravia German protectorates. That night he slept in Tomas Masaryk's bed. Two days later, he flew to Vienna where he once again stayed at the Hotel Imperial. The disappearance of central Europe's only genuine democracy was met in official circles by nearly universal silence. Leaders in England, France, and the Soviet Union hoped that by sacrificing Czechoslovakia, war with Germany would be averted. Otto Habsburg refused to be silent. His denunciation was published in *Time* magazine. "I condemn with the utmost energy the violence with which Germany subjugated Bohemia and Moravia. I condemn also the military occupation of Slovakia by a German army." Central Europe knew peace was not at hand. Churches in neighboring Poland and Rumania filled to overflowing as their governments prepared for war.

Four days after the invasion of the Sudetenland, President Eduard Beneš resigned. As Czechoslovakia faced its worst crisis in its twenty-year history, he announced, "I remain what I have always been, a convinced democrat, and therefore I am leaving the field. I feel it is for the best not to disturb the new European constellation that is arising." Beneš asked his government ministers to do their duty and remain at their posts. His successor, Emil Hácha, was in failing health, even before suffering a heart attack after meeting Herman Goering. With his ashen face resembling a death mask, he pleaded with his fellow citizens to accept their fate. Public address systems in Prague urged citizens to go about their business and be both "good Czechs and good Germans."

Sophie Hohenberg Nostitz-Rieneck had been an Austrian and a Czech, but Adolf Hitler dictated she and her family were German. In an instant her past and future were taken from her. Twice she felt orphaned, once in 1914 with the assassination of her parents, and again in 1938 with the theft of her nationality and country.

Hitler's Gestapo wasted no time in making their way to the home of Franz Ferdinand's daughter. The Nostitz-Rieneck mansion was searched from top to bottom, and the four children placed under house arrest. Sophie and Fritz were taken to a formidable bank building on the far side of Prague that had been transformed into Gestapo headquarters. During hours of interrogation, Fritz, the robust forty-five-year-old former officer in the Austrian Imperial Army, proved unflappable. Sophie also refused to be frightened. She had not flinched at the Gestapo headquarters in Berlin, and she refused to be intimidated by Himmler's minions in Prague. The couple was finally released, but the Gestapo had not finished with them.

American diplomat George Kennan wrote that the Czechs had two choices, collaborating with evil or committing heroic suicide. The Gestapo returned to the Nostitz-Rieneck home to make Sophie and her husband a similar offer. Fritz was summoned to his own library and offered a commission in either the Wehrmacht Home Guard, or the Gestapo. Imprisonment for him and his family was the alternative.

Fritz's late father had been a loyal Czech, but also a leader of Sudetenland Czechs of German ancestry. Recruiting his son to work with the Nazis would be popular in the Sudetenland, and allow him to be kept under close supervision, and even closer surveillance. It was a bitter surrender. Once Fritz joined the Wehrmacht Home Guard, he, Sophie, and their family became prize hostages.

Czechs who fled, bribed their way out of the country, or attempted to escape through snow-covered woods or mountain passes condemned family and friends left behind to imprisonment and death. Josef Korbel, a Czech diplomat who fled with his wife and daughter, had twenty-five members of his family arrested and die in concentration camps. Korbel's daughter Madeline Albright became the first female secretary of state of the United States.

Sophie supported her husband's bargain with the devil, hoping it might save Max and Ernst. She immediately wrote Heinrich Himmler requesting they be released from Dachau into the custody of her husband. After a long delay, she was informed Hitler and Goering vetoed her request. Ernst in particular was singled out as a "desecrator of Nazi iconography."

Prague became a city in purgatory. Fear, numbness, harassment, and suicides became a part of everyday life. Jews and Gypsies were declared non-citizens and joined thousands of deportees sent to Theresienstadt, an ancient Sudetenland fortress named for a Habsburg Empress. Franz Ferdinand's imprisoned assassin had died there. Ten thousand children would pass through its gates never to be seen again.

The Nazis quickly declared war on Czech culture. Books were burned; radio broadcasts censored; newspapers, theatres, and even Prague's National Opera House were closed. Museums and university libraries were emptied of paintings, tapestries, manuscripts, and books. The crown jewels of Bohemia's ancient kings were shipped to Berlin, and the ancestral homes of the Lobkowitz, Starhemberg, Kinsky, and other ancient families were systematically plundered.

Konopiste, Sophie Nostitz-Rieneck's birthplace and the former home of the man the Nazis referred to as the "decadent Franz Ferdinand," was an early target. The castle had been scrupulously maintained as a museum by the Czech government. With the exception of the pilfering by President Masaryk's family and other Czech officials, its interior looked much the way it had the day Sophie and her brothers were expelled. That quickly changed. Konopiste was emptied of its art, oriental rugs, Meissen china, priceless antiques, dozens of family portraits of Habsburg and Chotek ancestors, and hundreds of silver-framed family photographs. The Duchess of Hohenberg's entire library was packed into forty-two large wooden crates and transported out of the country. The castle's cutlery was melted down to extract its high gold and silver content, but its great dining hall and dining service was left intact to entertain distinguished visitors.

Franz Ferdinand's famous collection of medieval armor was sent to the newly created Wehrmacht Museum of Military History located in Prague. The museum was not open to the public. It was only a temporary home until Adolf Hitler could build a museum in Linz to house it. The Archduke's historic firearm collection was sent to the Imperial Hunting Museum in Berlin. Military paintings and other artifacts from the Archduke's army career were made available on "permanent loan" to the clubs, offices, dormitories, and private homes of Gestapo officials. Konopiste's furniture was reserved to furnish the home of the newly appointed Deputy Reich Protector of Bohemia and Moravia, Reinhard Heydrich. The castle and grounds where Sophie Nostitz-Rieneck had been born were turned into a training school for the Gestapo.

Adolf Hitler proudly called Heydrich "the man with an iron heart." Tall, blond, and blue-eyed, he became the architect of Hitler's final solution, a Nazi god of death responsible for the genocide of millions of Jews. Heydrich promised Hitler, "We will Germanize the Czech vermin." His own deputy described him as having "an ice cold intellect untouched by pangs of conscience.... Torture and killing were his daily occupations."

In private, Heydrich was a devoted family man to his wife, Lina, who had recruited him to join the Nazi Party, and their three young children. They lived on the outskirts of Prague in a beautiful chateau stolen from Ferdinand and Adele Bloch-Bauer. Adele was the famous "woman in gold" in Gustav Klimt's painting. Frau Heydrich proudly filled her home with furniture and treasures stolen from Konopiste. Waited on by slave laborers from the nearby Theresienstadt and Auschwitz concentration camps, Lina bragged to friends she lived like a princess in a magical fairy tale. Her fairy tale began unraveling when her husband, the "Butcher of Prague," was assassinated by Czech exiles flown into the country by Edvard Beneš and his government in exile.

Heinrich Himmler shed tears when he learned of the death of his favorite killer; Hitler lamented he was "irreplaceable." The Führer threatened to deport the entire non-German population from the country, but settled for the arrest, torture, and murder of five thousand Czechs. The village of Lidice near Prague was leveled to the ground, its men shot, and its women and children sent to concentration camps. Himmler gave his favorite deputy a flowery eulogy at a massive state funeral in Berlin. In the reign of terror that followed, Prague's time in purgatory ended, replaced by a Nazi hell. Sophie, Fritz, and their fellow Czechs tried to survive by being invisible.

Hitler celebrated his fiftieth birthday reviewing a four-hour military parade in Berlin. The cadaverous Czech President Hácha grimly stood at his side. Later that day, Hitler confided to intimates, "Gentlemen, the first half century of my life is now over... I am now at the very peak of my vitality and vigor, and no other German will possess the strength or authority to complete what I have set out to achieve." One week later in a broadcast beamed across Germany, the dreamer from Linz immodestly reflected on his life and achievements. Cynics labeled it Hitler's peace speech.

> I have brought back to the Reich provinces stolen from us in 1919. I have led back to their native country millions of Germans who were torn away from us and in deep misery. I have re-established the thousand-year-old historic unity of the German *Lebensraum*... I have endeavored to attain all this without spilling blood and without bringing my people, and consequently to others, the misery of wars. I who twenty-one years ago was an unknown worker and soldier of my people, have attained this... by my own energy, and can, therefore claim to be included amongst the greatest achievers the world has ever known.

Four months later, on September 1, 1939, Germany invaded Poland, and Britain and France declared war on the Reich. When Hitler realized a Second World War had begun, he surprised his subordinates by growing uncharacteristically quiet. A long period of uncomfortable silence followed, unnerving those around him. Finally, Hitler turned to his Foreign Minister, Joachim Ribbentrop, and asked, "What now?"

CHAPTER SEVENTEEN
THE ELEVENTH COMMANDMENT

"All the pale horses of the Apocalypse have stormed through
my life; revolution and famine, currency depreciation and
terror, epidemics and emigration."   —STEFAN ZWEIG

"Trust God. But never try to understand God."
            —ARCHDUCHESS MARIA-THERESA HABSBURG

The month the Second World War began, nearly one thousand pris-
oners, including Max and Ernst Hohenberg, were transferred to the
Flossenbürg Concentration Camp located in the Bavarian mountains.
Dachau was needed temporarily for the training of military personnel.
Flossenbürg was almost directly across the mountains from Falkenau,
one of Fritz's Sudetenland estates. Its inmates, primarily career criminals,
brutalized the political prisoners, communists, homosexuals, Jehovah's
Witnesses, and other conscientious objectors brought from Dachau.

Flossenbürg's inmates worked at a nearby aircraft manufacturing
plant or in deep granite quarries. Hitler's massive building projects required a steady supply of cut stones and masonry. Ernst and Max were
again assigned latrine duty, minus tools or handcart. The human waste
from the overflowing toilets was to be removed with their hands. No
humiliation was to be spared Franz Ferdinand's sons.

Winter came early that year with freezing rain, record snowfall,
and temperatures dropping to forty degrees below zero. Europe's winter

of 1940 was the coldest and longest on record. Dysentery and typhoid fever broke out at Flossenbürg. The contagious diseases spread so rapidly that guards retreated to a barbed-wire perimeter outside the camp. There, warmed by large fires, they waited for everyone inside to die.

Ernst, Max, and a seventy-year-old Viennese political prisoner named Dr. Friedrich Mittmeyer cared for the sick and dying. Almost no food or medical supplies remained in the camp. Burned charcoal was used as a disinfectant. Prisoners too weak to feed themselves were spoon-fed broth heated from frozen grass one mouthful at a time. The dead were buried in mass graves using pitchforks. When guards reentered the camp that spring, they were disgusted to find anyone alive. Casualties had been in the thousands; but newspapers and *Time* magazine reported the death of only one prisoner, Prince Ernst Hohenberg.

Ernst had not died, but his family did not learn he was alive for several months.

Flossenbürg's few surviving political prisoners returned to Dachau. To Max's surprise, he was ordered by his guards to write his autobiography. He imagined the only possible purpose for such a document was to use it against him in an upcoming trial. No other Dachau prisoner was asked to write such a document. At the end of his exhausting workdays, with almost no light to write, he carefully reconstructed his life on paper as his fellow prisoners slept around him.

Weighing and parsing each word, he used all his training as a lawyer to fill the pages with accurate nothingness so that no content could come back to haunt him. The exercise became a calculated game of chess, something to have fun with and discipline his mind. He wrote about his visits to Germany, the healthy animals he saw there, the well-kept farms, the polite people, the clean streets. Everything was painted in the most positive terms. Politics were never mentioned, nor were his thoughts and feelings about anything of substance. It became an act of passive revenge against his captors. He decided to bore them to death.

Sometime after completing his sanitized memoir, he was summoned to a meeting with the camp's commandant. Max was informed that if he signed a document agreeing to never discuss what he had seen, heard, or experienced at Dachau or Flossenbürg, he would serve the rest of his sentence under house arrest at Artstetten. Ernst was to remain at Dachau.

No Nazi mind-game could have been more devastating. To leave his younger brother behind was worse than a death sentence. Max did not believe he would have survived his ordeal without Ernst by his side. His brother assured him he, too, would soon be released, but his words lacked conviction. Ernst had been labeled a terrorist. The label worked its sinister dark magic. It made him a non-person.

Maximilian Hohenberg may have never felt more alone than on the train ride from Munich to Vienna. When he arrived unannounced at Artstetten, his family did not recognize him. Elisabeth asked about Ernst. After a long pause, her husband whispered, "He was alive when I left him." Max's young sons joyfully greeted him, wearing mandated haircuts combed to the left to better resemble the Führer, and dressed in the handsome uniforms of the Hitler Youth movement. It was a bittersweet homecoming.

Depression overwhelmed him. His house arrest confined him to a few crowded rooms at Artstetten, but his mind remained imprisoned with Ernst at Dachau. Once a week he was required to leave Artstetten and report to the local Gestapo Headquarters. There he had to document anyone he had seen or spoken with, and what had been discussed. He complained to Elisabeth that he was expected to spy on himself. Each headquarters visit triggered flashbacks to Dachau and Flossenbürg. With his brother in Dachau, Czech brother-in-law serving in the Wehrmacht Home Guard, two sons living in Germany, and his younger sons forced to join the Hitler Youth movement, there seemed no escape from the Nazis.

Poland, Denmark, Norway, Holland, Luxembourg, Belgium, and

France all fell to Hitler's armies. In November 1941, Hungary, which had once made up half of the Habsburg Empire, allied itself to Germany. The treaty was signed by Hitler at the Vienna's Belvedere Palace. Weeks earlier, Bulgaria had signed its own German military alliance there. Vienna's Neues Wiener Tagblatt celebrated the beginnings of a new "intercontinental order."

When Belgium was invaded, Nazi paratroopers landed within miles of the home of exiled Empress Zita and her eight children. The Habsburgs were warned of the approaching paratroopers by their cousins, the Belgian royal family. Zita, with her six youngest children, fled to Portugal. Her two oldest sons, Otto and Charles, headed to Brussels, then Paris. There they helped nearly twelve thousand Austrian Jewish exiles, the entire Belgian cabinet, and the Luxembourg royal family get exit visas to Spain and Portugal to escape the invading Nazis. The Luftwaffe bombed the castle where the exiled Habsburgs had lived, but they missed their targets. The Habsburgs reunited in Portugal and received asylum in the United States. President Roosevelt befriended Otto, who urged him to recognize Austria as Hitler's first victim, not his willing collaborator.

According to Albert Speer, Hitler's favorite architect, the Führer briefly visited Paris, France, on June 28, 1940. By fate, design, or synchronistic coincidence, the date was the anniversary of the 1914 Sarajevo assassination, and the signing of the 1918 Treaty of Versailles. Hitler toured the Paris Opera House, the Eiffel Tower, and other landmarks. Speer remembered Hitler telling him, "It was the dream of my life to be permitted to see Paris. I cannot say how happy I am to have that dream fulfilled today." The architect wrote in his memoirs:

> For a moment I felt something like pity for him: three hours in Paris, the one and only time he was to see it, made him happy when he stood at the height of his triumphs.... In the course of the tour Hitler raised the question of a Paris victory parade. But after dis-

cussing the matter with his adjutants... he decided against it... [saying], "I am not in the mood for a victory parade. We aren't done yet."

Hitler told Speer the parade should be scheduled for 1950, when the wars were over. The day he visited Paris, the Luftwaffe bombed England's Channel Islands of Guernsey and Jersey. The islands were quickly occupied by German troops. Within weeks, Greece and Yugoslavia were invaded.

Yugoslavia surrendered after only fourteen days of fighting. When German troops entered Sarajevo, they discovered the perfect gift for Hitler's fifty-second birthday. In an elaborate ceremony recorded for posterity, they removed the commemorative plaque marking the site of Franz Ferdinand's assassination. The event was shown in movie newsreels across occupied Europe. At its conclusion the Führer himself was shown happily receiving the gift. He recognized, perhaps more than anyone else, that the assassination had made possible his rise to power and his wars of racial terror.

Belvedere Palace was once again in the news. Yugoslavia's defeated government was summoned to Vienna to sign a treaty with their Nazi conquerors. Rumanian diplomat Raoul Bossy noted that Hitler entered the Palace's circular Chinese room preceded by three loud knocks. It was the same signal once used by the Habsburg court to announce the entrance of the Emperor. He wrote of the banquet that followed, "The shades of Archduke Franz Ferdinand d'Este, last owner of the palace, and his ancestors must have shuddered then in indignation and then must have done so again seeing Hitler, who never ate meat, attentively dice with his knife the vegetables served to him... the silence was oppressive.... It was truly a funereal meal."

That spring, Maximilian Hohenberg was called to the local Gestapo Headquarters and notified that one of his sons had been skipping his mandated Hitler Youth meetings. Max was warned to control the boy, or the Gestapo would do it for him. Word also came from Vienna that his Habsburg grandmother, Maria-Theresa, was in failing health. After repeated requests to Gestapo officers, he was granted permission to visit her. The visit may have saved his sanity and his soul.

Max did not travel alone. His four-year-old son, Peter, was his traveling companion. The Hohenbergs' youngest child had been reminded by his mother to be a good boy, sit still, be quiet, and say nothing. Two images remained in Peter's mind years after their journey. The first was the castle-like turrets on the front of the impressive house on Favoritenstrasse. The second was a tea cozy. It sat on a writing desk between his father and great-grandmother, but no tea was ever served.

As the adults whispered back and forth, Peter became fixated on the cozy. He could hear nothing of their soft-spoken words. Everything was said in quiet whispers. When the visit came to a close, his great-grandmother asked if there was anything he wanted. He told her he would very much like to ask why she had a tea cozy on the table without serving them tea. She gently lifted up the cozy and revealed a telephone. Then she gingerly placed the cover back over the phone and whispered, "It is so *they* cannot listen to our conversation." Maria-Theresa Braganza Habsburg refused to surrender her sense of humor to the Nazis.

The Archduchess was nicknamed the melancholy beauty of the Habsburg court by those who knew her life story but not her dry wit. Her handsome father had once been King of Portugal, yet died in penniless exile. She was the third unhappy wife of Emperor Franz Joseph's younger brother Karl Ludwig. Court watchers claimed Karl Ludwig's chief recreations were mistreating the three women he married. Despite years of marital neglect and verbal abuse, her faith, resilience, and sense of humor remained intact.

Peter never forgot the visit with his great-grandmother, a great lady from another time and place. She taught him to find humor in life's absurdities, even under a tea cozy. The visit helped Maximilian regain control over his life. Maria-Theresa's parting words were to remember the eleventh commandment, "Trust God. But never try to understand God." She told him if he wished to keep his sanity and outlast his enemies, nothing else was more important. Following the visit to the house on Favoritenstrasse, Max's spirit rose. During his weekly meetings at the local Gestapo Headquarters, he surprised his interrogators by presenting them with an ever-growing list of missing, stolen, and looted items taken from Artstetten. Using his skills as a lawyer and diplomat, he turned the tables on the Nazi bureaucrats and employed legalistic jargon to politely, but persistently, inquire about restitution.

That Christmas he and Elisabeth celebrated the birth of their sixth child, a boy they named Gerhard. In recognition of delivering another member of the master race to the Reich, Elisabeth was presented the "Mother's Silver Cross Medal" by the Nazi Party. The shining blue and white medallion featured a mounted swastika over a cross, and a facsimile signature of Adolf Hitler. She refused to wear it.

In Württemberg, her mother—who had borne twelve children— was also belatedly recognized for her maternal service to the Fatherland. Nazi officials delivered to her the Mother's Gold Cross, First Class Medal. Elisabeth's father, Maximilian Prince of Waldburg, defiantly returned it, telling authorities, "My wife is not a cow the Nazis can decorate!" Few people had such courage.

One week before the twenty-third anniversary of the Sarajevo assassinations, Germany invaded the Soviet Union. Months earlier, Adolf Hitler had sent Joseph Stalin a Christmas message reading, "Best Wishes for your personal well-being as well as for the prosperous future of the people of the friendly Soviet Union." Stalin replied, "The friendship of the peoples of Germany and the Soviet Union, cemented in blood, had every reason to be lasting and firm."

The surprise invasion and quick implosion of Joseph Stalin's armies caused millions to despair. Among them was Austria's best-selling author Stefan Zweig. He had fled to England, then to the United States, and finally to Brazil. There the homesick writer took up residence in Petropolis, a mountain city with strong Austrian roots. It was named for Archduchess Maria-Theresa's Brazilian uncle whose mother, a Habsburg princess, was born in Vienna. The city's German architecture, gothic cathedral, and mountain location reminded Zweig of Austria.

Twenty-two nations in Europe, North Africa, and the Middle East had fallen to the Nazis. Only England to the west and the Soviet Union in the east had not surrendered. The Nazis seemed on the threshold of total victory. The thought of a united Europe under the heel of Adolf Hitler caused Stefan Zweig and his wife to commit suicide. Two days earlier, he finished writing his final book, *The World of Yesterday*. In many ways, it was a four-hundred-page suicide note. Among his final words, he wrote:

> I myself have lived at the time of the two greatest wars known to mankind… the first on the German side and the second among Germany's enemies. Before those wars I saw individual freedom at its zenith, and then I saw liberty at its lowest point in hundreds of years; I have been acclaimed and despised, free and not free, rich and poor. All the pale horses of the apocalypse have stormed through my life; revolution and famine, currency depreciation and terror, epidemics and emigration; I have seen great mass ideologies grow before my eyes, and spread, Fascism in Italy, National Socialism in Germany, Bolshevism in Russia, and above all the ultimate pestilence that has poisoned the flower of our European culture, nationalism in general. I have been a defenseless, helpless witness of the unimaginable relapse of mankind into what was believed to be long forgotten barbarism.

Zweig's capitulation to pessimism expressed the depression and resignation felt by many; but exiled German author Thomas Mann wrote, "He should have never granted the Nazis this triumph." The

Hohenbergs' response to the Russian invasion was markedly different. To Max, the invasion brought hope. He believed Hitler was repeating Napoleon's blunder of trying to conquer an unconquerable country. The night terrors tormenting him since Dachau began to fade away. Ernst refused to believe the initial optimistic reports from the Nazis about the invasion, but feared he would not be alive long enough to see the invasion fail. For their sister, Sophie, the invasion made her worst nightmare a reality. Czechoslovakian colleges and universities were closed and students of "German" descent drafted into Hitler's army. Within days of the news, Sophie and Fritz's twenty-year-old son, Erwein, and eighteen-year-old son, Franz, were drafted into Adolf Hitler's army. Her eldest children went from being schoolboys to soldiers, sacrificed as cannon fodder to the Nazi war machine.

CHAPTER EIGHTEEN
APOCALYPSE

"To live in fear every hour of every day is terrible. To never
know what would happen next. To want to speak out against
evil which was the right thing to do, but to know to speak out
was to jeopardize everything and everyone you loved. I don't
know how they did it. It was a time of endless fear."

—MAXIMILIAN AND ELISABETH HOHENBERG'S
YOUNGEST SON, GERHARD

"There is no way out unless I drive a bullet through my brain."

—ADOLF HITLER

Following twelve weeks of military training, and eight weeks at the
German War College, Erwein and Franz Nostitz-Rieneck were sent to
Münster in lower Saxony to be taught the intricacies of tank warfare.
Thirty years after Franz Ferdinand's death, his first two grandsons be-
came lieutenants leading panzer divisions against Russia, the country
the Archduke warned Austria to never fight.

On June 28, 1942, another anniversary of the Sarajevo assassinations, Hitler ordered German panzers invading Russia to turn south
toward the city of Stalingrad. It was a fatal mistake. Six months later,
German and Russian armies were locked in a death struggle over a
thousand-mile battlefront from the Baltic to the Black Sea. The
164-day Battle of Stalingrad changed the destiny of Adolf Hitler, his
war, the Hohenbergs, and the world. Winter and the Russian army

stopped then annihilated Germany's armies. Max Hohenberg's son Georg, fifteen at the time, later remembered:

> In the beginning of the war when the Germans were winning, almost everyone in Austria seemed to think the war was wonderful. Most believed Hitler's victories were glorious acts of revenge for 1918. After Stalingrad, almost overnight, many discovered they had been anti-Nazi all along. Suddenly they remembered they were Austrians, not Germans.

Sophie's two sons survived the debacle that was Stalingrad. Cousins, friends, schoolmates, and eight hundred thousand of their fellow soldiers did not. The Soviet Union suffered one million casualties. Joseph Stalin's massive armies wasted no time in pushing Hitler's shattered forces west. Erwein and Franz and millions of others were caught between the opposing furies of two of history's greatest mass murderers.

The winter chill of Stalingrad was felt quickly in German Silesia, today northwestern Poland. That was where Maisie Hohenberg and her young son were staying. Silesia stood directly in the path of the advancing Russian armies as they smashed, burned, and raped their way to Berlin.

Days before the war had begun, Maisie's parents were recalled to London. Her mother pleaded with her to join them, but she refused to leave without Ernst. Her family was in more danger than she realized. Her father, Captain George Jervis Wood, was an undercover agent for MI-6, British Military Intelligence. Attempts by his wife and daughter to free Ernst had unwittingly endangered his own covert activities.

Once Captain and Mrs. Wood left Austria, Fritz Nostitz-Rieneck traveled to Vienna. He brought Maisie and her young son Ferdinand to Prague, then to a country estate in the Sudetenland, and finally to the north German countryside of Silesia to stay in the care of distant Hohenberg cousins.

Count and Countess Friedrich Schaffgotsch were among Germany's wealthiest industrialists and largest land owners. Like the Duchess of Hohenberg's father in Württemberg, some Germans were untouchable, even in Hitler's Third Reich. Their magnificent castle was protected by an ancient moat on one side, a private lake on the other, and unassailable wealth and privilege. Yet for Maisie Hohenberg it was a lonely, frightening time. She was raising a small son without a father, living with a family she did not know, in a country that had imprisoned her husband, speaking a language she had never mastered, and forced to read lips because of her increasing deafness.

Ernst had been transferred to his third concentration camp, Sachsenhausen-Oranienburg, twenty-two miles north of Berlin. The camp's outward appearance was similar to Dachau, but its security tighter. Sachsenhausen was ringed by a higher stone wall, an electrified fence, and ferocious attack dogs. Heavily armed sentries kept watch from tall towers. The prison had no night. Bright lights lit the entire compound twenty-four hours a day inside and out.

Heinrich Himmler ordered the administrative offices of all the Reich's concentration camps moved there. So, too, were many high-value prisoners. Austrian Chancellor Kurt Schuschnigg, Lutheran Pastor Martin Niemoller, the grandson of Otto von Bismarck, the last Crown Princess of Bavaria, the former prime ministers of Spain and France, and captured Polish and Soviet generals were held there in isolation. Joseph Stalin's oldest son, and many others, died within its walls. Maisie, fearful that Ernst could not survive much longer as a Nazi prisoner, redoubled her efforts to free him. Determined to be independent, and not a burden, she began working in a local nursery earning money to buy stationary and stamps for the countless letters she wrote. At the behest of Count Schaffgotsch, she petitioned Silesian native and Dresden Gestapo Chief Udo Gustav von Woyrsch for assistance. He eventually wrote back apologizing that he was unable to help. Ernst remained imprisoned under orders from "the highest possible German authorities." Maisie knew his coded language referred to Himmler, Goering, and Hitler himself. Her single hope was that one of them in a moment of sanity or mercy might free Ernst.

As Hitler's armies retreated more and more, cracks began to appear in German solidarity, and in the Schaffgotsch family itself. Maisie learned that a nephew of Count Schaffgotsch had been an early supporter of Adolf Hitler. His brother was not. Aside from their political differences, the second brother had married the daughter of a prominent Jewish banker in Berlin and moved with her to Silesia. As Hitler rose to power, the Nazi brother told his family that his Jewish sister-in-law was in danger. He offered to transport her to safety through southern Germany and Austria to Switzerland. The two entered the train together, but she was never seen again.

No one ever learned whether she had been turned over to the Gestapo, or whether her own brother-in-law had thrown her from the train. Silesia's ancient aristocratic families, including his own, stopped speaking to him. He steadily rose in the ranks of the Nazi Party, but became a non-person within his own family.

In the spring of 1943, the Countess of Schaffgotsch joined an elderly cousin for lunch at the Hotel Metropole. Her cousin dined at the hotel every noon with his wife, friends, and family members. It was his habit to ask young officers passing by if they would like to join them for a meal. One day the nearly blind Schaffgotsch cousin failed to recognize the Nazi whose sister-in-law had disappeared. He cheerfully asked him, "Would you like to share lunch with us?" Everyone at the table was shocked and embarrassed, but no one dared leave.

The high-ranking Nazi who had been ostracized for so long was delighted at the invitation and happily joined them. By the end of the meal, he extended an offer to help anyone at the table who might ever need his assistance. Only the Countess Schaffgotsch spoke up, asking for his help in freeing Prince Ernst Hohenberg from Berlin's Sachsenhausen Concentration Camp. The Nazi, who was soon leaving for the capital, promised he would do what he could. No one believed him, but the Countess rushed home and urged Maisie to write one more letter.

Ernst Kaltenbrunner, the Chief of Reich Security, controlled all access to Heinrich Himmler. His name was familiar to Maisie. He was the Nazi who had thrown Elisabeth and her out of his office days after the Anschluss. Maisie boldly wrote him. With the German army in retreat on all fronts, his response was more cordial. Kaltenbrunner told her if she made a direct appeal to Heinrich Himmler, he would pass it on to him.

Two Gestapo officers soon visited Schaffgotsch Castle. Maisie feared the worst but was told that her husband would soon be freed and returned to Vienna. She was also handed her first uncensored letter from Ernst since his arrest. It ended with the words, "Every day and every hour my thoughts are with you… I embrace you and send you a thousand kisses."

Maisie never learned whether it was the shadow of Stalingrad, the influence of Countess Schaffgotsch's Nazi cousin, infighting within the Nazi bureaucracy, the five-year crusade of the Hohenberg women, or the tightening noose around his own neck that finally convinced Heinrich Himmler to sign the release order.

She thanked the Count and Countess, quickly packed, and left the sanctuary that had been home for her and her son during most of the war. Within months, the advancing Russian army looted and burned the magnificent castle, Count Schaffgotsch was dead, and his family scattered.

A letter postmarked from Berlin, 12 April 1943, was waiting for Maisie in Vienna. It read, "I arrive tomorrow morning the 13th, at the Franz Joseph Bahnhof [train station] at 8:45. A thousand hugs, Ernst." Five dark years after he disappeared into Gestapo hell, a ghostly Ernst slowly emerged from the train. Maisie was stunned by the skeletal appearance of her thirty-nine-year-old husband. Ernst's health was broken, his heart damaged, his spirit crushed. Only glimpses of his sense of humor revealed his former self. It took time for Ernst and his six-year-old son to know each other and for him to adjust to the bright sights and loud noises of the city. He longed to return to the country-side, but was forbidden from leaving Vienna. There he was required to work long hours in a war factory. The constant Nazi surveillance and stress of the city stole his remaining strength.

Saturdays he was required to report to the Gestapo Headquarters of Baldur von Schirach, Reich Governor of Greater Vienna. There he was questioned about his weekly activities. His parole forbade him from having contact with anyone who had been a prisoner in a con-centration camp, or anyone else the Nazis considered an enemy of the state. Ernst could not see, write, or meet his brother, Max. They had also lost contact with their sister and family in Prague, and she had lost contact with her sons fighting on the eastern front. None of them knew who was alive or dead.

That February, death came to the Hohenbergs' eighty-eight-year-old grandmother. Old and new Vienna attended her funeral, even high-ranking Nazis. Max, Ernst, and their wives were there, but the terms of their parole did not allow them to fraternize with each other. Even though their Habsburg grandmother was given a state funeral, most of the mourners, including old friends, ignored them.

Eighteen days later, Maisie gave birth to their second child. He was named Ernst after his father, but there was little time for joy. The next week the American and British air forces began bombing Vienna day and night. On the seventh anniversary of the Anschluss, the largest Austrian air raid of the war took place. Otto Habsburg urged President Roosevelt not to carpet-bomb Austria, but his pleas were ignored. The Hofburg balcony where Adolf Hitler had spoken to 300,000 cheering Viennese was reduced to rubble. Two thousand animals at the Vienna Zoo were killed. Belvedere Palace, the Spanish Riding School, the Imperial Stables, the Art Museum, and the Acad-emy of Fine Arts were all damaged.

The city's world-famous State Opera House, the Burgtheatre, and the train station where Hitler had first set foot in Vienna burned to the ground. Twenty percent of Vienna was destroyed, 87,000 homes, including Archduchess Maria-Theresa's house and entire neighborhood on Favoritenstrasse; but she was not there to see it. Her body rested beneath the city's simple Capuchin Church alongside her late husband, his two previous wives, eighteen empresses, and twelve Habsburg emperors, including Franz Joseph.

In Prague, the city's medieval streets, towers, bridges, and castles remained untouched by the war, but that was about to change. General George Patton's invading American army approached it from the west. From the east came the avenging Soviet armies of Marshal Ivan Konev. Sophie tried to reassure her young son and daughter they would be safe, but no one knew which army would reach the city, and what would happen when they did. Fritz and his Home Guard were ordered to defend Prague to the last man. Months earlier, 200,000 Polish men, women, and children had been killed in Warsaw when they rebelled against their German occupiers. In revenge, the ancient capital of Poland was razed to the ground.

For the rest of Sophie's life, mention of the war always turned her thoughts to February. The war ruined the month for her. People thought it the shortest month of the year. To her, it seemed the longest. The war, February, and death were forever linked in her mind to the passing of her grandmother in February 1944, and twelve months later, to the death of her son Franz. He was killed in February 1945 fighting the Russians in Poland. The tiny village where he died was named Sophienberg.

The official letter informing her that the most gentle of their four children had been killed on the Russian front stated, "Your son died for the Führer and the Fatherland." The words brought her no comfort. Franz Assisi Maximilian Nostitz-Rieneck died three weeks after his twenty-second birthday. Her firstborn son, Erwein, was somewhere on the war's eastern front, but Sophie didn't know whether he, too, was dead.

In Berlin, Adolf Hitler's delusions blocked any attempts to save Germany from destruction. Days after the 1941 Japanese attack on Pearl Harbor, he had declared war on the United States, dismissing it as "nothing more than a mass of immigrants from many nations and races." Now German armies in the west were being decimated by an American-led invasion force as diverse as the nation they represented. To his east, armies of Slavs and other ethnic groups dismissed by the Nazis as racially inferior were annihilating soldiers of Hitler's master race.

Adolf Hitler promised at war's end to build a wall around the Reich to keep non-Germans from entering the country. But no walls could save Nazi Germany. Hitler ordered no retreat on any fronts, but retreated to his own childhood fantasies of cowboy-and-Indian dismissing the advancing Russians as "Redskins." To boost the morale of his soldiers fighting on the collapsing eastern front, he ordered 300,000 copies of Karl May's western fairy tales sent to them. They were too busy fighting for their lives to read.

Baldur von Schirach traveled from Vienna to Berlin to tell the Führer the war had to end soon, "one way or the other." Schirach was promptly rebuffed, but his suggestion brought a wisp of reality to Hitler. After their meeting, Adolf Hitler turned to an aide and said, "How does he imagine we do that? He knows exactly as I do there is no way out, unless I drive a bullet through my head."

CHAPTER NINETEEN
THE WHOLE COUNTRY WAS
AS IF UNDER A SPELL

"I can't believe how all this could have happened. It is enough
to make one lose faith in God."　　　—EVA BRAUN
in a last letter to a friend
written from Adolf Hitler's bunker

"We may all perish, but we shall take the world with us."
—ADOLF HITLER

On July 20, 1944, Hitler narrowly survived an assassination attempt at
Wolf's Lair, his military headquarters in East Prussia. A bomb hidden
in a briefcase wounded twenty people. Three died, Hitler survived.
The conspiracy was headed by trusted Prussian aristocrats from his
General Staff who planned to kill the Führer, seize power, and end the
war. Seven thousand suspected conspirators were arrested. Five thousand military officers, aristocrats, industrialists, educators, government ministers, and religious leaders were shot, hanged, or beheaded.

Following his near murder, Hitler's paranoia increased and his
physical and mental health deteriorated. He increasingly raged at
those unable or unwilling to follow his orders. With military disaster
looming, Heinrich Himmler sought answers in astrology, numerology,
and religion. He told a friend, "I know that I am generally regarded as
a heedless pagan, but in the depths of my heart I am a believer; I be-

lieve in God and providence. In the course of the last year I have learnt to believe in miracles again. The Führer's escape on the twentieth of July was a miracle." Herman Goering did not believe in miracles. He turned to morphine.

On March 19, 1945, Hitler had the official Nazi newspaper, *Völkischer Beobachter*, publish an order for all German military personnel and civilians to destroy anything and everything that could be useful to the enemy. This included infrastructure, factories, housing, and food. It was in effect a demand that Germany commit suicide. "Not a German stalk of wheat is to feed the enemy, not a German mouth to give him information, not a German hand to offer him help. He is to find every footbridge destroyed, every road blocked—nothing but death, annihilation and hatred will meet him."

Two months earlier, Hitler had retreated fifty feet below ground to a three-thousand-square-foot bunker in Berlin. Reality was not allowed to enter the bunker with him. He told those who followed him there, "In the future anyone who tells anyone else the war is lost will be treated as a traitor, with all the consequences for him and his family. I will take action without regard to rank and prestige."

The only exemption to his mandate was to Hitler himself. He spent hours blaming the Jews for starting the war, and hours more denouncing his generals and allies for losing it. Eventually his audience was reduced to sycophants, true believers who shared his delusions. He ranted, "We shall never capitulate. Never. We may all perish, but we shall take the world with us." His mistress, Eva Braun, wrote a final letter from the bunker to her best friend, "I can't believe how all this could have happened. It is enough to make one lose faith in God."

Hitler who as a child had dreamed of being an architect and rebuilding his hometown of Linz had instead become an architect of death, destroying everyone and everything he touched. Linz still held his imagination. He ordered an architectural scale model of the city carried from his Chancellery office to the bunker. An eyewitness said,

"No matter at what time, whether during the day or night, whenever he had the opportunity during those weeks, he was sitting in front of this model [as if it were] a promised land into which we would gain entrance."

At the end of his life, Hitler's mind also returned again and again to the Vienna of his youth. Following a final meeting with Baldur von Schirach, his anger and anti-Semitism quickly overcame momentary nostalgia for the city. He told his weary listeners:

> After 1918 the average Viennese found himself reduced to extreme poverty. But before the war it was wonderful: never shall I forget the gracious spectacle of the Vienna Opera, the women sparkling with diadems and fine clothes. In 1922 I was again at the opera, and what a difference! In the places of the cultured society of old there now sat the Jewish riff-raff; the women stretched out their hands to show off their jewelry, a heart rending site! I never once saw the Imperial box occupied. I suppose the Emperor Franz Joseph was not musical. I am an implacable enemy of the Habsburgs, but the sight of this mob sprawling to the very edge of the Imperial box was disgusting, and it angered me immensely.

As von Schirach had earlier predicted, one way or another, the war would soon end. With aerial bombing destroying larger and larger parts of Germany, Max and Elisabeth brought their two older sons home from Württemberg. To escape the prying eyes of local Nazis, Franz, Georg, and their next-oldest son, Albrecht, were sent to Vienna's Stubenbastel secondary school. Franz soon returned to Württemberg to avoid the draft. Georg, who was fifteen at the time, later remembered:

> We knew exactly who was a Nazi and who was not, but we still had to be very careful with the other students and the teachers. You felt like you knew who you could trust, but you were never

completely sure. By 1945 we had to keep changing schools because they kept getting bombed. We were just happy to be alive with so much destruction and death around us. My father taught us about the importance of laughter. He used to say, "To be able to laugh is to be able to stay sane." To us laughter was like oxygen. The only problem was you couldn't laugh when you were too frightened, so we tried very hard not to be too frightened.

Georg and Albrecht never knew from day to day whether their school would be standing, bombed, or closed forever. Then on March 29, 1945, the oldest Nazi they had ever seen entered their classroom to make an announcement. The Russians had reached the outskirts of Vienna. Students were told the time had come for them to defend the Fatherland. They were ordered to enlist in either the Wehrmacht or the Gestapo. In the final days of the war, Max and Elisabeth's sons were presented with the same choice their Uncle Fritz had been given at its beginning.

It was three days before Easter—Holy Thursday, Maundy Thursday, or in the Austrian Christian calendar Mourning Thursday, the day set aside to commemorate Christ's last supper. Georg and Albrecht both wondered if they would be alive by Easter. The brothers signed up for the Wehrmacht, were given shovels, and told to begin digging ditches in the streets. At day's end they laid their shovels down and began the long walk home to Artstetten. They made up their mind they would survive, or die together, as a family.

The village of Artstetten was filled with rumors that the Nazis were carrying out executions and massacres. Maximilian received an order to report to the Commandant of the Gestapo—alone. Elisabeth went to Gestapo Headquarters in his place demanding to know the purpose of the meeting. A ferocious argument followed with the Commandant refusing to discuss the matter, and Elisabeth refusing to leave his office.

A compromise was finally reached. Max met with the Commandant's wife in a public place away from Gestapo Headquarters. She informed him that he and a number of other prominent Austrians were about to be killed. He immediately went into hiding. Years after the events, Elisabeth wondered whether the Commandant was trying to warn Maximilian or planned to assassinate him, and whether his wife was working with or against her husband. Fear, heroism, and treachery were everywhere.

The advance guard for Joseph Stalin's troops was known for their reputation for savagery. Princess Ileana of Rumania, whose castle stood in the path of the Russian invaders, later wrote:

> The Soviet army was not like anything which had been seen since the days of Genghis Khan's Tartar hordes... with frightening and unhuman simplicity they took what they wanted at the point of a gun, and they shot at people with that complete lack of feeling which a normal man has when he shoots at a cardboard target... not even old women were spared. The terrifying part was the methodical brutality in which everything was done.... They robbed rich and poor alike. They had no standards by which to distinguish between one individual and another.

Once German troops retreated, Max returned to his home. There he waited with his wife and children for the Soviet army to appear. Despite the Soviets' barbarous reputation, he and Elisabeth greeted them as liberators. His view of communists had been tempered by the political prisoners he came to know and admire at Dachau and Flossenbürg. Max believed everything depended on the character of the man, not his political beliefs. His reputation may have preceded him.

The few pieces of their belongings remaining at Artstetten were quickly looted by Soviet troops, but he and his family were treated with gruff respect. The Hohenbergs had been born in palaces. Most of their new overseers had been born as peasants, but they shared a common enemy—Adolf Hitler. Max's son Georg later said his father may have been the only Duke in the history of the Soviet Union the communists regarded with respect.

Soviet troops arrived in Vienna the day after Easter to a very different reception. Some German units fought in brutal hand-to-hand combat. Others fled. Even as thousands died, Stalin's soldiers made time to take anything of value they could find, but they discovered a city with no water, no gas, no electricity, and almost no food.

Incredibly Ernst Hohenberg, like his young nephews, had been inducted into the Wehrmacht Home Guard and ordered to defend Vienna. Like them, he quickly deserted. The day the Red Army moved into the city, he and Maisie waited in their apartment to be killed or liberated. They managed to send their sons to the safety of Upper Austria, but Ernst was unable to travel. His heart condition required medicine only available on Vienna's black market. Even that collapsed in the chaos of the Russian advance.

When fighting in their neighborhood became too intense, they fled their apartment with only the clothes on their backs. Gunfire and looting seemed everywhere. Russian and German troops, deserters, marauders, and rapists fought each other and anyone else they could prey upon. A building porter recognized Maisie and agreed to hide them, but they were found by Russian troops and were again forced to run.

For fourteen days, Ernst and Maisie ran, hid, fled, and ran again until they found shelter in a basement crowded with other refugees. There was no light and almost no air, but the cramped cellar offered safety from the violence above them until a fire broke out. People panicked. The heavy door that kept them safe also trapped them.

Ernst found an exit through a collapsed wall into an adjoining basement. Once again they became fugitives. Embers and burning ash rained down on them. Smoke burned their eyes and choked their lungs. Finally, they returned to their ransacked apartment where they were harassed and threatened by soldiers and drunken deserters taking what they wanted at the point of a gun. Maisie later said they were terrified the entire time, never knowing from moment to moment if they would be killed.

Once they were able to escape Vienna, they traveled as far away from the Soviet army as possible. First by train, then by truck, and finally over steep mountain passes by foot, weeks of stops and starts ended with a joyful reunion with their two children. With the help of British soldiers, Ernst, Maisie, and their sons crossed the Austrian border into the tiny neutral country of Lichtenstein. The Hohenbergs' cousin Prince Franz Joseph II was the ruler there. Only then did Ernst receive the medical attention he needed.

———

The spring of 1945 was unusually beautiful in Prague, but the threat of violence continued in the skies over the city. Konopiste Castle witnessed one of the last air battles of the Second World War. A fleet of American B17 bombers was attacked by Messerschmitt jets, one of the Nazis' final wonder weapons. Nine crewmembers of a B17 bomber were captured and taken to Konopiste for interrogation after crashing their plane. Everyone knew the war would be over in days, but on April 19 Gestapo officers shot and killed each airman with single bullets to the head. The nine Americans were buried in a common grave two miles from Konopiste.

Four days later in the burning ruins of Berlin, Heinrich Himmler met Swedish Diplomat Count Folke Bernadotte. With bitter resignation he told him, "I admit Germany is beaten," but then his dark mood lifted. The defeat, he assured Bernadotte, would be blamed on traitors who stabbed Hitler in the back, much as the Kaiser had been in the First World War. Himmler was confident that the Führer's legend would grow. The Swedish diplomat listened in grim silence as the Nazi predicted someday history would remember Adolf Hitler as the greatest German of them all.

Himmler was not alone in believing Hitler's reputation would survive Germany's defeat. In a final meeting with his military commanders, the failed artist from Linz continued blaming others for the disaster. "If the German people lose the war; it will have proved itself unworthy of me!" Hitler didn't specify whether he was referring to the nearly seven million German soldiers and civilians who died in the war, or those who survived to face the consequences of the defeat. Like Count Bernadotte to Himmler, the Führer's listeners said nothing. Privately Hitler confided to his personal pilot that his tombstone should read, "He was the victim of his generals." Everyone was blamed for Hitler's downfall, for the war, for the defeat, for the destruction, and for the deaths, except Hitler himself.

Hitler's order of the day on the 15th of April to his dwindling army revealed his obsessions and delusions:

> Anyone ordering you to retreat... is to be taken prisoner at once, and if necessary killed on the spot, no matter what his rank may be. If every soldier at the eastern front does his duty in the coming days and weeks, the last onrush of Asia will be broken, exactly as in the end the penetration of our enemy in the west will fail in spite of everything. Berlin will remain German. Vienna will be German once more, and Europe will never be Russian.

On the following day, the Battle of Berlin began. Soviet troops encircled the city. Hitler continued ordering German armies that no long existed to fight them. He climbed the stairs of his bunker one last time on April 20, his fifty-sixth birthday, to present Iron Crosses to child soldiers defending the city. That night Soviet artillery unmercifully bombarded the city that would soon be theirs. Sometime in the early morning hours of April 29, Hitler learned Benito Mussolini and his mistress had been captured and assassinated. Their mutilated bodies, beaten, kicked, and repeatedly shot, were publicly hanged in a Milan square for the entire world to vilify. Hours later,

Hitler decided to put his own affairs in order. He married his mistress, Eva Braun, and dictated his will, blaming the Jews for starting the war, and declaring Herman Goering and Heinrich Himmler traitors for secretly negotiating an end to it behind his back. Both men were angrily dismissed from all positions in the government and the Nazi Party.

Even in the depths of defeat, his optimism survived. Hitler's testament declared, "A seed has been sown in German history that will one-day grow to usher in the rebirth of the National Socialist movement in a truly united nation." In his last hours, Hitler continued searching for an audience worthy of him and his racist ideology. His final words were dedicated to followers who survived him along with generations to come:

> I hope my spirit will continue to dwell among them and accompany them always.... Let them never, above all, allow fear to preside over their actions, placing the honor of the nation above everything that exists on earth. May they always remember that our task, the consolidation of a National Socialist state, represents the work of centuries to come.... Above all, I enjoin the government and the people to uphold the race laws to the limit and to resist mercilessly the poisoner of all nations, international Jewry.

Adolf Hitler and Eva Braun committed suicide on April 30, 1945, sitting next to a photograph of his mother. In parts of Germany and northern Europe, it was the eve of Witches Night, an ancient pagan holiday commemorating the vanquishing of demons, witches, and ghosts before the coming of spring. On the Christian calendar it was the Feast of St. Walpurga, who was famous for exorcising demons from those possessed by the devil.

May 1, 1945, Hamburg Radio reported the news of Hitler's heroic death defending the Fatherland from Bolshevik invaders. Newspapers across the globe followed their lead. The *Philadelphia Inquirer*'s banner headline read, Hitler is Dead Nazi radio reports Führer killed fighting Russians. One week later, Germany unconditionally surrendered.

Journalist Dorothy Thompson, who had interviewed Hitler before the war, was in the ancient city of Jerusalem when she learned of his death. On May 7, 1945, she wrote in the *St. Louis Post Dispatch*,

> By insisting that Germany fight on for months after the war definitely was lost, he brought about the utter ruin of Germany itself, leaving the country a wilderness of rubble without government, communications or food.... The evil that he did lives after him... Jewry's worst enemy has been defeated and his country literally brought to dust, but the seeds of hatred he sowed throughout the world will flourish still.... Throughout the root of Nazism is unabridged nationalism which elevates a nation into a god, there is no sign that such nationalism is abating, and though Nazism is also the embodiment of a reign of terror, terrorism is not extirpated with Hitler's fall. Our civilization therefore confronts in victory an undiminished crisis.

Another article from the same newspaper reported the destruction of Eagle's Nest, Hitler's famous mountain retreat facing Austria. A neighbor from the nearby village was quoted as emphatically declaring, "Nobody believes Hitler is dead." For the rest of their lives, many Germans and Austrians refused to believe the truth about his suicide, his military blunders, or the Holocaust.

Brunhilde Pomsel was a typical German woman of her time, except for her work during the war. She was secretary to Nazi Minister of Public Enlightenment and Propaganda Joseph Goebbels. She was also in the Hitler bunker at the time of his suicide. Pomsel took Goebbels's dictation and transcribed his correspondence, including personal, political, and military observations, for his private diary. Some days, a single diary entry numbered eighty-five typewritten pages.

Frau Pomsel knew Adolf Hitler, Eva Braun, Hermann Goering, Heinrich Himmler, Albert Speer, and the entire leadership of Nazi Germany. At the time of her death at the age of 106 in 2017, she looked back on her life and reflected:

> I wouldn't see myself as being guilty unless you blame the entire German population for ultimately enabling that government to take control. That was all of us; including me.... The whole country was as if under a spell.... I wasn't interested in politics... I know no one believes us today—everyone thinks we knew everything. We knew nothing. It was all a well-kept secret. We believed it. We swallowed it. It all seemed entirely plausible... I didn't do anything but type in Goebbels's office. And I had no idea of what was behind all that. Well, very little anyway.

CHAPTER TWENTY
PHANTOMS AND PATRIOTS

"I shudder to visualize what is actually happening in this period to millions now and what is going to happen in this period when famine stalks the earth.... From Stettin in the Baltic to Trieste in the Adriatic an Iron Curtain has descended across the continent. Behind that line lies all the ancient capitals of the ancient states of central and eastern Europe, Warsaw, Berlin, Prague, Budapest, Belgrade, Bucharest and Sofia... mass expulsions of Germans on a scale grievous and undreamed of are taking place."

—WINSTON CHURCHILL,
Iron Curtain Speech, Westminster College, Fulton, Missouri

"The Lord said vengeance is mine. They held to that belief. They taught us there is only one judge above all of us, above the Nazis, and we were not that judge."

—GEORG HOHENBERG

Sophie and Fritz Nostitz-Rieneck's former Sudetenland estate of Falkenau was the location of the last European battle of the Second World War. The date was May 8, 1945. General George S. Patton's soldiers found themselves in a firefight with German soldiers guarding a slave labor camp built there. None of the Americans wanted to die in the closing hours of the war; but some Germans chose death rather than a world without Hitler. Patton's battle-hardened veterans had seen action in North Africa and Sicily; landed on Omaha Beach on

D-Day; and survived the Battle of the Bulge. American casualties of this final battle included the sons and grandsons of the American immigrants scorned by Adolf Hitler. They died five thousand miles from their homes freeing one thousand sick and dying women prisoners in the Sudetenland countryside of Czechoslovakia.

Four days earlier, Czech partisans in Prague had attacked retreating German military units in the city. The Germans decided they would rather surrender to the American army in the west than fight the approaching Soviet troops from the east. Hours of chaotic street fighting slowed their withdrawal, but they finally joined forty thousand other German troops and laid down their weapons to the Americans. Days later the captives were repatriated to the Russians. The Allies had agreed to return German soldiers who fought on the Russian front to Joseph Stalin's Red Army. He wanted revenge for the millions killed by the Nazis.

In Prague, Fritz took off his Wehrmacht Home Guard uniform for the last time. Czechoslovakia—occupied by the Nazis for six years—a country betrayed by its friends and allies, its own president, government, and army, survived by becoming a nation of collaborators. Fritz faced no retribution or allegations from Czechs who had endured the occupation with him. Still there was little sense of relief. He and Sophie had heard nothing from their son serving in the German army. Erwein, in fact, was closer to home than they could have imagined. On the 8th of May, the day American and German troops were fighting to the death at Falkenau, the day the war in Europe ended, Erwein surrendered his panzer division to the Americans seventy miles north of Prague. He was then quickly transferred to the nearby Soviet army and sent east to a Russian slave labor camp.

To have lost one son in the war, and to have another survive only to disappear into the vastness of the Soviet Union, was almost too much to bear. When Sophie and Fritz learned that Max, Ernst, and their families had survived, they prayed God had one more miracle for their family, Erwein's safe return.

Eduard Beneš, Czechoslovakia's former president who had abandoned the country seven years earlier, returned with vengeance rather than prayers in his heart. Perhaps hoping to deflect from his own failed leadership, Beneš declared an intention to "liquidate... the German problem in our republic once and for all."

One year earlier, Harold Nicolson—a British member of parliament—learned of Beneš's plans for a postwar Czechoslovakia and summarized them in his diary. It was an ethnic cleansing policy borrowed from Adolf Hitler, and a land collectivization program inspired by Joseph Stalin. Jan Masaryk, son of the country's first president and Beneš's future Foreign Secretary, told Nicolson:

> Czechoslovakia will become a neighbor of Russia and must get on good terms with her. This will entail some switch of home policy in the direction of State Socialism and the nationalization of mines and forests.... They must expel most of the nasty Germans, but are quite prepared to keep the nice ones provided that they become good Czech citizens.

When the war ended, Beneš's position hardened. Czechoslovakia's new Justice Minister declared, "There are no good Germans, only bad, and even worse ones. They are a foreign ulcer in our body." The bitterness of the times was reflected in the words of a leading Czech Catholic cleric who pontificated, "Once in a thousand years the time has come to settle accounts with the Germans, who are evil and to whom the commandment, 'Love Thy Neighbor' does not apply."

Adolf Hitler's ethnic cleansing policies were turned against his "master race." In a speech on October 28, 1945, Beneš presented his "final solution to the German Question" announcing all "Sudetenland" Germans were to be banished from Czechoslovakia. His "reslovakinization" program revoked the citizenship of Czechs with German ancestry, confiscated their homes, farms, and assets, and ordered them out of the country. For identification, ethnic Germans were forced to wear a large N for "Nemec" sewn into their clothes. The Czech slur meant "German mute." Nearly one out of every three Czechs, more than three million citizens, were expelled from their homeland.

Beneš may have created the largest forced dislocation of any population during the twentieth century. Among his targeted Sudetenland deportees was the Nazi "collaborator" Oskar Schindler, who rescued over 1,200 Jews during the Holocaust, and Sophie and Fritz Nostitz-Rieneck with their children.

Prior to the outbreak of the war, Fritz had placed all his assets in his wife's name, hoping something might be saved for his family. It made no difference. Everything they owned was confiscated. Hitler had revoked their Czech citizenship against their will, making them citizens of the German Reich. Beneš refused to return it. With Beneš's help, Hitler's vendetta continued to curse them.

Fritz was despondent that his collaboration with the Nazis condemned his family to exile, but the new Czech government made him a surprise offer. He was promised that if he divorced his "Habsburg" wife he could retain his citizenship, keep any seized assets, and resume the life he and his ancestors had enjoyed in Czechoslovakia for centuries. The Count was also assured that the courts would grant him full custody of their underage children.

Government agents repeatedly referred to his wife of thirty-five years as the "Habsburg princess," much like Adolf Hitler and the Nazis. Fritz told Sophie it was clear Beneš's bureaucrats were incapable of knowing who he or his wife were, or the difference between a Habsburg and a Hohenberg. He informed the government that the entire Nostitz-Rieneck family would leave Czechoslovakia together.

The official expulsion paperwork detailed the date and time of their departure, as if the family had been staying at a hotel now waiting for the next guests to arrive. Bed sheets, linens, towels, and other household items had to be purchased anew, beds made up, dishes, pots, and pans washed and scrubbed. Even new soap had to be left in soap dishes. Once government inspectors approved the house for its new occupants, the family would be provided a safe conduct pass during their deportation. Thousands without safe conduct passes were being attacked, beaten, raped, and killed by mobs as Czech police looked the other way.

Each member of the family was allowed to pack a suitcase the size of an overnight bag, the same order given to Sophie decades earlier when she was expelled from Konopiste. For the second time in her life, she lost her home, and her homeland. Sophie packed few clothes. She filled her single suitcase with family photos and treasured mementos of her absent sons. The most difficult part of leaving the house, church, neighborhood, city, and country she loved was leaving without Erwein and Franz.

Sophie's family, like millions of other Czechs of German ancestry, was not told their destination. Many held in former prisons and concentration camps were brutalized, murdered, or committed suicide there. The rumors never stopped. At one point Sophie was told they were going to Dachau, then that they would be held at the Theresienstadt Concentration Camp, the same prison where the assassin of her parents had died. Finally, they joined thousands of other deportees in a long convoy of military trucks and were taken to a detention camp outside of Karlsbad—today Karlovy Vary.

The Czech city, eighty miles northwest of Prague, was named for a fourteenth-century Habsburg Emperor. Hot springs and its Art Nouveau architecture once made it a favorite holiday destination for Beethoven, Chopin, Goethe, Gogol, and even Sigmund Freud and Emperor Franz Joseph. In happier times Sophie's family had passed through the city on their way to their country estates; but it had become a city of ghosts. Nearly its entire population had been deported due to their German roots. In Brno, the country's third-largest city, twenty-three thousand were expelled. Six thousand died during the "evacuation."

The trip from Prague to Karlsbad usually took three hours. War-ravaged roads, breakdowns, and harassment caused the journey—one without food, water, or bathroom breaks—to last two days. Sophie's family arrived hungry, dehydrated, and exhausted. They didn't know it at the time, but Erwein had been imprisoned in the city before being sent as a prisoner of war to Russia.

The ethnic and political fault lines in Czechoslovakia were being replicated across Europe. Berlin, Vienna, and most of the continent was being divided into separate Russian, American, British, and French occupation zones. Destinations for refugees were often arbitrary and final. Eight hundred thousand Czechs were sent to eastern Germany in a zone occupied by the Russian army. They never returned. Halfway around the world in a speech at a small Missouri college, Winston Churchill decried what he called an "Iron Curtain" descending across Europe. Parts of Austria, including Artstetten, and most of eastern Europe, fell behind the Soviet zone of military and political occupation.

Artstetten soon became a popular tourist attraction for military officers, party officials, and even ordinary soldiers from the Soviet Union curious to see the former home of Archduke Franz Ferdinand. Elisabeth was pressed into service as their tour guide. She told stories about the Archduke's affection for Russia, his desire for peace, and shared family tales about the castle's surviving paintings.

One portrait was never shown. It hung unobtrusively in the dark corner of a seldom-used hallway. The painting was of Alexandra, Russia's last Empress, wife of Nicholas II His Imperial Majesty the Emperor and Autocrat of All the Russians. During Franz Ferdinand's 1902 visit to St. Petersburg, Nicholas showed him several paintings of the Czarina and asked which he preferred. As a parting gift, Nicholas presented the portrait to him.

A Russian officer wandered down the hallway and noticed the dust-covered painting. He asked about its history. Elisabeth dismissed it as an obscure Habsburg Archduchess, but he frowned and gruffly said, "This is not an Archduchess! A Russian officer recognizes a portrait of a Russian Empress!" Then he smiled an ironic smile. Knowing the Czarina, her entire family, and much of the country's aristocracy had been murdered during the Bolshevik Revolution, the Duchess promptly moved the picture to the attic. It did not see the light of day for ten years—the length of the Soviet occupation of Austria.

Russian officers and soldiers sometimes came to Artstetten for another reason: to play with the Hohenberg children. They enjoyed carrying the youngest children on their shoulders, learning German words, and teaching them Russian phrases. Many talked of being homesick for their own children.

Despite the friendly interactions, their Soviet occupiers seemed unable to alleviate the hunger, malnutrition, and starvation Churchill accurately predicted would follow the war. Destroyed farms, harsh winters, summer droughts, and crop failures caused food production to fall to levels not seen since the summer before Franz Ferdinand's assassination. Some claimed it was another of Hitler's parting gifts.

Hunger was a constant companion at Artstetten. Elisabeth Hohenberg tried to set an example by not complaining about how little there was to eat, or the lack of variety in what appeared on their table. Only years later did she reveal her true feelings. When certain foods were served, she would smile, and politely but firmly say, "No, thank you. I never want to take another bite of that again!" For the rest of her life, she never deviated from her "do not eat" list of postwar hardship cuisine.

One day a knock at Artstetten's door solved a Dachau mystery. The visitor was the Gypsy boy, now a young man, whom Max had hid in a tool box from his pursuing Nazi guard. The man brought his family and offered a gift to thank Max for saving his life. After a few brief words, the man and his family quickly disappeared, but the large goose left behind provided the Hohenbergs the best meal they had eaten since before the war.

The Austrian consul in Karlsbad finally arranged for Sophie and her family to be released into Maximilian's custody. To her surprise, her brother had become mayor of the village of Artstetten. The Russians appointed him to the position since he was one of the few Austrians who had not collaborated with the Nazis. In time, he would be re-elected by the people themselves, but Russian military and civil authorities remained in firm control. Sophie and Fritz used the opportunity of living under the Soviet army of occupation to enlist help in locating Erwein. Many promises were made, but their son was only one prisoner in a country holding millions. Even Stalin was unsure of the identity, location, and number of prisoners held in his slave labor camps.

Leopold Figl, who had been imprisoned with Max and Ernst at Dachau, became Chancellor of Austria. He tried to use his influence to locate and free Erwein, but even he could not penetrate the bureaucratic maze of Joseph Stalin's prisons. No one knew for certain whether Erwein was alive or dead. Sophie and Fritz prayed, wrote letters, and spoke with anyone who might provide information. Nothing seemed to help, but they refused to give up hope.

One family reunion that did take place was when Ernst, Maisie, and their two sons returned to Artstetten. There were few tears, but much laughter. Ernst's wit remained strong despite his five years of imprisonment. He looked twice his age and his health never fully recovered, but he found the energy to mock his frail body and tease everyone around him.

Maisie privately grieved for the lost time that could never be recovered, but the family relished being together. Sixty years after the Hohenberg reunion, Maximilian and Elisabeth's youngest son, Gerhard, remembered:

> Time together was a gift and they did not waste it complaining. They were genuinely fond of one another, survived the war, and still had each other. They were from a generation that did not complain.

From time to time they would mention what had been, or what they once had, but without anger or bitterness. I can never remember them looking back unless they used humor to poke fun at themselves or their fellow Austrians.

A favorite Hohenberg joke concerned the patriots and phantoms of the Anschluss. For years the greatest source of pride for many Austrians was that they had witnessed Hitler's triumphal entrance into Vienna. People outdid themselves bragging that they cheered the Führer's car as it passed or heard him speak from the balcony of the Hofburg Palace. They waxed eloquently about where they stood, the parts of his speech that moved them to tears, and the magic of seeing, hearing, and being a part of that historic day.

Then, no one was there.

When the war turned against Hitler, no one admitted to being in Vienna that day. No one had heard the speech. No one knew anything about it. After a pause, Max or Ernst would dryly add, "It must have been a city of phantoms." The punch line was accompanied by genuine laughter.

They knew exactly where they were the day Hitler was rapturously cheered by over a quarter million screaming Austrians. Ernst was being arrested by the Gestapo in the apartment of his father-in-law. Max was behind the locked doors and rattling windows of his hiding place trying to say good-bye to Elisabeth and their children. None of them could hear his words as cheers from the city's Heroes Square shook Vienna, and all of Europe. Within an hour, Max had joined his brother in jail. The stories were told without bitterness. Max's son Georg later reminisced that when the family came together the reunions resembled the sights, sounds, and laughter of a Viennese cabaret:

They kept their sense of humor and their faith. There is no doubt they believed in a higher power and that helped them survive. Even in the darkest times, they could laugh. Since they laughed, their children laughed. That was the best medicine. That was a great gift from heaven. They had seen enough vengeance in their lives and wanted none of it. The Lord said vengeance is mine. They held to that belief. They taught us there is only one judge above all of us, above the Nazis, and we were not that judge.

Vendettas were left to others. In the fall of 1945, the victors of the Second World War met at Nuremberg to put the losers of the war on trial. The names of many of the defendants were familiar to the Hohenbergs. Arthur Seyss-Inquart, who ordered Max and Ernst's arrest hours following the Anschluss, and Ernst Kaltenbrunner who first imprisoned, then later helped free Ernst, were found guilty of crimes against humanity. Both men were hanged.

Baldur von Schirach and Albert Speer, the only two Nazis leaders to condemn Hitler from the witness stand, were each sentenced to twenty years in prison. Schirach, leader of the Hitler Youth movement at the age of twenty-four, was denounced at Nuremberg as the poisoner of a generation of children. As Reich Governor of Greater Vienna, he deported 65,000 Viennese Jews to Auschwitz. He admitted during the trial, "I put my morals to the side, when out of misplaced faith in the Führer, I took part in this action. I did it. I cannot undo it.… It was the most all-encompassing and diabolical genocide ever committed by man… Adolf Hitler gave the order… Hitler and Himmler together started this crime against humanity which will remain a blot on our history for centuries." During his two decades of imprisonment, Schirach served less than one day a piece for the 65,000 Jews he sent to Auschwitz. His tombstone reads, "I was one of you."

Heinrich Himmler, the coward who refused to meet Sophie face-to-face, whose letter to Maisie confirmed Ernst and Max's imprisonment at Dachau, and whose signature six years later informed her that Ernst would be released, committed suicide within hours of his arrest. Elisabeth Hohenberg's nemesis at the Hotel Imperial, Hermann Goering, remained arrogant and unrepentant. He denounced Schirach and Speer as traitors, and he denied any knowledge of the Holocaust. Goering was condemned to death for conspiring to initiate the war and for crimes against humanity. Hours before he was to be hanged, he also took his own life. His body was cremated at Dachau, carried in a trash can to a local river, and unceremoniously dumped there.

Gustav Krupp, the wealthy ammunitions manufacturer who armed Germany in both world wars, was indicted at Nuremberg as a war criminal, but never tried. Declining mental and physical health, and perhaps his wealth, saved him. Krupp had built Kaiser Wilhelm's U-boats, helped finance the 1933 election that brought Hitler to power, and used slave labor from concentration camps to build Hitler's weapons. He died peacefully in his bed at Schloss Blühnbach. The Austrian castle in the Tyrolean Alps had once been owned by Archduke Franz Ferdinand, but sold by his family at bargain rates to pay his debts after Sarajevo.

Many Nazis did not live to see the full fruits of their evil labor, but with the help of Eduard Beneš and his accomplices, Hitler's dream of ethnic cleansing became a reality. Despite genocide, the Holocaust, and millions of military and civilian casualties, the expulsion of ethnic "Germans" from Czechoslovakia, Rumania, Hungary, and other European countries not only increased Germany's population, but made it more homogenous. Post World War II, Germans and other Europeans found themselves living in countries less ethnically and religiously diverse than at any time in centuries. Adolf Hitler and his Nazis had succeeded in shattering the Habsburg dream of uniting Europe under the umbrella of a multicultural empire.

The Hohenbergs, meanwhile, refused to live in the past, but were not yet ready to forget the Habsburg dreams of their father.

CHAPTER TWENTY-ONE
ANSWERED AND UNANSWERED PRAYERS

"This war would have never come unless, under American and modernizing pressure, we had driven the Habsburgs out of Austria and Hungary and the Hohenzollerns out of Germany. By making these vacuums we gave the opening for the Hitlerite monster to crawl out of its sewer onto the vacant thrones."
—WINSTON CHURCHILL

"I hope it doesn't sound too pretentious if I raise my voice to speak out."
—MAXIMILIAN HOHENBERG

On their first holiday together since the war, Maximilian and Elisabeth traveled to Rome for an audience with Pope Pius XII. The trip was a spiritual and personal pilgrimage. As Vatican Secretary of State, Eugenio Pacelli had tried to free the Hohenberg brothers from Dachau. They wanted to thank him. But the Pope took the opportunity to thank them for standing up against the Nazis when even the Catholic Church had not. Max showed Elisabeth the ruins of ancient and modern Rome, including the Palazzo Venezia where he'd had his final meeting with Mussolini. From its shuttered balcony Mussolini declared war against England and France in 1940. Max's predictions about the Italian dictator's fate had all come to pass.

Since the Austrian government seized Nazis' property following the war, and the Nazis seized all Hohenberg properties before the war,

Ernst had to sue to have his family home and estates returned to him. Eventually his lawsuit succeeded, and he reclaimed Radmer and the forests and mountain properties he loved. One-third of the land was turned over to his sister. She, Fritz, and their children moved into a small cottage near the mountain village of Eisenerz, a short distance from Ernst and Maisie's home. Sophie filled the cottage with family photographs, and filled her days and nights seeking information about Erwein. She believed in her heart that her firstborn son still lived.

In February of 1948, a communist coup overthrew Czechoslovakia's government. President Beneš had been outmaneuvered by his communist allies just as earlier he had been outmaneuvered by the Nazis. Two weeks later, Jan Masaryk, the country's Foreign Minister, was found dead beneath a window of his apartment in Prague Castle. The son of the country's first president was either a victim of suicide or assassination. Eduard Beneš resigned the presidency and died in quiet retirement. The last sparks of Czechoslovakia's once-thriving democracy were extinguished.

That April, Max and Ernst were asked by other concentration camp survivors to return to Dachau for a reunion. Plans were being made to turn the empty camp into a memorial to the Holocaust. To the surprise of their families and friends, the brothers agreed. They felt a kinship, an almost spiritual brotherhood, with their fellow survivors. Ten years after their arrest and imprisonment, they returned to Germany's first concentration camp. They silently walked the grounds as free men, side by side, alone with their thoughts. When they arrived home, they said nothing about the camp, but it seemed a healing experience for them.

Other reunions never took place. For Sophie Nostitz-Rieneck, the war had not ended as long as her son remained a prisoner somewhere in the vastness of the Soviet Union. The war finally came to an end when she was notified that Erwein died at his Ukrainian prison camp on September 11, 1949. He was twenty-eight years old and had been alive the entire five years his family had searched for him. The letter informing her of his death gave no details.

One year later, she received an unexpected visitor. A prisoner of war from the Ukrainian camp where Erwein died was finally released. He made his way to Czechoslovakia, then to Artstetten, and finally to Eisenerz. His bunk bed had been next to Erwein's and he wanted Sophie to know that, in his last hours, her son's faith never left him. He had prayed on his rosary until his final breath.

That gift allowed Sophie to live again. The visitor did not describe the slave labor camp where they had been imprisoned, or the back-breaking work they endured, the brutal guards, or the harsh Ukrainian winters. He just wanted her to know that her son was a good man and did not die alone. Erwein died with his faith and a friend at his side. The soldier's words brought her comfort and peace. Sophie never again thought of her son's death without remembering the gift Erwein's friend had given her.

Alois, Sophie's surviving son, married a Waldburg cousin. When they had children of their own, they named their youngest son Erwein Franz, in memory of the brothers Alois lost in Hitler's wars. He devoted the rest of his life to helping families find the graves of fathers, brothers, and sons killed in the war so they might be reburied closer to home. Alois never found where either of his own brothers were buried; but he was able to bring closure to other grieving families.

Without having their graves near her, Sophie created her own private packet of memories for each of her lost sons. She began with their first childhood drawings and their schoolwork she had carried with her when she left Czechoslovakia. Every letter they wrote to her was included, ending with her last picture of each of them as draftees in the German army. On Franz's packet she added the letter that informed her, "Your son died for the Führer and the Fatherland." They were empty words to her, but being a soldier had been part of his short life. The last piece of paper she put in the packet and tied with a string was a Bible quote, "The Lord Gives and the Lord Takes away. Blessed be the name of the Lord." Sophie had lost two sons, but not her faith. She never doubted they would meet again in a better place.

Maximilian had two crosses carved above the tombs of their parents at Artstetten. The cross above Franz Ferdinand's sepulcher was for the Archduke's first grandson, Erwein Maximilian Franz Nostitz-Rieneck. Above the Duchess of Hohenberg's sepulcher was placed a cross for Franz Assisi Friedrich Ernst Nostitz-Rieneck.

In March of 1954, forty-nine-year-old Ernst Hohenberg traveled to Graz, the birthplace of his father, for a reunion with other Dachau survivors. The evening before their meeting he checked into the Steinerhof Hotel in good spirits. That night he suffered a massive heart attack and died. Maximilian was in Vienna with his son Peter when they received the call. He brought Ernst's body back to Artstetten Castle to be buried near their assassinated parents. The youngest of Archduke Franz Ferdinand and the Duchess of Hohenberg's three children was the first to die. Hitler and his Third Reich continued claiming victims.

Ernst's death was reported in newspapers and magazines around the world including the *New York Times* and *Time* magazine. Under the headline SON OF FRANZ FERDINAND, one of Vienna's leading newspapers wrote:

> The family was blessed to have him in their lives and that he was able to experience life with his two children. His name and entire life was a symbol of the shock and tragedy of Sarajevo. The bitter years he spent in concentration camps took a toll on his heart that brought about his death before he reached his fiftieth birthday. The intellectual power and gentle tolerance of this nobleman during his time of pain and suffering were never broken.

All the surviving members of the Hohenberg family traveled to Artstetten to bid him farewell. The funeral Mass was held in the church where the Archduke and his Duchess had been buried forty years earlier. The adjoining sepulchers of the Hohenbergs' parents were carved with lions, lambs, and doves of peace, the symbols of their love. Four decades and two world wars had passed. Sophie, Maximilian, and Ernst had grown up and married. Children had been born. Children had died. Now Ernst rejoined his parents for the final time at Artstetten.

The funeral Mass of the Catholic Church and the liturgical prayers were identical to those used in 1914 for their parents. The family selected a six-word epitaph to carve on Ernst Hohenberg's tomb. It read, "He was a loyal, honest Austrian."

Later when Sophie Nostitz-Rieneck thought of Ernst's funeral at Artstetten, what she may have most remembered was the next generation of Hohenbergs who were there. They had all grow into adulthood. Her youngest child was a married woman of twenty-five expecting her first child.

The year of Ernst's death, Franz Janacek also died, breaking another link with the past. He had been in service to the Hohenberg family since before any of them had been born. With the death of Ernst, the loss of her oldest two sons, Franz Janacek's passing, and the next generation of Hohenberg children grown and having children of their own, Franz Ferdinand's daughter must have felt much older than her fifty-three years.

Nine months after Ernst's funeral, the Soviet Union finally agreed to end its decade-long occupation of Austria. Communist autocrats in Moscow continued to control the rest of eastern Europe, including Czechoslovakia for thirty-five years; but the end of the occupation offered Austria and the Hohenbergs a fresh beginning.

The 1955 treaty restoring Austrian independence was signed in Vienna's Belvedere Palace by former Chancellor Leopold Figl. Like Max and Ernst Hohenberg, Figl had once been labeled an enemy of the state by the Nazis and imprisoned for high treason by Adolf Hitler.

Sophie Nostitz-Rieneck and Maximilian Hohenberg thought the location of Belvedere an excellent site for the historic event. Their mother and father had always loved the palace, and the signature on the treaty by a fellow Dachau survivor would have delighted Ernst. Their younger brother had always liked Leopold Figl and the palace where they spent much of their happy childhood. The event seemed to exorcize any association of it with Adolf Hitler.

Once the Hohenbergs were free of their Russian overseers, Elisabeth and Maximilian surprised their sons by removing two walls at Artstetten to reveal a secret room. Before the war, a hallway had been boarded up and plastered over to create a storage space to hide priceless paintings, furniture, and family heirlooms. The Nazi and Russian looters who ransacked Artstetten and the youngest of the Hohenberg children had no idea the room was there. When everything was brought into the light of day, they always remembered the event as a second Christmas.

Among the hastily packed artifacts was the collection of ceramic lambs Franz Ferdinand had given his wife throughout the thirteen years of their marriage. When Sophie Nostitz-Rieneck learned her father's gifts to their mother had been saved, no other buried treasure could have made her happier.

The past surrounded and touched the Hohenbergs nearly every day of their lives, but their children thought little about what had happened before they were born. Georg Hohenberg remembered an epiphany he experienced during a stroll he took with his father. He told his mother about it, but confided in no one else until years later:

> We often walked in the gardens of the Belvedere Palace because it was the nearest park to the apartment we kept in Vienna. My father often laughed and said we only moved 500 meters to our apartment from our former home in the Belvedere. I knew he had lived there. It was just a fact of life, but as a child I never thought much about

it. Once though he pointed out a window and said, "That is my mother's sleeping room where I was born." It was a very touching and fascinating moment, to think that he was born there, and spent his childhood in that beautiful palace.

Suddenly it made the past real and unreal at the same moment. Slowly, I started to understand how much he had lost in his life, and how little I had lost. He was in the place of his birth, yet on the outside of everything he had ever known. It had all been turned upside down. Nothing was the same. To be somebody, then to be nobody would be a horrible thing. Everything was different from what one imagined, but he didn't seem to feel that way. Over the years I had the opportunity to enter Belvedere Palace many times. My father did too, but he never returned to the palace where he was born.

Maximilian Hohenberg did return to public life beyond the village of Artstetten. He issued a statement that read, "My family has lived in Austria for 700 years, so I hope it doesn't sound too pretentious if I raise my voice to speak out about the large issues facing the land of my birth." His decision was prompted in part by the haunting words placed within the gates of the Dachau memorial, "May the example of those who were exterminated here between 1933 and 1945 unite the living in their defenses of peace and freedom and in reverence of human dignity."

The visit he and Elisabeth had made to Rome also played a part. Pope Pius XII had granted Max special permission to see the Vatican's famous collection of maps. Looking at the maps of Europe, he lamented the political boundaries dividing the continent. The gentle curator quietly said political and religious leaders divided Europe, and it would take political and religious leaders to unite it. His words echoed the sentiments written at Dachau. Max believed no one was in a better position to make them a reality than Otto Habsburg, but first he had to end his cousin's Austrian exile.

Otto Habsburg briefly returned to the country following the war, but French occupation authorities deported him. The country's 1919 constitution continued to read, "Members of the House of Habsburg are banned from entering the land unless they specifically renounce their membership of this House and all its associated claims of sovereignty and declare themselves loyal citizens of the Republic." The injustice of having to renounce membership in one's own family, the pain of being a patriot yet considered an enemy of the state, and the loneliness of being an exile from one's own country spoke to the heart and soul of the Hohenberg experience. Max once again took up his quest to end his cousin's exile.

Nostalgia for a glorious past, wounds from the Anschluss years, and a decade of communist occupation lingered deep in the Austrian soul. Max believed that if given the opportunity Otto Habsburg was in a unique position to heal his country and bring it together as the young Queen Elisabeth's recent coronation had done in England. For many Austrians, the Habsburg heir to the vacant throne represented a bridge from the past to the future; but the past meant different things to different people. Otto's early warnings and denunciations against Hitler, his work to help Jews and others escape the Nazis, and his defense of Austria as Hitler's first victim made him a hero for some. But for allies of the Nazis, Anschluss supporters, Nazi collaborators, and deniers of the Holocaust, he was the enemy, an uncomfortable reminder of their past.

Max traveled throughout Austria campaigning for a restoration of the constitutional monarchy, but he discovered Hitler's hate had not died with him. The fervor and scorn once reserved for the country's Jews was directed at him and his Habsburg cousins. Despite verbal abuse, attacks on his personal character, and physical threats, he refused to give up. More than once his goal seemed within reach. Austria's Fed-
 ·l Chancellor, Julius Raab, spoke publicly in favor of restoring Otto's
     nship. A war of words erupted in parliament and the nation's

newspapers. The country's Interior Minister, Oskar Helmer, assured Max that the majority of Austrians supported his crusade, but an angry vocal minority prevented a resolution to the stalemate.

As 1961 drew to a close, Otto Habsburg asked that all efforts to restore the constitutional monarchy end. After forty-three years of exile he renounced any claims to the vacant throne and asked to simply return to Austria as an ordinary citizen. As Max feared, despite overwhelming public support, opponents continued blocking Otto's return. The former Crown Prince announced he would take his case to the Austrian courts.

Exhausted, disappointed, and depressed, Max retired to Artstetten to spend a quiet Christmas with his family. On January 8, 1962, Sophie Nostitz-Rieneck received a telephone call. Her fifty-nine-year-old brother had suffered a massive heart attack. He died the following day. Maximilian Hohenberg's death did what he had always hoped Otto Habsburg would do. For one brief moment, Austria became united again.

Eighteen miles of mourners choked the roads leading to his Artstetten funeral. Aristocrats stood with Socialists. Atheist and agnostics walked alongside Catholic priests, nuns, and bishops. Dachau's Jews, Roma, and Jehovah's Witnesses offered prayers for his soul. Over one thousand people unable to be seated in the church quietly stood outside in the rain until the funeral Mass ended. Royal relatives traveled from Luxembourg and Liechtenstein. Archduke Hubert Salvator, a grandson of Emperor Franz Joseph, represented the Habsburg Imperial Family. Otto von Habsburg asked the government for permission to attend, but his request was rejected. All the living Hohenbergs were there, but Max's sister, Sophie, must have felt very alone.

Journalists celebrated the contradictions, heights, and depths of his life. Vienna's conservative *Weiner Presse* wrote, "He was a Habsburg, who was not permitted to be one, instead he became Austria's first concentration camp victim. His life ended today, but it began at Belvedere Palace in 1902." The death caused the anti-monarchist Socialist newspaper *Arbeiter Zeitung* to salute all the Hohenbergs:

> They had every reason to turn on the Imperial House. But they declined to kick the fallen. That the old Habsburg had ceased to exist was precisely why they came out for it. Nor did this keep them from being correct citizens of the republic.... Their convictions were monarchists, but they lived their lives faithful to the law.

A third paper reported:

> Today we are joining with his concentration camp comrades one last time to remember Maximilian Hohenberg.... In the same way his parents were the first two victims of World War I, their sons were the first two political prisoners taken to Dachau. He was a man who was not just true to his own house and family, but always to Austria his entire life. This memory will stay with us forever.

Four years after Maximilian's death, the Austrian Constitutional Court restored Otto Habsburg's citizenship. Following nearly half a century of exile, the Hohenbergs' cousin was finally able to legally reenter his own country. Sophie Nostitz-Rieneck welcomed her cousin home.

CHAPTER TWENTY-TWO
THE GOOD FIGHT

"It is not the wounds of life that matter. It is what we do with
them."   —SOPHIE NOSTITZ-RIENECK

"I have fought the good fight. I have finished my course. I have
kept the faith."   —2 TIMOTHY 4:8

In 1981, Archduke Franz Ferdinand's daughter, who had outlived her
younger brothers, two of her four children, and—after fifty-three years
of marriage—her husband, Fritz, decided to return to Czechoslovakia
for a visit. Alois, her surviving son, his wife, and children traveled with
her. They found their former country estates at Falkenau and Heinrichgrun overgrown and in ruins. The crumbling Nostitz-Rieneck coat
of arms could still be seen over the main portal of the Falkenau house.
In Prague, their Maltese Square home had become the offices of the
Czech Republic's Ministry of Culture. Musical concerts were sometimes played there. The books in the mansion's world-famous library
were gone, but the shelves were not empty. The National Museum's
own library had replaced it.

Sophie and her family retraced the well-worn path to the Our
Lady of Victories Church. There she showed her grandchildren the
famous Infant of Prague statue. She lit a candle and offered prayers
for the living and the dead. They also traveled the thirty miles from
Prague to Konopiste Castle. Sophie and her family dutifully bought

tickets to enter the home where she had been born. No one recognized the former princess as she joined a large group of tourists shuffling through the castle.

The monotone tour guide rushed from room to room making attempts to amuse the tourists with fabrications about the Archduke, the Hohenbergs, and Konopiste. Sophie quietly whispered corrections to her family about nearly everything the guide said. The lies told about his grandfather angered Alois, but as Sophie's own mother had done with her father, she gently touched his arm soothing him with a smile. The visit seemed to please her. It allowed her the opportunity to share the truth about her parents and the Hohenbergs' story with the next generation of her family. Truth was important to her.

Following Fritz's death, Sophie had moved to Salzburg to be near family, including Max's widow, Elisabeth. They shared stories about their children and grandchildren, and often laughed and teased each other. The dark sad times were seldom mentioned, but that was the laser focus of questions by inquiring journalists. Newspapers, authors, and historians came to interview Sophie, causing Elisabeth to ask, "Why do you keep speaking with them? They never print what you say. They distort your stories, and only write what they want to write." Sophie always had the same answer. "The real story has never been told. Maybe the next interview will print the truth."

When her grandson attended law school in Salzburg, he came to live with her. Three decades later, Count Friedrich Nostitz-Rieneck's memories of their time together remained vivid:

> My grandmother told me many stories of her youth, of her parents, and of her whole life.... Yet I never heard her speak badly of anyone, never the Serbs who killed her parents, not the Czechs who naturalized her home two times, nor the Germans who took her two sons to die in a war that was not their war.... To live the life she lived without bitterness was a great example to us....

She kept too busy to hate. She loved to read. She loved music and sports. She loved nature, gardens, and being outdoors, but mostly she loved to laugh.... My favorite memory of her was her laughter. She laughed as if she was a young girl.

I remember once when I lived with her I woke up at 2:00 a.m. and heard her TV on from my little room upstairs. I thought it can't be. My grandmother never has problems sleeping. I slowly went down the stairs and saw her in her room watching ice hockey. It was two in the morning and she was watching the Czech Republic play Canada. She loved ice hockey perhaps because she played it as a child at St. Moritz with her father. She loved football too. I remember talking with her when the Czech Republic was playing Germany. She always rooted for the Czechs even after she lost her home there two times.

I can't say she hated Germany, but she never rooted for any of their sports teams. My grandmother's generation had known so much loss, so many tragedies, yet they still found fun, beauty, laughter and goodness in life. Next to her bed she always kept a photograph of my great-grandparents entering the car in Sarajevo, minutes before they were murdered. On the backside she wrote, "The last steps of my beloved parents—before the assassination on June 28, 1914." It was a shocking abrupt end to the happy life she and her brothers had known.

Such wounds never heal, yet my grandmother taught us the wounds don't have to destroy a person. It is not the wounds of life that matter. It is what we do with them.

Two years later, the three great matriarchs of the family, eighty-one-year-old Sophie Countess of Nostitz-Rieneck; Elisabeth, the seventy-eight-year-old Dowager Duchess of Hohenberg; and Ernst's seventy-three-year-old widow, Maisie, journeyed to Artstetten for a family wedding. Maximilian's granddaughter Princess Sophie

Hohenberg married Baron Jean-Louis de Potesta of Belgium. She was the namesake of her Aunt Sophie and goddaughter of Max's wife, Elisabeth. The celebration was one of the last times the three remarkable sisters-in-law would be together.

In 1985, Maisie, the Countess Maria-Theresa Wood Hohenberg, died at her home in Radmer. She had been in poor health since her son Ferdinand, who had been confined to a wheelchair since he was a young man, died at the age of fifty-one. Although the youngest Hohenberg woman of her generation, she was the first to die. Maisie returned to Artstetten for the last time and was buried beneath the chapel next to Ernst.

On the fifty-fifth anniversary of the Anschluss, Max's widow, Elisabeth, also died and was interned at Artstetten. The identical sepulchers of the four Hohenbergs, Maximilian and Elisabeth, Ernst and Maisie, stand side by side, together in death as they had been in life. Just steps away are the tombs of Archduke Franz Ferdinand and the Duchess of Hohenberg.

The anniversary of the Anschluss in 1989 also claimed the life of former Empress Zita Habsburg. Two hundred royal relatives from near and far attended her massive funeral in Vienna; among them were the Hohenbergs. The death of the Empress was reported in news stories around the world. The *St. Louis Post-Dispatch* wrote:

> Empress Zita, 97, was buried in the Habsburg family crypt beneath the Capuchins Church after a requiem mass in St. Stephen's Cathedral, in which prayers were read in many of the vast empire's languages—German, Hungarian, Czech, Slovene, Polish, and Italian.... Communist ruled Hungary's state television, along with five West European countries, broadcast the funeral live.... The Habsburg empire has become popular again, for its past glories, but also for the political lesson it is thought able to teach central Europe—which has known little but disasters since the Empire col-

lapsed—and to a western Europe looking for new forms of multi-lateral political organizations.

Five months later, Zita's son Otto was instrumental in sponsoring a picnic through the Pan-European Organization, the continent's oldest European unification movement. Attendees met on both sides of the Austro-Hungarian border across from the Hungarian town of Sopron. Picnic-goers were encouraged to bring food, wine, and wire cutters. At two thirty in the afternoon, the border crossing was opened. Hundreds of thousands of eastern Europeans fled into Austria.

Sophie Nostitz-Rieneck lived long enough to see some, but not all, of her father's dreams realized, and some of the nightmares of her own life wiped away. In 1989, the Velvet Revolution peacefully overthrew the communist regime in Czechoslovakia. The country's new president, Vaclav Havel, offered a public apology for the expulsion of the nation's Sudeten "Germans."

Communist regimes collapsed across Europe. The Solidarity Movement in Poland voted the communists out of office. By the end of December, revolution in Rumania ended forty-two years of communist rule there. Cracks in the Iron Curtain made at the Sopron Picnic culminated in the fall of the Berlin Wall, the reunification of Germany, and calls for European unity.

Temperatures fell to near freezing across Austria the last October of Sophie's life. The cold weather was a reminder that winter was approaching. She had always tried to live in the present. That fall, after moving into the home of her daughter, she more and more revisited the past. But it was not the past of Adolf Hitler, the Nazis, or the wars that followed Sarajevo. Those memories did not linger in her soul. Nor did the ancient castles and palaces where she once lived. They had become museums, vanished, or were in ruins. Dachau and the other concentration camps where her brothers had been imprisoned were silent and empty. The battlefield in Poland where one of her sons died was overgrown, indistinguishable from the surrounding landscape. The Russian gulag where her other son was buried in an unmarked grave had long ago disappeared from maps. Those physical places did not haunt her mind or trouble her sleep. It was the vibrant men and women she loved in life and who loved her who remained alive in her heart. Her grandson said of her:

> My grandmother's generation had so many losses, so many tragedies, yet they found beauty and laughter and goodness in life, even at the end of her life. She saw nearly everything swept away, but never gave up. I think that generation was sustained by faith and loyalty, a sense of humor, and a deep commitment to family. These were things she inherited from her parents that provided her the resilience to survive. But her faith, her religion remained the single most important thing in her life. She never doubted that one day she would be reunited with all those she loved. Her ability to withstand the insanity of life and still be standing was a miracle rooted in that faith and family.

There were many anniversaries in Sophie Nostitz-Rieneck's life. Some she cherished, others were too sad or too painful to relive. October 28 was a day she dreaded. It was the date in 1914 when Gavrilo Princip was convicted of assassinating her parents, and four years later when Czechoslovakia declared its independence from the Austro-Hungarian Empire. Eduard Beneš announced his ethnic cleansing policy on October 28, 1945. That was the date Sophie, her family, and millions of other Czechs of German ancestry learned they were to be expelled from their homes. On October 27, 1990, one day before those anniversaries, the eighty-nine-year-old daughter of Archduke Franz Ferdinand and the Duchess of Hohenberg died peacefully in her sleep.

She was not buried at Artstetten Castle with her parents, brothers, and sisters-in-law, but in the family crypt of her son-in-law in the

Austrian village of Thannhauser. Sophie and Fritz, her husband of fifty-three years, rested side by side. On the Mass card handed out to family and friends who came to bid her "auf wiedersehen" were two photographs. One was a smiling photo of her surrounded by the flowers she loved. The other was a photo of the Infant of Prague statue found at Our Lady of Victories church in Czechoslovakia. She had selected the prayer and a favorite Bible quote for the card. Taken together, they reflect the life she led. "I am with God. I die, but my love for you will not die. I will love you from heaven as I have on earth... I have fought the good fight. I have finished my course. I have kept the faith."

CHAPTER TWENTY-THREE
THE DESTINY OF ONE FAMILY

"From tears of war the daily bread of future generations will grow."
—ADOLF HITLER

"Sarajevo, Konopiste, and the Hitler years cast a longer and longer shadow over him."
—PRINCESS SOPHIE HOHENBERG DE POTESTA
on her father

"When we see names in history books the people behind the names aren't real. Yet they were once real and continue to influence us today." —PRINCE GERHARD HOHENBERG

When Maximilian Hohenberg died in 1962, the title Duke of Hohenberg passed to his oldest son, Franz. He had married Princess Elisabeth, the daughter of the Grand Duchess of Luxembourg, a niece of Empress Zita, in 1956. The brilliant wedding, in Luxembourg's centuries-old Notre-Dame Cathedral, was attended by family, friends, and royal relations from across Europe. Franz inherited his father's handsome features, charm, and intelligence; his Aunt Sophie's love of music and culture; and his Uncle Ernst's wit, love of nature, and restless hyperactivity. Like the rest of his generation, he also inherited the traumatic legacy of Sarajevo, Adolf Hitler, and a decade of communist occupation.

Following his father's death, Franz discovered a family secret he never suspected. Maximilian Hohenberg had been homesick for his childhood home of Konopiste his entire life. Copies of his private correspondence documented his efforts to have something, almost anything of Konopiste, returned to his brother, sister, and himself.

In 1945, Max thought his prayers might be answered. Artworks stolen by Adolf Hitler from across Europe were discovered in the Alt-Ausee salt mines south of Salzburg. Max had a hunch and carefully followed the story. In addition to Michelangelo's famous statue of the Madonna of Bruges, Jan van Eyck's Ghent Altarpiece, and masterworks by Vermeer, Hitler had also hidden forty cases of artifacts from Konopiste.

Maximilian wrote dozens of letters to the military officers who later became known as the "Monuments Men." He pleaded to have family portraits, paintings, photo albums, and books from his mother's private library returned to him. They were the legacy Franz Ferdinand and the Duchess of Hohenberg meant for their children, and for the grandchildren and great-grandchildren they would never know.

His words were eloquent and heartfelt, without rancor, bitterness, or self-importance, but they were rejected. Eventually all the Hohenbergs' treasures found in the Austrian mountains were returned to Czechoslovakia. In 1947, Konopiste was reopened as a museum. In his father's last will and testament, Maximilian asked his son to do everything in his power to return Konopiste and its artifacts to the family. His father had never mentioned, or even hinted, any of this to anyone during his lifetime. Shocked, even burdened by the request, Franz decided to travel to Czechoslovakia to visit the castle of his father's dream.

During the visit, Franz Hohenberg entered a world that his father had always kept from him. It was a past Franz was never again able to escape. When he returned to Austria, he told his brothers, "Now I really don't understand our father." He was amazed someone who had lost so much—loving parents, total security, a close-knit family, a home like Konopiste—and had also been arrested, publicly humiliated, and imprisoned in Hitler's concentration camps could live a life without anger or bitterness. His father never spoke of those losses or scars, but somehow they became rooted in Franz's own soul. The Konopiste visit changed him. Franz's youngest daughter, Sophie, explained:

> My father could tell one joke after another. He loved the arts and nature, but he was also sensitive, almost fragile in some ways. As he grew older Sarajevo, Konopiste, and the Hitler years cast a longer and longer shadow over him. He felt if he had experienced the same kind of loses as his own father, he would have crumbled. That reality began to almost haunt him.

Franz returned to the castle many times. But in 1977, he died of a heart attack before reaching his fiftieth birthday. No member of the next generation of his family had been able to join him there before his untimely death. Following the collapse of communism, Franz's youngest daughter, Princess Sophie, and her husband, Baron Jean-Louis de Potesta, finally visited Konopiste. Although named for her great-aunt who had been born there, she never imagined she would feel anything seeing the house. Years later she reminisced:

> I didn't expect to be moved. I felt no links to the house. To me it was only a building with bricks and stones, but I was surprised. Love lingered in every room. It could still be felt. It surrounded and embraced you. This was a home, a real family home, a genuine sanctuary for the loving father, mother, and children who once lived there. Even the Nazi murderers and thieves, and Hitler's blind hatred for our family, could not steal the love from that house.

Princess Sophie later returned to the Czech castle with her three children. They were near the ages of Franz Ferdinand's orphans, Sophie, Max, and Ernst, when they had been expelled from the castle. Following that visit, she decided to try to reclaim Konopiste for her family. Years of legal battles in local, national, and international courts resulted in her claims for repatriation of the castle being rejected. But in 2013 she said,

> The fight itself is important. Not necessarily the result. It is import-
> ant that people know the truth. It is important for others to know
> what happened, what was done, and how it was done. If I don't
> succeed, someone from the next generation will continue because
> ultimately this is a fight about justice and truth.

On June 28, 2014, four generations of the Hohenberg family gath-ered at Austria's Artstetten Castle. The one hundredth anniversary of the Sarajevo assassinations bought together the descendants of Arch-duke Franz Ferdinand, his beloved wife, the Duchess of Hohenberg, and their Habsburg cousins. They shared family stories, reminisced, and laughed. Young and old relatives attended a solemn peace Mass at the nearby Basilica of Maria Taferl officiated by their cousin the Car-dinal Archbishop of Vienna, Christopher Schönborn.

The sanctuary of the Basilica holds a memorial to the fallen in the two world wars. If visitors look carefully, they can also find an etching of the Archduke and Duchess of Hohenberg, their heads bowed in prayer, tucked unobtrusively into one of the stained-glass windows. Before the family went their separate ways, prayers were offered for peace, and on behalf of loved ones living and dead. The Hohenbergs gathered not to grieve, but rather to give thanks for the founders of their family and the love that made their lives possible.

Georg Hohenberg, like his father, Maximilian, an Austrian dip-lomat, entertained family and guests with tales of his diplomatic ad-ventures. His stories brought good cheer but conjured up more than a few ghosts. When he was stationed in Argentina, he found himself working with pro-Nazi Austrians who had fled there after the war, Austrians who fled the Nazis before the war, and Austrian and Czech cousins who escaped the Nazis during the war. He said it took a Ho-henberg to keep all the Austrians in Argentina sorted out.

Once at a large reception in Venice he found himself standing on a balcony next to a small boy struggling to see over the railing. He lifted him up to share the magnificent view of the Grand Canal. An older woman bolted from the reception, yanked the child from his hands, and quickly vanished among the guests. He couldn't imagine what she had been thinking until another guest whispered an explanation. The lady was a member of the Serbian royal family. The boy was her son. She must have imagined the grandson of Archduke Franz Ferdinand was about to avenge the Sarajevo assassination by throwing the young Serbian prince from the balcony. Georg confessed he didn't know whether to feel badly about the woman's behavior or to laugh. Since he was a Hohenberg, he laughed; but being a diplomat, it was a quiet laugh only he heard.

A favorite story shared by Gerhard Hohenberg, Georg's brother, concerned an encounter with the Duke and Duchess of Windsor. Gerhard was once seated next to the Duchess at a dinner party on the island of Malta. She effortlessly switched from English to German in midsentence when she discovered his identity. Her dress, manners, and jewels were impeccable. He looked across the table at the Duke of Windsor. During his nation's worst crisis, the Duke had abdicated the throne of England to marry the chattering woman seated next to him.

Gerhard was struck at how small the former King was, not just in physical stature, but in other ways. He and the Duchess seemed to have spent their adult lives attending parties and avoiding responsibilities. Resting in the nearby harbor, within sight of the dinner party, was the still magnificent British Mediterranean Fleet. At one time every sailor, admiral, and soldier in the British Empire saluted the Duke as Edward VIII by the Grace of God, of Great Britain, Ireland, and of the British Dominions beyond the Seas, King, Defender of the Faith, Emperor of India.

Captain George Jervis Wood, Maisie Hohenberg's father, served as the Duke's personal military aide throughout the Second World War.

His stony silence regarding the couple as individuals and as members of the royal family spoke volumes. Others who knew Edward said of the dethroned Prince Charming that he was at his best in the best of times, and at his worst during the worst of times. Gerhard couldn't help contrast the legacy of the Duke and Duchess's love story with that of his own family.

Georg Hohenberg's last diplomatic posting was as Austria's Ambassador to the Vatican where he was quickly befriended by Pope John Paul II. The two had much in common. The Pope's father was a captain in the Austro-Hungarian army who named his son Karel, the Polish version of Karl, after the last Habsburg Emperor. In 2004, the Pope moved the late Emperor one step closer to Catholic sainthood. For his virtuous life and peace efforts to end the First World War, Karl was recognized by the Catholic Church as a "Servant of God." A crowd of fifty thousand people from across central Europe celebrated the televised event from St. Peter's Square. Ambassador Hohenberg, his family, and Habsburg cousins were there. Archduke Franz Ferdinand had stood as Karl's godfather. Following the death of Karl's dissolute father, he became the guardian of the future Emperor and his younger brother. The founder of the Hohenberg dynasty said at the time, "I will do everything in my power to bring them up as good Christians, Austrians, and Habsburgs." He succeeded. Looking back on the story of his remarkable family, Ambassador Hohenberg stated:

> It helps to take the long view of history, of justice, and of life. As a retired diplomat, I see things through different eyes. My grandfather Franz Ferdinand struggled throughout his entire life. My parents struggled too. They didn't accomplish everything they wanted to accomplish. And our generation won't either, but with the next generation, there is always hope.

Prince Gerhard Hohenberg, Archduke Franz Ferdinand's youngest grandson, had the last word on his family's past, present, and future. Sitting at a small outdoor café in Vienna across a windy street from St. Stephen's Cathedral, he said:

> Some years ago I visited a dear friend in southern Austria who had recently been widowed. She asked me to stay for lunch and if her grandson might join us. I of course agreed. Throughout the meal the young boy, who was very nice and polite, kept staring at me. He hardly spoke. He just sat there the entire time looking at everything I did. After he left she told me he wanted to see for himself if people like me really still exist. He couldn't believe he saw the grandson of Franz Ferdinand, someone from the history books who had been killed in 1914. It was very funny. When we see names in history books the people behind the names aren't real. Yet they were once real and continue to influence us today. People don't realize that our family still exists, but we do. The history of Austria and the history of our family is a history of real people and real miracles. We have always believed in miracles and will always believe in miracles. We survived Sarajevo and the wars that followed. We survived Hitler and the Nazis, Stalin and the Communists. We survived the twentieth century. How could we not believe in miracles?

ACKNOWLEDGMENTS

Writing is a solitary activity, but writing nonfiction is a team sport. There have been many people who have shared this journey with me. This is a collective thank you to friends, librarians, historians, archivists, and others in the United States, Austria, Belgium, Bosnia-Herzegovina, England, Luxemburg, and Germany who helped in large and small ways to tell this story.

The roots of this book began when I was a small boy. My mother introduced to me to Kurt von Schuschnigg, a professor of Political Science at St. Louis University. She told me this quiet, shy man had once been the Chancellor of Austria, was arrested by Adolf Hitler, and then imprisoned in Germany at the Dachau Concentration Camp. I didn't know what a chancellor or concentration camp was, where Austria or Germany were, or the name Adolf Hitler, but that introduction created a lifetime of curiosity and questions. This is where that curiosity led me.

As a young teacher I visited Dachau in Germany, and Vienna's Imperial War Museum in Austria. I learned of the 1914 assassination of Archduke Franz Ferdinand, the only political assassination to spark a world war. His last words to his dying wife, "Sophie, don't die, live for our children," haunted me. I wondered, what became of his orphan children? No one seemed to know.

I only began to learn the answer to that question in 2007. That year an article in the *New York Times* titled, "Princess and Heir of

Franz Ferdinand Fights to Repeal a Law and Gain a Castle," caught my attention. I began a correspondence with the Princess, Sophie Hohenberg de Potesta of Luxemburg, the great-granddaughter of Archduke Franz Ferdinand.

In 2011, when I was serving as the Fulbright Chair of the Gender and Women's Studies Program at Alpen-Adria University in Klagenfurt, Austria, the Princess and I finally met. She introduced me to her uncle, Prince Gerhard Hohenberg, the youngest living grandson of the Archduke, her cousin Count Fritz Nostitz-Rieneck, and HRH Georg, Duke of Hohenberg. Together they introduced me to other members of the Hohenberg, Nostiz-Rieneck, and Habsburg families. Without them, this book would never have been possible.

My wife, Mary Jo Harwood, has been with me throughout this long writing and research project. Without her patience and support, there would be no book. Diane Day and Merry Zylstra patiently and loyally read through endless drafts of this story offering invaluable insights, suggestions, and encouragement. Heather Painter in the United States, Germany, and Austria, in English and in German, provided invaluable research, help, and assistance. A special nod to Jeanne Norberg my first editor on my first book who taught me to write, and whose loyalty and friendship saved my life more than once.

Lastly I want to thank my agent, Rita Rosenkranz, and my editor at Diversion Books, Keith Wallman, for believing in this story as much as I did.

NOTES

CHAPTER ONE
HITLER AT THE HOTEL IMPERIAL, 1938

1.   to the Hotel Imperial in the heart of Vienna.: Toland, John. *Adolf Hitler*, 454, Doubleday & Company, Garden City, 1976.
2.   seized his Austrian homeland without a shot fired.: Weyr, Thomas. *The Setting of the Pearl: Vienna Under Hitler*, 32, Oxford University Press, Oxford, 2005.
2.   these dual ambitions.: Hitler, Adolf. *Mein Kampf*, 3, Trns. Ralph Manheim, Houghton Mifflin, New York, 1999.
2.   a powerful attraction for him.: MacDonogh, Giles. 1938: *Hitler's Gamble*, 72, Random House, New York, 2009.
2.   about his five fateful Vienna years.: Toland, 455.
3.   and tonight I am here.: Ibid.
3.   five children fled the same hotel to go into hiding.: Hohenberg, Princess Sophie de Potesta.
3.   the sons of Franz Ferdinand.: Ibid.
3.   a challenge the competitive rivals readily embraced.: Ibid.
4.   to immigrate to the United States.: Bloch, Eduard. "My Patient Adolf Hitler: A Memoir of Hitler's Jewish Physician," *The Journal of Historical Review*, May–June 1994. (Vol. 14. No 3) pp. 27–35.
4.   also provided his personal protection.: Kellerhoff, Sven Felix. "Wie Hitler seinen jüdischen Kompaniechef schützte". Die Welt, 7 July 2012; Weber, Thomas. *Hitler's First War*, 344, Oxford University Press, Oxford, 2010.
4.   the women who loved them would fight back.: *New York Times*, 23 March 1938, 38, col. 1. "Habsburg Princes Arrested by Austrian Nazis."
4.   "all mystery, mystery, mystery.": Whittle, Tyler. *The Last Kaiser: A Biography of Wilhelm II German Emperor and King of Prussia*, 129, Times Books, New York, 1977. The future King Edward VII wrote his mother Queen Victoria Prime Minister Salisbury was "sure that poor Rudolph…was murdered."
4.   lynchpin of central Europe for six hundred years, never fully recovered.: Brook-Shepherd, Gordon. *Uncrowned Emperor: The Life and Times of Otto von Habsburg*, 16, Hambledon and London, London, 2003.
5.   Archduke Franz Ferdinand, as his successor.: Ibid.

5. a role not suited for his brittle personality.: Zweig, Stefan. *The World of Yesterday: Memoirs of a European*, 239 (translated from German by Anthea Bell), Pushkin Press, London, 2009.

5. lacked the thing most valued by the Viennese—charm.: Ibid.

5. in a rented palace, might someday be Emperor.: Pauli, Hertha. *The Secret of Sarajevo: The Story of Franz Ferdinand and Sophie*, Collins, 44, London, 1966.

5. "I don't want to see it.": Ibid., 43–44.

5. gracefulness his sorely missed cousin Rudolph epitomized.: Hohenberg, Prince Gerhard. Even the German Empress Frederick, mother of the future Kaiser, told an Austrian diplomat, "You cannot think how I admire your good-looking, witty and elegant Crown Prince Rudolph, when I compare him with my clumsy, loutish son Wilhelm!" Kürenberg, *The Kaiser*, 57.

5. the melancholy shadow of the dead Crown Prince.: Pauli, 29.

5. did nothing to make Franz Ferdinand's life easier.: Ibid.

5. the way a younger generation worshipped Rudolph.: Kubizek, August. *The Young Hitler I Knew: The Definitive Inside Look at the Artist Who Became a Monster*, 44–45/52 (Translated by Geoffrey Brooks), Pen & Sword Books, Yorkshire, 2019.

6. a time Franz Joseph had not sat on the throne.: McGuigan, Dorothy Gies. *The Habsburgs: The Personal Lives of a Royal Family that Made History for Six Centuries*, 388, Doubleday and Company, New York, 1966.

6. stubbornly outliving five younger heirs.: Ibid.

6. he represented stability and permanence.: Unterreiner, Katrin. *Emperor Franz Joseph 1830–1916: Myth and Truth*, 28, Christian Brandstatter Verlag, 2006.

6. the bureaucratic labyrinth of the Habsburg's Ministry of Finance.: Kubizek, 52–53.

6. and a bullying martinet at home.: Ibid., 56.

6. intimidated, mocked, and beat his children.: Jones, J. Sydney. *Hitler in Vienna 1907–1913: Clues to the Future*, 193, 25, Cooper Square Press, New York, 2002.

6. "I became a little revolutionary.": Hitler, Adolf, 14–15.

6. her son was a "lost soul.": Delaforce, Patrick. *Adolf Hitler: The Curious and Macabre Anecdotes*, 11, Fonthill Ltd., London, 2012.

7. selling out German Austria to its ethnic inferiors.: Kubizek, 226.

7. from the Empire's largest ethnic minority.: Ibid.

7. rather than the many Austrian palaces at his disposal.: Brožouský, Miroslav. *Konopiste Chateau*, 35, The Institute for the Care of Historic Monuments of Central Bohemia in Prague, 1995.

7. ethnic and religious groups poisoning Austria.: Kubizek, 226.

7. glorified in Dr. Pötsch's lectures, but in the wedding bed.: Jászi, Oscar. *The Dissolution of the Habsburg Monarchy*, 32–33, Chicago, University of Chicago Press, 1971.

7. over fifty million citizens ruled by Franz Joseph.: Marek, George R. *The Eagles Die: Franz Joseph, Elisabeth, and Their Austria*, 4, Harper and Row, New York, 1974.

7. Lorraine, Salzburg, Styria, Carinthia, Silesia, and Modena their ruling Duke.: Brook-Shepherd, Gordon. *Archduke of Sarajevo: The Romance and Tragedy of Franz Ferdinand of Austria*, 290, Little, Brown & Company, Boston, 1984.

8. making them a minority in their own homeland.: Jones, 7.

8. "nations this monster of Habsburg marriages built up.": Kubizek, 114.

8. Not so his unpopular heir.: Marek, 39.

8. the Habsburg most hated by Adolf Hitler.: Kubizek, 226.

8. the object of his youthful scorn.: Hitler, Adolf. H.R. Trevor-Roper, ed. *Hitler's Private Conversations*, 30, Farrar, Straus, & Young, New York, 1953.

8. the Slavization, marginalization, and destruction of German Austria.: Hitler, *Mein Kampf*, 92–93.

8. hundreds of thousands of animals during his travels on four continents.: Aichelburg, Wladimir. *Erzherzog Franz Ferdinand von Österreich—Este und Artstetten*, 19, Verlagsbüro Mag. Johann Lehner Ges.m.b., Wien, 2000.

9. close personal friends who were Americans.: Storer, Maria Longworth. *The Recent Bosnian Tragedy: A Personal Recollection of the Archduke Franz Ferdinand and his Wife, the Duchess of Hohenberg*, 674–678, Catholic World, Vol. 99, August 1914, No 593.

9. electoral laws to protect their interests.: Brook-Shepherd, Gordon. *Archduke of Sarajevo*, 290–291.

9. "in or out of office.": Pauli, 200.

9. of his "multinational State" at least "half way.": Viktoria Luise, *The Kaiser's Daughter: Memoirs of H.R.I. Princess of Prussia*, 12–13, Englewood Cliff, Prentice-Hall, 1977.

10. by dealing with the utmost fairness to all.: Cavendish-Bentinck, William. *Men, Women, and Things: Memories of the Duke of Portland*, 394, Faber & Faber, London, 1938.

10. but cleansing and desirable.: Hitler, *Mein Kampf*, 3. On the night war was declared, the French Ambassador to Germany said to the English Ambassador, "There are three people in Berlin tonight who regret that war has broken out; you, me and Kaiser Wilhelm," Whittle, *The Last Kaiser*, 271.

10. the war he had prayed for was at hand.: Ibid., 158–159.

CHAPTER TWO
THE ARTIST, THE ARCHDUKE, AND THE EMPEROR

11. boarded a train in 1907 from his hometown of Linz.: Jones, 1.

11. in the capital of the mighty Habsburg Empire.: Ibid., 2.

12. a traditionalist who embraced modernity.: Illies, Florian. (translated by Shaun Whiteside and Jamie Lee Searle) *1913—The Year Before the Storm*, 27, Melville House, Brooklyn, 2013.

12. designer of the first hybrid petroleum and electric automobile.: Brooks, Tim. "Ferdinand Porsche—Famed for First Hybrid, Beetle, and Link with Hitler," 1, *The National*, February 12, 2012.

12. reading dispatches and signing papers.: Horthy, Nicholas Admiral. *Memoirs,* 52–53, Simon Publications, Safety Harbor, 2000.

12. "and one couldn't see anything.": Linsboth, Christina. *Two Rulers in an "Automobile,"* World and Worlds of the Habsburgs, A Schloss Schonbrunn Kulturand und Betreibsges, m.b.H. project, Wien, 2007–2008.

12. stability, permanence, and continuity.: Lansdale, Maria Horner. *Vienna and the Viennese,* 279, Henry Coates & Company, Philadelphia, 1902. Kaiser Wilhelm II, Germany's Emperor and a royal snob, claimed the Habsburg court the most eloquent in all of Europe.

13. "shebang, did make sense in a way.": Hitler, *Mein Kampf,* 13.

13. and the times pass on regardless.": Kurlander, Eric. *The Perils of Discursive "Balkanization" Petronilla Ehrenpreis, Krieg und Fridenszible im Diskurs,* H-Net Reviews in the Humanities & Social Studies, February 2007.

13. his nearby home and office at Belvedere Palace.: Illies, 27.

13. in a crowded tenement in the heart of the city.: Jones, 6.

13. "I find everything very beautiful.": Ibid., 3.

13. an enchantment out of *The Thousand and One Nights.*": Hamann, Brigitte. *Hitler: Portrait of the Tyrant as a Young Man,* 26, Taurus Park, London, 2010.

14. medley of nations together in any set form.: Ibid., 8.

14. Stalin also lived there at one time.: Jones, 248.

14. as a thirteen-year-old runaway.: Ibid., 3.

14. experienced during her visit as a girl.: Cawthorne, Nigel. *Hitler: The Psychiatric Files: The Madness of the Führer,* 20, Arcturus Publishing Ltd., London, 2016.

14. tapestry of languages, religions, foods, music, dress, and traditions.: Hamann, 304–305.

14. but for the upward mobility his Empire offered.: Ibid., 326.

15. "for the first time in my young life, at odds with myself.": Hitler, *Mein Kampf,* 20.

15. What dreams he dreamt, I do not know.: Bloch, 3.

15. rather feed his dreams with music than his body with food.: Kubizek, 183.

15. Both boys were survivors.: Ibid., 49.

16. quit school without graduating at the age of fifteen.: Ibid., 30–31.

16. his solitary friend was a listener.: Ibid., 148.

16. "The whole of Vienna is waiting for you!": Ibid., 145.

16. proof of his persuasive verbal skills.: Ibid., 150.

16. clasping an ivory-tipped ebony walking stick.: Ibid., 150–151.

16. the "wretched shabby" room where his friend lived.: Ibid., 153.

16. talked as if he were taking art classes.: Ibid., 157.

17. he dreamed of rebuilding Linz and Vienna.: Ibid.

17. "all with the greatest seriousness.": Ibid.

17. he suddenly seemed "unbalanced.": Ibid., 160.

17. "They twice turned me down.": Ibid., 52.

17. as a customs official for the Habsburg government.: Ibid., 157.

17. "Nothing found favor in his eyes.": Ibid., 234.
17. his friend was a musician, not a soldier.: Ibid., 234.
17. "did not deserve a single soldier.": Ibid., 204.
18. urged August to flee to Germany.: Ibid., 205.
18. to join the army reserves.: Ibid.

CHAPTER THREE
CAN THIS BE A JEW?

19. traveled to Vienna to celebrate the anniversary.: "The Austrian Emperor's Jubilee," 712, The *Japan Weekly* Mail, Vol. 49, June 20, 1908.
19. Hitler loved all things German.: Hitler, *Mein Kampf*, 12–13.
19. a horrendous thunderstorm broke over the city.: *Japan Weekly*.
20. "three generations of German princes.": Ibid.
20. and high ideals of "monarchial principles.": Ibid.
20. the struggle for the destiny of the whole nation.: Hitler, *Mein Kampf*, 141.
21. "an exhaustingly kind ruler and emperor.": Trosclair, Wade. *The Limits and Conceptions of Austrianness: The Bohemian-German Press During Franz Joseph's Jubilee in 1908*, 14, Dissertation, Central European University Nationalism Studies Program, Budapest, Hungary, 2013.
21. "in their own mother tongues.": Unowsky, Daniel L. *The Pomp and Politics of Patriotism: Imperial Celebrations in Habsburg Austria 1848–1916*, 141, 144, Purdue University Press, West Lafayette, Indiana, 2005.
21. "guardian angel, custodian, and patron saint.": Trosclair, 13.
21. "exotic dress and appearance" of the revelers.: Unowsky, 141–144.
21. when he heard other languages, especially Czech.: Hamann, 321.
21. "and above all Galician Jews still a German city?": Kubizek, 229.
22. the nobility, the capitalist and the Jews.: Hitler, *Mein Kampf*, 23.
22. "not only the buildings but also the people.": Kubizek, 229.
22. Archduke's Czech marriage were his Habsburg relatives.: Pauli, 196.
22. a lady-in-waiting to his cousin, a Habsburg Archduchess.: Ibid., 126. Franz Ferdinand did not have a particularly high opinion of his own relatives, any more than they did of him. In private he described most of them as "cretins" and with these words, "They're stupid and thick-headed in so far as they're not crackpots!" Kürenberg, 277.
22. and the Archduke's own family did not approve.: Ibid., 83.
22. a royal wife after being a mere servant.: Ibid., 96–97, 100.
23. "with her Slav deceit, for our kindness!": Hohenberg, Prince Gerhard. Empress Elisabeth, who was herself Bavarian, once bluntly told Emperor Franz Joseph, "Above all, no more inbreeding! You should be glad that for once fresh blood comes into the family, instead of Spanish or Bavarian." Kürenberg, *The Kaiser*, 272. Franz Joseph was not interested in new blood, only blue blood. He saw selecting the correct royal marriage partner as a dynastic duty.

23. and detested any semblance of a normal family life.: Stephanie of Belgium, Princess. H.R.H., *I Was to Be Empress*, 153, Ivor Nicholson & Watson, London, 1937. Franz Ferdinand was a close friend of his cousin Crown Prince Rudolph, friendly with Stephanie, and painfully aware of her unhappy marriage. Stephanie may have been the only member of the Habsburg family more unpopular than Franz Ferdinand.

23. "he is stupid, but he has no feelings.": Hamann, Brigitte. *Bertha von Suttner: A Life for Peace*, Translated by Ann Dubsky, 233, Syracuse University Press, 1996.

23. remained his companion for the rest of his life.: Unterreiner, Katrin. *Emperor Franz Joseph, 1830–1916: Myth and Truth*, 88, Christian Brandstätter Verlag, Wien, 2006.

23. his loyal stepmother remained at his side when he died.: Pauli, 216–217.

24. their children could never inherit the throne.: Hohenberg, Prince Gerhard.

24. and fifteen stiff and scowling Habsburg Archdukes.: Pauli, 143.

24. and two younger stepsisters.: Ibid.

25. and eventually dominate Europe.: Kubizek, 226.

25. and destroy Franz Ferdinand and his wife.: Hohenberg, Prince Gerhard.

25. "The older I get the more I like children.": Unowsky, 141.

26. to Franz Joseph before, during, or after their performance.: Hohenberg, Prince Gerhard.

26. visiting his favorite bench in Schönbrunn's public gardens.: Kubizek, 207.

26. Hitler could crystallize his thoughts and vent his rage.: Ibid.

26. of which he dreamed in his lonely hours.: Ibid., 229.

27. "Is this a German?": Ibid., 230.

27. looked like every other citizen.: Ibid.

27. retold the story to his roommate for hours on end.: Ibid.

27. from his eight weeks of military service.: Ibid., 232–233.

27. "how little he wanted to be alone.": Ibid., 234.

27. postcards from Hitler complaining of his "hermit"-like existence.: Jones, 99–101.

28. annexed by Austria into the Habsburg Empire.: Ibid.

28. example of the "Slavization of Austria.": Hamann, Hitler, 103–104.

28. once again sold out its German citizens.: Pauli, 228–229.

28. feared the annexation would antagonize Russia.: Ibid., 254.

28. still be the greatest tragedy for the Austrian monarchy.: Ibid.

28. also the leader of the government's peace party.: Cassels, 90.

28. "to pave the way for revolution?": Ibid.

29. prevailed against his vehement arguments.: Ibid.

29. the event lingered in the capitals of Europe.: Ibid.

29. and devoted cousin and friend, Willy.: Levine, Don Isaac. *Letters from the Kaiser to the Czar*, 222–226, Frederick A. Stokes Company, New York, 1920.

29. Hitler had moved with no forwarding address.: Kubizek, 240.

30. "born of this dying imperial Vienna.": Ibid., 163.

CHAPTER FOUR
THE LION AND THE LAMB

31. but the tragedy was ignored by the Habsburg court.: Hohenberg, Prince Gerhard.
32. glorious triumphs in the Empire's long history.: Unowsky.
32. "love binds people and ruler.": Ibid.
32. "with the collective singing of the state hymn.": Ibid.
32. declare martial law there.: Trosclair, 14.
32. "and had become the most cruelly destroyed.": Ibid.
32. but poverty and hunger followed.: Jones, 126–127.
32. the smallest rent payment, he became homeless.: Ibid., 127.
33. "could not concern myself much with the people around me.": Hitler, *Mein Kampf*, 40.
33. "obtain an opportunity of continuing my education.": Ibid., 41.
33. morality as a symptom of stupid, sheep-like patience, etc.: Ibid., 39.
33. our nation is pitifully poor in *human beings*.: Ibid., 40.
34. "leave the building at once or be thrown off the scaffolding.": Ibid.
34. "which is as dirty and false as he himself.": Ibid., 90.
34. allowed in ten languages with no interpreters.: Ibid.
34. grisly discovery of frozen bodies near its locked entrance.: Hamann, 153.
35. where to find food, and how to earn money.: Jones, 135.
35. often their last meal until the next morning.: Ibid.
35. caused most travelers to avoid him.: Hamann, 155.
35. outside the Hotel Imperial, a night he never forgot.: Toland, 455.
35. Franz Ferdinand's nephew and heir.: Ibid.
35. seemed to have the world at his feet.: Ibid.
36. after their son Max was born there.: Hohenberg, Prince Gerhard.
36. hostess and undisputed mistress of the house.: Ibid.
36. but court protocol forbade her to use it.: Ibid.
36. an opportunity to play in the empty guardhouses.: Ibid.
36. in simpler carriages, they were ignored.: Ibid.
37. just as he and their mother had done.: Hohenberg, Princess Sophie de Potesta.
37. we sensed we were in a different category.: Brook-Shepherd, 93.
37. Eckartsau and Blühnbach for fall hunting.: Ibid.
38. the straitjacketed life her Aunt Sophie lived in Vienna.: Ibid., 109–110.
38. simply pressing his arm and saying, "Franzi, Franzi.": Ibid.
38. kept in a glass case at Artstetten Castle.: Hohenberg, Prince Gerhard.
38. provided him a lifetime of financial security.: Ibid.
39. more than anything else, it was a family home.: Hohenberg, Princess Sophie de Potesta.
39. sailing on the Nile River seeking the warmth of the Egyptian sun.: Pauli, 51.
39. evergreen sent from Konopiste eased his homesickness.: Ibid.
39. "I won't cut down their inheritance.": Ibid., 57.

39. both times their Christmas trees came from Konopiste.: Ibid.
40. and dynastic solidarity with Russia.: Taylor, A.J.P. *The Struggle for Mastery in Europe 1848-1918*, 494, Oxford, 1954.
40. elevating her status in the Empire and abroad.: Brook-Shepherd, Archduke of Sarajevo, 109.
40. she was warmly accepted by the Rumanian royal family.: Ibid., 183–186.
40. in grand style by the German Emperor and Empress.: Viktoria Luise, 12–13.
40. "marrying a lady in waiting or even chambermaids.".: Brook-Shepherd, 168.
40. would have to "face facts" and accept Sophie.: Brook-Shepherd, Gordon. *Uncle of Europe: The Social and Diplomatic Life of King Edward VII*, 261, Harcourt, Brace & Jovanovich, 1976.
40. the personal intervention of Pope Leo XIII, to permit their marriage.: Pauli, 126.
41. that I am so happy was all your doing.: Pauli, 154.
41. vipers of the Habsburg court, his nephew and political heir, Karl.: Hohenberg, Princess Sophie de Potesta.
41. slow, painful death from cancer.: Bloch.
42. grave in the Catholic cemetery outside of Linz.: Ibid.
42. writer he considered their superior, William Shakespeare.: Delaforce, 214–215.
42. and Shylock his favorite villain.: Ryback, Timothy W. *Hitler's Private Library: The Books that Shaped his Life*, xi, xii, xiii, Vintage Books, London, 2010.

CHAPTER FIVE
THE GRANITE FOUNDATION

43. would destroy the Empire and the peace of Europe.: Hohenberg, Prince Gerhard.
43. he also needed ideas and allies.: Ibid.
43. Popovici's book became their bible.: Pauli, 215.
43. the federal government holding them together.: Arco-Zinneberg, *Graf Ulrich, Meine Reise un die Erde*, 100, Jahre Weltreise de Thronfolgers, 33, Verlag J & Sandler, J.H. Donau, 1993.
44. the oligarchs of Hungary, and Adolf Hitler.: Pauli, 120.
44. "destined to become simply large Bohemian landlords.".: Brook-Shepherd, 115.
44. entered into by a princess of the royal house.: Ibid., 64.
44. need for political reforms led to his untimely death.: Thiele, Johannes. *Crown Prince Rudolph 1858–1889: Myth and Truth*, 40–45 (Translated by Martin Kelsey), Christian Brandstätter Verlag, Vienna, 2008.
45. worst fears about the future of German Austrians.: Hitler, 92–93.
45. working-class neighborhood north of the city center.: Hamann, 41.
45. other Jewish philanthropists paid for its construction.: Ibid., 158–159.
45. many Jewish residents, and they befriended him.: Hanisch, 272. In Hitler's Linz childhood, Czechs and Communists were generally viewed with sus-

picion, as were Jesuit priests due to their education and perceived political power. In Albert Speer's autobiography, he wrote that Hitler told him his first awareness about race as a child was his dislike of his Czech classmates in Linz, 99. He concluded even then that Czechs must be stopped from immigrating into German Austria.

45. and politically meddling Jesuit priests.: Hamann, 29.

45. They split the profits 50-50.: Hanisch, 272.

45. the shabbily dressed antisocial artist.: Ibid., 240.

46. with prayers, doctors, nurses, and Jesuit priests.: Hohenberg, Prince Gerhard. Franz Ferdinand had few memories of his biological mother, Princess Maria Annunciata. Archduchess Maria-Theresa, who became his stepmother when he was seven, was to him his "real" mother, his "Dearest Mama."

46. to learn everything and at the end knew nothing.: Hohenberg, Princess Sophie de Potesta. Franz Ferdinand was an introvert who as a public figure was expected to be an extrovert. Franz Ferdinand would today, in all probability, be labeled as a student with a hyperactive activity disorder.

47. "my time in Vienna was especially fruitful and valuable.": Kubizek, 179.

47. "magnifying glass by the light of the moon.": Hamann, 11. Hitler was an avid reader. Like many German and Austrian children, he enjoyed Karl May's fictional tales of the American west, despite the fact that May had never been to America and had never seen a cowboy or Indian his entire life.

47. "contained more than the human mind could grasp.": Kubizek, 181.

47. preferred spending his time talking politics.: Hanisch, 298.

47. "preserve and cultivate its nationality and language.": Hamann, 91.

47. and continually fueled his self-righteous indignation.: Hanisch, 271.

47. and muttered more Jews than in Jerusalem.: Illies, 91.

47. who enjoyed baiting and mocking him.: Hanisch, 242.

48. waved his arms, and screamed at them.: Ibid.

48. from the room he and Kubizek once rented.: Hamann, 240–243.

48. campaigned for the union of Austria with Germany.: Ibid., 246.

48. his being arrested and expelled from parliament.: Ibid., 248.

48. crusade as a step toward annexation by Germany.: Ibid., 240.

48. "Away with Rome means away from Austria.": Ibid., 252.

48. and politically loyal Catholics against him.: Ibid., 304–305.

49. and political dominance were threatened.: Ibid., 285. Hitler later incorporated many of Schönerer's and Lueger's techniques and speaking points into his Nazi Party speeches, rallies, and programs.

49. rave blissfully when he talks to them.: Ibid., 241–243.

49. "to get accustomed to the German environment.": Ibid., 277.

49. mayor of the world's sixth-largest city.: Ibid., 286.

50. mesmerized by the mayor's political skill and acumen.: Ibid., 323–324.

50. the battle cry heard at his massive political rallies.: Ibid., 327. Lueger said of his selective Jewish friendships, "I decide who is a Jew." Hitler also made exceptions to his anti-Semitism when it suited him. He not only allowed his

mother's Jewish doctor and Jewish commanders during the First World War to peacefully immigrate to America, but had as a frequent visitor to the Eagle's Nest a young girl, Berhardine Nienau, known to have a Jewish grandmother. She referred to him as "Uncle Adolf." Martin Bormann stopped the visits causing Hitler to complain, "There are people who have a true talent for spoiling my every joy." Hoffman, 166.

50. and one-third of its university students were Jewish.: Ibid., 286.

50. a kind of terrorism here which couldn't conceivably be worse.": Jones, 11.

50. "wore the effigy of a hanged Jew on their watch chains," but hung no Jews.: Czernin, Ottokar Count. *In the World War*, 50, Cassel & Company, London, 1919.

51. The Archduke, however, genuinely admired him.: Ibid.

51. saluted their nuptials as a "triumph of the heart.": Pauli, 149.

51. "which would inevitably lead this state to destruction.": Jones, 153–154.

51. and won his court case against Hanisch.: Hamann, 171.

51. "Yours, always faithfully, Adolf Hitler.": Bloch, Hamann, 62.

51. "In everlasting thankfulness, Adolf Hitler.": Ibid.

52. and watercolors directly to Jewish dealers.: Hamann, 173.

52. but his skill at self-delusion and his lies were his own.: Ibid., 380.

52. he could not understand why luck had turned against him.: Hauner, 8.

52. "and if I grasp it, I cannot understand it.": Hamann, 62.

52. the high number of men being called into the army.: Ibid., 393, 395.

52. "under no circumstances do I want to serve in the Austrian army.": Ibid., 395.

52. "where they found fame and honor.": Hitler, 125.

52. "the most German of all German cities.": Ibid.

53. "the granite foundation of all my acts.": Ibid.

53. but never left me.: Ibid.

CHAPTER SIX
THE SPY, THE DRAFT DODGER,
AND THE PEACEMAKER

54. influence of Wagner's music and Hitler's words.: Hamann, 395–396.

54. and his newly recruited disciple.: Ibid., 398.

55. on that Babylon of races!: Ibid., 399.

55. "Letters left behind.": Asprey, Robert. *The Panther's Feast,* 260, G.P. Putnam's Sons, New York, 1959.

55. but the suicide of Austria's spy chief was different.: Jones, 244.

55. "lengthy and brilliant" reports from him.: Asprey, 263.

55. "overexertion resulting from severe neurasthenia.": Ibid., 262.

55. doubted the version of events unfolding in Vienna.: Ibid., 278–279.

56. "A flood of reproaches flooded over me.": Ibid., 279–280.

56. "The damage he caused was slight.": Ibid., 280.

56. Austria would be nearly defenseless.: Ibid., 293.

56. was a delicate task that would take time.: Ibid., 287–288.
56. war "between Germanism and Slavism.": Taylor, A.J.P., 496.
57. and Catholic Austria to continence such a scandal.: Clark, Christopher. *The Sleepwalkers: How Europe Went to War in 1914*, 102–103, Penguin, London, 2012.
57. labeled him a draft dodger.: Hamann, 394.
57. to study architecture, but never applied.: Jones, 251–252.
57. But I don't believe that at all.: Hamann, 399.
57. to Vienna to claim the Habsburg crown.: Pauli, 242–243.
58. "accession to the imperial throne as long as possible.": Ibid.
58. but he feared his blind spot for all things military.: Hohenberg, Prince Gerhard.
58. uniforms he himself sometimes designed.: Carter, Miranda. *George, Nicholas, and Wilhelm: Three Royal Cousins and the Road to War*, 101, Alfred A. Knopf, New York, 2009.
58. and the fate of his Empire, to his generals.: Hohenberg, Prince Gerhard.
58. one of the reasons Adolf Hitler hated the dynasty.: Cassels, 126. Austrian Prime Minister Kurt von Stürgkh a member of Conrad von Hötzendorf's war party, declared in his memoirs, "I firmly believe… that if Franz Ferdinand had come to the throne and been convinced that some other alliance would have been more profitable for Austria-Hungary, it would not have cost him one heart pang to abandon Germany and her Kaiser." Stürgkh was himself assassinated in 1916.
58. tore the Habsburg's multinational Empire asunder.: Hamann, 402.
59. a major factor in his decision to flee Vienna.: Ibid., 393–394.
59. and even on the Empire's own allies.: Bostridge, Mark. *The Fateful Year: England 1914*, 168, Penguin Books, London, 2014.
59. He hung up on the General.: Hohenberg, Prince Gerhard.
59. "and struggle as long as I live!": Ibid.
59. profile of a 1914 Austrian woman.: Pauli, 247.
59. "Christian zeal and integrity of her character.": Storer, Maria Longworth, 674–675.
60. "a rather dubious light on Franz Ferdinand.": Pauli, 247.
60. "through the eyes of his wife.": Ibid., 193.
60. "changed while I have a word to say.": Ibid., 222.
60. visit with King George V and Queen Mary.: Brook-Shepherd, *Royal Sunset: The European Dynasties and the Great War*, 274, Doubleday, Garden City, 1987.
61. "he has changed for the better.": Ibid.
63. never spent another night in the Imperial Palace.: Hohenberg, Prince Gerhardt.
63. they were searching for was in their city.: Hauner, 11. Resistance to military service was not tolerated in either Austria or Germany. The neighboring countries worked together to search for and arrest anyone they considered draft dodgers.
63. "the object of evading military service.": Ibid.

CHAPTER SEVEN:
FATE

65. and of course I would pay the fine willingly.: Jones, 321.
65. "see fit to allow him to report in Salzburg.": Hauner, 11. Hitler seemed to have an innate ability to charm people to his side, and even gain their sympathy when he needed them.
65. "and unable to bear arms.": Ibid., 12.
65. where he was certain destiny waited for him.: Jones, 228. Hitler could be quite superstitious, and like Franz Ferdinand, believed in destiny and fate.
65. Häusler had moved out of the room they shared.: Hamann, 191.
66. a human-interest story printed in the *London Times*.: Illies, 149.
66. "to despise the joys of family life.": Stephanie, 153.
66. before a firing squad and Charlotte's insanity.: O'Connor, Richard. *The Cactus Throne: The Tragedy of Maximilian and Carlotta*, 329, 275–276. Despite the tragedies associated with the castle, it is not in any way gloomy, but radiates warmth.
66. held some memory of the doomed couple.: Hohenberg, Prince Gerhard.
67. "We must simply trust God.": Pauli.
67. preferred traveling with his dogs rather than his family.: Hohenberg, Prince Gerhard.
67. promised to visit them again at Konopiste that June.: Ibid.
67. a post that had been vacant for eighteen years.: Illies, 178.
67. province he never wanted as part of the Empire.: Brook-Shepherd, 222.
67. their resentment of their expansion into the Balkans.: Ibid., 235.
68. "When it happens, take them, they are for you.": Ibid.
68. "The crypt at Artstetten is finished now.": Ibid.
68. with Franz Ferdinand to ask him further questions.: Ibid.
68. showed them his favorite view of his rose garden.: Hohenberg, Prince Gerhard.
68. unless their parents hosted a formal dinner.: Ibid.
69. Sophie, received a special invitation.: Ibid.
69. Duchess would leave for Bosnia in a few days.: Ibid.
69. "death to the Habsburg dynasty.": Cassels, Lavender. *The Archduke and the Assassin; Sarajevo June 28, 1914*, 161, Dorset Press, New York, 1984.
70. "and the filthy Bohemian sow!": Brook-Shepherd, Archduke of Sarajevo, 221 / Gerd, Höller. *Franz Ferdinand von Österreich-Este*, Graz, 1982.
70. keys to his nephew Karl if he did not return.: Dedijer, Vladimir. *The Road to Sarajevo*, 165, Simon & Schuster, New York, 1966.
70. in his arms following her 1901 birth.: Brook-Shepherd, 104.
70. stay with his wife and children if anything happened to him.: Dedijer, 165, 262, Simon & Schuster, New York, 1966.
70. except there would never be another like it.: Hohenberg, Prince Gerhard.
71. "would never understand my absence.": Brook-Shepherd, 233.

71. "some Serbian bullets waiting for me.": MacMillan, Margaret. *The War That Ended Peace: The Road to 1914*, 550, Random House, New York, 2013.
71. "my place is at my husband's side.": Pauli, 276.
71. "foresaw the catastrophe a hundred times.": Czernin, 46.
71. "appalled him from beginning to end.": Pauli, 268.
71. the one occasion when he did not get his way.: Brook-Shepherd, 269.
72. when he performed official duties.: Pauli, 265.
72. to search for his replacement.: Clark, 117.
72. hectoring for a war against Serbia.: Pauli, 283.
72. advance publicity for any trip by Franz Ferdinand.: Ibid., 275.
73. Railroad Street, Mastajbeg Street, Appel Quay, Franz Joseph street, Prince Rudolf Street.: Cassells, 144.
73. "a virtual challenge to fate.": McMeekin, 5.
73. did not have direct control over them.: Ibid.
73. but the 525th anniversary of the Battle of Kosovo.: Pauli, 270. Bilanski and Bosnia's military governor Oskar Potiorek were political rivals, but neither was a supporter of Franz Ferdinand. Bilanski was considered an ally and "close confidant" of the conservative bureaucracy surrounding Emperor Franz Joseph. Thrice the Archduke had blocked Potiorek's promotion in the army, believing he was all talk and no action. His disastrous performance in the First World War confirmed the Archduke's assessment.
73. killed the Turkish leader of the conquering Islamic army.: Ibid.
74. including the police force responsible for guarding Franz Ferdinand.: Ibid.
74. "Let's hope nothing happens.": Ibid.

CHAPTER EIGHT
INSCRUTABLE DESTINY

76. were to be assassinated that morning.: Special Correspondent, *New York Times*. "Bishops Lanyi's Death Recalls 'Death Vision,'" October 18, 1931.
76. this prince of peace becoming Austria's Emperor.: Ibid.
76. 28 June 1914. Half past 3 a.m.: Ibid.
78. and attaching a drawing of what he had seen.: Ibid. This is one of the most documented cases of what some people call extrasensory perception. The fact that Lanyi was a bishop and relayed his dream verbally and in writing to others prior to the actual events taking place helped make it so famous.
78. "I thought something like this might happen.": Smith, D.J. *One Morning in Sarajevo: June 28, 1914*, Weidenfeld & Nicolson, London, 2008.
78. probably be given a medal in Vienna and a government job.: Brook Shepherd, AofS, 248–249.
78. road to Mayerling shortly before his tragic death.: Kürenberg, 280.
78. "the replacement doesn't like me either.": Remak, 139. Franz Ferdinand was famous, some might say infamous, for his dark humor.

79. bomb, the injuries, or the near assassination.: Ibid.

79. "they throw bombs at me. It is an outrage!": Cassels, 178.

79. "All right, you can go on.": Ibid., 251. Rebecca West wrote in her book *Black Lamb and Grey Falcon* of meeting a man, who as a boy, had been at the reception for Franz Ferdinand at the Sarajevo City Hall. He told her, "We could not take our eyes off the Archduke... we were all Silent... we all felt awkward, because we knew that when he went out he would certainly be killed. No, it was not a matter of being told... we knew if one man had thrown a bomb, another man would throw another bomb, and another after that if he should fail. I tell you it gave a very strange feeling to the assembly," pp. 332–333.

79. "most illustrious visit with utmost enthusiasm.": Ibid.

79. "over the failure of the attack.": Ibid.

80. "Live for the children.": Ibid.

80. "Excellent sale of both horses.": Ibid.

80. "order which I myself could not maintain.": Pauli, 288. Istvan Tisza, Hungary's Prime Minister, also saw God's hand in the Archduke's assassination and was himself assassinated four years later.

81. fallen beneath the bullets of Slavic fanatics.: Hitler, *Mein Kampf,* 158–159.

81. "Now will you consent to my marriage proposal?": Gady, Franz-Stefan. "The Scandalous Affair That Started World War I," *The National Interest, A Quarterly Journal of International Affairs and Diplomacy*, May–June 2014.

81. "victim to the brutal hands of a murderer.": Pauli, 288.

81. who left at once for Chlumetz.: Nostitz-Rieneck, Count.

81. "Our childhoods were over.": Ibid. Members of the Nostitz-Rieneck and Hohenberg family tell slightly different versions of the traumatic hours following the assassination of their great-grandparents. This may reflect the confusion, shock, and pain of the events. They agree the children were told conflicting stories of what had happened to their parents in Sarajevo and did not learn about their deaths until the following day.

82. to tell them of their parents' deaths.: Ibid.

82. "Mama would have lost her mind.": Ibid.

82. the parents reach beyond the grave.: Brook-Shepherd, 253.

82. with regard to the position of the children.: Pope-Hennessy, James. *Queen Mary 1867–1953*, 483, Knopf, New York, 1960.

83. "has caused quite a stir in Germany.": Ziegler, Phillip. *King Edward VIII*, 42, Knopf, New York, 1991. Even when young Edward, Prince of Wales, seemed to identify with his German heritage as much, if not more, than his English ancestry.

83. "it's a great deal less worry.": Aronson, Theo. *Crowns in Conflict*, 101, Salem Publishers, Manchester, 1986. Wilhelm came to genuinely like and trust Franz Ferdinand.

83. reached out to them in any way.: Hohenberg, Prince Gerhard.

83. but those, too, had disappeared.: Pauli, 289. This was confirmed with a conversation I had with H.R.I.H. Archduke Christian Habsburg in Washington, DC, on October 21, 2011.

83. "event has solved a very difficult problem.": Penfield, Frederick Courtland. United States Ambassador to Austria-Hungary, United States Department of State Papers Relating to the Foreign Affairs of the United States, June 30, 1914, National Archives Microfilm Publications, Microfilm No 695, Supplement 2, 1917, The World War.

84. We are all in such utter misery.: Daisy, Princess of Pless. *What I Left Unsaid*, 145, Cassel & Company, London, 1936. Younger members of the aristocracy and others from their generation like Kurt Schuschnigg had a more favorable view of Franz Ferdinand than did older traditionalists.

84. and allowed it to happen.: McMeekin, Sean. *July 1914: Countdown to War*, Basic Books, 28, New York, 2014.

84. children of Vienna silently paid their respects.: Brook-Shepherd, 264.

84. coffins in the Hofburg Palace's Imperial Chapel.: Ibid.

85. and Crown Prince Rudolph's widow, Stephanie.: Artstetten Museum, May 18, 2011. Banners from the flowers are kept on display at Artstetten.

85. subterranean elements in Franz Joseph's government.: Pauli, 273.

85. "To Our Last Best Hope, In Loyal Devotion.": Beatty, 190.

85. not recognized as a Habsburg by the court.: Lafore, Laurence. *The Long Fuse: An Interpretation of the Origins of the World War*, 208, J.B. Lippincott, 1965.

85. haunted him for the rest of his life.: Pauli, 294.

86. "And how were the maneuvers?": Remak, Joachim. *Sarajevo: The Story of a Political Murder*, 265, Criterion, New York, 1959.

86. immovably established until Franz Joseph's death.: Windisch-Grätz, Prince Ludwig. *My Memoir*, 49–50, Houghton Mifflin Company, Boston, 1924.

86. and engulf them in world catastrophe.: Czernin, 49.

86. "whose course could no longer be arrested.": Hitler, 159.

86. and sweep away the mongrel Habsburg Empire.: Ibid., 162. Franz Joseph viewed his "mongrel Habsburg Empire" differently than Adolf Hitler. Yet each man recognized the unique role it played in Europe. The Emperor wrote, "The Austro-Hungarian Monarchy is not a fanciful work of art, but an absolute necessity for the present and future existence of her peoples. It is a refuge for those nations of central Europe which, without a common home, would have a deplorable existence and be tossed about by all their more powerful neighbors; whereas as long as they are joined together, they themselves constitute an imposing power," p. 440, Kürenberg.

87. "it would break into a thousand fragments.": Hitler, 159.

CHAPTER NINE
A KIND OF DULL CATALEPTIC STATE

89. The next man will have to be a man of war.: Pless, 146–147.

89. "drift on in a kind of dull cataleptic trance.": Churchill, Winston. *The World Crisis 1911–1914*, 192, Thornton Butterworth Limited, London, 1923.

89. Franz Joseph reluctantly declared war on Serbia.: Nostitz-Rieneck interview.
89. "not place himself on the side of regicides.": Alexander, H.R.H. Prince Regent. *Serbia's Part in the War Vol.1: The Rampart Against Pan-Germanism*, 122, Simpkin, Marshall & Hamilton, London, 1918.
90. better, or change for the worse?: Beatty, 184.
90. "thousands and thousands of men to their deaths.": Mager, Hugo. *Elizabeth: Grand Duchess of Russia*, 269, Carroll & Graf Publishers, New York, 1998.
90. "but it fulfills all its functions.": Cowles, Virginia. *The Last Tsar*, 70, Putnam, New York, 1977.
90. "being permitted to live at this time.": Hitler, 161.
90. everything else receded to shallow nothingness.: Ibid., 150.
91. Money quickly became a problem.: Hohenberg, Princess Sophie de Potesta.
91. but received no funds to support them.: Ibid.
91. "can be no question of payment.": *Time* Magazine. Yugoslavia: Embalmments, March 29, 1920.
91. obligated to assist his children?: Nostitz-Rieneck, Count.
92. the financial security of her orphaned grandchildren.: Hohenberg, Prince Gerhard.
92. "Wouldn't it be better to give them property?": Nostitz-Rieneck. Archduke Karl and the Hohenbergs' grandmother Archduchess Maria-Theresa were the lone members of the Habsburg family and court to safeguard the interest of Franz Ferdinand's royal orphans.
92. Styrian-mountain land to the Hohenberg children.: Ibid.
92. "a matter of secondary interest.": Alexander, 122.
92. "would have had me shot after Lemberg.": Sondhaus, Lawrence. *Franz Conrad von Hötzendorf: Architect of the Apocalypse*, 168, Humanities Press, Boston, 2000. Shortly after Hitler's armies invaded Russia in the Second World War, he praised von Hotzendorf as "the most intelligent commander of the First World War."
93. "and we chose the most terrible.": Czernin, 33.
93. and unnecessary war in modern times.": Kiegard, Karl von. "Frederick Wilhelm Exclusive Interview with the United Press," United Press International, November 20, 1914.
93. looking death straight in the eye.: Hauner, 121. Hitler relished his time in the army, and found the adrenalin rush of combat frightening, but exhilarating. While Hitler fought in the German army on the western front, his childhood friend and former Vienna roommate August Kubizek fought in the Austrian army on the eastern front. Rudolph Häusler, his former Munich roommate, also fought in Franz Joseph's army.
93. sacrifices being made on distant battlefields.: Nostitz-Rieneck, Count.
94. "pray for our parents and for us.": King, Greg, and Sue Woolmans. *The Assassination of the Archduke: Sarajevo 1914 and the Romance That Changed the World*, St. Martin's Press, 257, New York, 2013.

94. her final gift to the children of Bosnia.: Nicoll, Leo S.J., and Anton Puntigam S.J. *Leven un Wirken eines Jesuisen in Bosnien*, 102, Dissertation, University of Vienna, 1970. Correspondence with author May 25, 2011. Puntigam wrote the Duchess of Hohenberg was the mother to every child she met. When she was assassinated, she was wearing flowers presented to her by a young Muslim girl from Sarajevo who the Duchess said reminded her of her own daughter.

94. a conversation the priest never forgot.: Ibid. Nedjo Cabrinovic was physically small, almost birdlike, with a gentle, friendly demeanor that contrasted with his talkative nature.

94. We will die for our ideals.: Ibid.

95. Maximilian did. Ernst refused.: Ibid.

95. because the letter had saved his soul.: Ibid.

95. "Somehow Hitler never got even a letter!": Carruthers, Bob. *Private Hitler's War 1914–1918*, 78, Pen & Sword Books, Barnsley, 2014.

95. "worth much more than any territorial gains.": Hauner, 13.

96. "instinct for self-preservation and the admonitions of duty.": Ibid., 13–14.

96. in which they have suffered so much.: *New York Times*, July 8, 1916.

96. Archduke Karl, and Archduchess Zita.: Hohenberg, Princess Sophie de Potesta. Archduchess Maria-Theresa had initially supported the war and was especially angered when Italy, the homeland of Franz Ferdinand's biological mother, declared war on Austria. She and two of her sisters hired a submarine to attack the Italian fleet, but it sank with no injuries without accomplishing its goal. She was briefly banned from the Habsburg court.

96. Army Chief of Staff Hötzendorf's battlefield blunders.: Russell, Gareth. *The Emperors: How Europe's Rulers Were Destroyed by the First World War*, 164, Amberley Publishing, Gloucestershire, 2015.

97. Franz Ferdinand's oldest son was the perfect messenger.: Hohenberg, Princess Sophie de Potesta, March 22, 2013.

97. On November 16, 1916, that abruptly changed.: Brook-Shepherd. *The Last Habsburg*, 49, Weybright and Talley, New York, 1968. Franz Ferdinand once complained, "I must wait, and be told less than the meanest boot boy in Schönbrunn. My position is like that of an expectant heir to an entailed inheritance who must look on quietly while the aged proprietor lets great properties be depreciated through dishonest management," p. 278, Kürenberg.

97. "and the cooperation of our enemies permit.": Vovk, Justin. *Imperial Requiem: Four Royal Women and the Fall of the Age of Empresses*, 324, University L.L.C. Bloomington, 2012.

97. scattered advisors back to Vienna.: Ibid.

97. "the most intelligent commander of the first World War.": Hitler, *Secret Conversations*, 44.

97. "what is the advantage in that?": Hohenberg, Prince Gerhard.

97. "a few wretched scoundrels agitating for peace.": Hauner, 14.

98. Franz Ferdinand had wanted and hoped for his son.: Hohenberg, Princess Sophie de Potesta.
98. named for the Duchess of Hohenberg.: Nicoll, March 22, 2013.
98. but declined for herself and her brothers.: Ibid. Many people found Puntigam obnoxious and clueless, but his childlike sincerity regarding faith, charity, and forgiveness connected with others including Franz Ferdinand's stepmother Archduchess Maria-Theresa, and two of the Archduke's three children.
98. its German ally were about to get much worse.: Hohenberg, Princess Sophie de Potesta.
98. "a chance of confronting upheaval with success.": Voyk, 324.
99. and frightened the Hohenberg children.: Nostitz-Rieneck, Count.
99. The Habsburgs' multinational empire imploded.: Gilbert, Martin. *The First World War: A Complete History*, 491, Henry Holt & Company, New York, 1994.
99. "is indispensable for Europe's equilibrium.": Kürenberg, 230.
100. Duchess was promptly torn down.: Nicoll correspondence. Following the war, Puntigam was the only Catholic priest expelled from Bosnia. Money raised for the Sarajevo memorials, but never used, was eventually given to the Catholic Church. Following the Sarajevo trial of the assassins, Puntigam was given the gun used by Princip to kill the Archduke and Duchess. He gave it to the Jesuit order, but kept Franz Ferdinand's bloodstained shirt, which he considered a sacred relic of the martyred Archduke. The shirt has since disappeared.
100. "I renounce all participation in the affairs of state.": Gady.
100. "Only an inner peace can heal the wounds of this war.": Brook-Shepherd, *The Last Habsburg*, 219.
100. "and continuous readiness to sacrifice himself.": Hauner, 15.
101. "the greatest villainy of the century.": Ibid.
101. There is no making pacts with Jews.: Ibid., 16.
101. the one that convinced him to enter politics.: Hitler, *Secret Conversations*, 44.
101. "Can cause the ruin of a whole people.": Ibid.

CHAPTER TEN
EXILES

102. No one came to their defense.: Nostitz-Rieneck, Count.
102. "protective care" of the government.: Ibid.
102. No such room was ever found.: Ibid.
103. her future husband, she received no property.: Ibid. Sophie later did receive one-third of her brother's land inheritance.
103. propaganda against landlords and aristocrats.: Ibid.
103. Emperor Karl and his family into Swiss exile.: Brook-Shepherd, *The Last Habsburg Emperor*, 234.
103. remained in loyal service to the orphans.: Nostitz-Rieneck. Franz Janaczek remained in loyal service to the family until his death in the early 1950s. He

always refused to write his memoirs or discuss any matters concerning Franz Ferdinand and his children.

103. and their aunt comfort and companionship.: Ibid.
104. last guest they would ever host at Konopiste.: Ibid.
104. countryside could be cleared of armed looters.: Ibid.
104. display any fear in front of their Czech "protectors.": Ibid.
104. a photo of their parents but was turned back.: King, Greg, and Sue Woolmans, 257.
104. but she was allowed to keep it.: Nostitz-Rieneck, Count.
105. Konopiste remained their true home.: King, Woolmans, 257.
105. for the call to return to Konopiste that never came.: Nostitz-Rieneck, Count.
105. rested the tombs of their mother and father.: Ibid. The burial chambers of the Archduke and Duchess are open to visitors at the Artstetten Castle museum.
105. Archduke Franz Ferdinand and the Duchess of Hohenberg.: Pauli, 303.
105. revolutionary activities in and out of the army.: Hauner, 17–18.
106. "his extraordinary talent as an orator.": Ibid., 18. In Ronald Hayman's book *Hitler & Geli* he discusses Hitler's training in public speaking during his army days, pp. 58–59.
106. "led to the donation of three hundred Marks.": Hitler, 322–323. Hitler's speeches had been tolerated by his roommates and the inhabitants of his homeless shelters, but never before had he received such an overwhelmingly positive response to his orations.
106. he officially joined the small party.: Hauner, 18.
106. "I thought of nothing else but revolution.": Range, Peter Ross. *1924: The Year That Made Hitler*, 117, Little, Brown & Company, New York, 2016.
106. unite Germany against its political and military enemies.: Hauner, 19. Hitler believed an entirely new political party was needed in Austria, but it wasn't until he connected with the small German Workers Party in Munich that he discovered an existing political party he could bend to his will.
106. "All non-German immigration must be prevented.": Ibid., 20. Anti-Semitism, fierce opposition to immigration, and appeals to nationalism were the cornerstones of Hitler's rise to power from its earliest days.
107. "a racial tuberculosis among nations.": Ibid., 18, 21.
107. "in view of the Archduke's marriage being morganatic.": Cavendish, William Duke of Portland. Letter to Thomas Masaryk, August 2, 1919, Artstetten.
107. "by the government for the benefit of the children.": Ibid.
107. Through their letter writing, they fell in love.: Nostitz-Rieneck, Count.
107. to begin her new married life.: Ibid.
108. Some had vanished.: Ibid.
108. but nothing that had been her mother's.: Ibid.
108. Her wedding day was touched by sadness.: Ibid.
108. but her face showed no joy.: Ibid.
108. son of the exiled German Emperor—committed suicide.: MacDonogh, Giles. *The Last Kaiser: The Life of Wilhelm II*, 327, Whittle, New York, 1977.

109. and the athletic life they enjoyed.: Nostitz-Rieneck, Count.
109. a daughter completed their family circle.: Ibid.
109. the estates around them vanished with the stroke of a pen.: Ibid.
110. President Masaryk kept none of his promises.: Hohenberg, Princess Sophie de Potesta.
110. "of members of the former royal family of Austria-Hungary.": Ibid.
110. by their Habsburg relatives or the state.: Ibid.
110. four years before the treaty was legally enforceable.: Ibid.
110. in the Bohemian countryside of their youth.: Ibid. Ernst, the youngest of the orphaned children, seemed the most emotionally fragile following Sarajevo.
111. and Ernst Hohenberg refused to join their ranks.: Ibid.
111. began to heal from the wounds of Sarajevo.: Special Correspondent *New York Times*. Vienna Monarchist Report on Progress, p. 8, February 7, 1935.
111. Emperor Karl to the vacant Habsburg throne.: Nostitz-Rieneck.
111. former palaces, farms, and estates had to be renounced.: Ibid.
111. on a collision course with Adolf Hitler.: Ibid.

CHAPTER ELEVEN
THE MOST GOLDEN TONGUED OF DEMAGOGUES

112. Mussolini being appointed prime minister of Italy in 1922.: Mack Smith, Denis. *Mussolini: A Biography*, 56–57, Vintage Books, New York, 1982.
112. failed and he was arrested for treason.: Kershaw, Ian. *Hitler: 1889–1936: Hubris*, 211, W.W. Norton & Company, New York, 1999.
112. "those who betrayed the country in 1918.": Hauner, 47.
113. with a new Mercedes automobile.: Ibid., 50.
113. Hohenberg brothers to visit their sister in Prague.: Royal Musings: News and Commentaries About the Reigning Royal Houses and the Former European Monarchies as Well, *Maximilian von Hohenberg to Wed*, July 8, 1926. In addition to the announcement of his engagement the article reported, "Last August a monarchist movement in Czechoslovakia wanted to turn the country from a republic into a monarchy with Maximilian as king." Royalmusingsblogspot.com., retrieved April 27, 2011.
113. phone calls, and visits to Austria.: Nostitz-Rieneck, Count.
114. joys of bachelorhood for domestic bliss.: Ibid.
114. childhood friend Princess Marie Lobkowicz Waldburg-Wolfegg.: Hohenberg, Princess Sophie de Potesta. Archduchess Maria-Theresa had earlier played family matchmaker between Karl Habsburg and his wife, Zita, resulting in one of the few happy Habsburg marriages and eight children.
114. the Princess's granddaughter brought the desired result.: Hohenberg, Georg Duke of.
114. "engaged today to Countess Elisabeth Waldburg-Wolfegg.": Royal Musings, July 8, 1926.

114. wedding photographs she could finally enjoy.: Hohenberg, Princess Sophie de Potesta.

114. widowed thirty-year-old former Empress Zita.: Ibid. The Hohenbergs' loyalty to their Habsburg cousins Karl and Zita stood in dramatic contrast to many of the Habsburg family who abandoned them with the collapse of the monarchy in 1918.

115. He was thirty-eight years old.: The *New York Times* article on Emperor Karl's death read, "Charles of Austria Dies of Pneumonia in Exile... Vienna is grief-stricken... News of death empties cafes and fills the streets with throngs of mourners... Charles was democratic... opposed German domination and sought a separate peace... Kaiser did not trust Charles."

115. Zita had eight children, five of them boys.: Hohenberg, Prince Gerhard.

115. Germany and Russia would fill by force.: Schofield, 93.

115. It also gave his life a new sense of purpose.: Hohenberg, Prince Gerhard.

116. There were few takers.: Roberts, Kenneth L. *Europe's Morning After*, 174, Harper & Brothers, New York, 1921. Austria's economy never fully recovered after 1918.

116. a Habsburg Archduke, arrested and jailed for fraud.: Gaillon, Eloise, and Jeffrey Post. "An Examination of the Napoleon Diamond Necklace," 353, *Gems & Gemology Magazine*, 2007. The Napoleon necklace once owned by Archduchess Maria-Theresa is now in the Smithsonian collection in Washington, DC.

116. provide his benefactors unparalleled profits.: Smith, Howard K. *Last Train from Berlin: An Eyewitness Account of Germany at War*, 340, Knopf, New York, 1942. Smith's book provides a remarkable firsthand account of life in Nazi Germany prior to 1941.

116. Two-thirds of Hitler's followers were under the age of forty.: Lower, Wendy. *Hitler's Furies: German Women in the Nazi Killing Fields*, Houghton Mifflin Harcourt, Boston, 2013.

117. "despite our love of the army.": Hauner, 89.

117. "cursed in your grave by future generations.": Ibid.

117. "brotherly German people of Austria.": Ibid.

117. granting him dictatorial powers.: Ibid.

117. placed on any German citizen traveling there.: Ibid.

118. the principle of "the superiority of the Aryan Race.": Grace Communion International, The Protestant Church in Hitler's Germany and the Barmen Declaration, p. 1, https://www.gci.org/history/barmen.

118. non-political matters were conceded to the Vatican.: Cornwell, John. *Hitler's Pope: The Secret History of Pius XII*, Viking, New York, 1999. Individual Catholics and Lutherans courageously spoke out against Hitler including Clemens August, the Catholic bishop of Münster, and Lutheran priest Martin Niemöller.

118. "an agitator of genius.": Thompson, Dorothy. *I Saw Hitler*, 29, 32, Farrar & Rinehart, New York, 1932.

118.   "news print is usually plain nonsense.": Ibid.

119.   "this superior race shall conquer the earth.'": Ibid.

119.   reclaiming the vacant throne for themselves.: Lamar, Cecil. *Wilhelm II Vol II: Emperor and Exile, 1900–1941*, 325, 331, University of North Carolina Press, Chapel Hill, 1996.

119.   behind closed doors to wealthy monarchists.: Ibid., 331.

119.   openly joined the Nazi Party.: Petropoulos, Jonathan. *Royals and the Reich: The Princes von Hessen in Nazi Germany*, 3, Oxford University Press, Oxford, 2008.

119.   "and we may want one in England before long.": Olson, Lynne. *Troublesome Young Men*, 66, Farrar, Straus and Giroux, New York, 2007.

119.   "the basic features of the Fascist state.": Ricks, Thomas E. *Churchill & Orwell: The Fight for Freedoms*, 86, Penguin Press, New York, 2017.

120.   "have to adopt totalitarian methods.": Messersmith, G.S. The Papers of G.S. Messersmith, February 23, 1935, University of Delaware, Box 4, F30.

120.   definitely be receiving treatment elsewhere.: Stiller, Jesse. *George S. Messersmith: Diplomat of Democracy*, 56, University of North Carolina Press, Chapel Hill, 1987.

120.   Hitler's anti-Semitism or his designs on Austria.: Ibid.

120.   "safeguarded only by the destruction of Austria.": Hitler, 1. Few people read *Mein Kampf* cover to cover, but even reading a few pages gave readers a road map of Hitler's mind-set and plans. Four people who apparently read the entire book were George Messersmith, Maximilian Hohenberg, Otto Habsburg, and Tomas Masaryk, first president of Czechoslovakia.

120.   and Jews known as the "Iron Ring.": Schofield, Victoria. *Witness to History: the Life of John Wheeler Bennett*, 93, Yale University Press, New Haven, 2012.

120.   as an alternative to Adolf Hitler.: Ibid.

120.   Sophie quietly supported their brother's efforts.: Ibid.

121.   Austrian towns declared themselves "Emperor Communities.": Trove.nia.gov.au/ndp/del/article/37838421.

121.   to a happy, certain, and great future.: Ibid.

121.   as if he was spitting on her grave.: Franklin D. Roosevelt Presidential Library and Museum. National Archives and Records, Documents papers 1933–1945. Memorandum on Austrian Situation, Box 23, p. 3.

122.   windows of his legendary sanctuary toward his homeland.: Riefenstahl, 210.

122.   from here I can look at Germany *and* Austria.: Ibid.

CHAPTER TWELVE
IMPENDING HORRORS

123.   "you've caught the Chancellor cleaning up.": Messersmith Papers, February 23, 1935.

124.   and became immediate best sellers.: Clare, George. *Last Waltz in Vienna: The Rise and Destruction of a Family, 1842–1942*, 127, Holt, Rinehart and Winston, New York, 1980.

124. "draw impressionable youth from Adolf Hitler.": Millard, 136.

124. the American press followed.: In Alistair Cooke's 1977 book, *Six Men,* he writes the American magazines *Time* and *News Review* delivered in England had "two sometimes three pages torn out" by English censors to keep the British public from reading about Edward and Mrs. Simpson.

124. "unofficial and devoted to pleasure.": Zeigler, Philip. *King Edward VIII,* 182, Knopf, New York, 1991.

125. for MI-6, the British Intelligence Service.: Sebba, 217.

125. "internal affairs (regarding) Jews or anything else.": Ibid.

125. described Mrs. Simpson as "charming and intelligent.": Messersmith Papers, December 6, 1936.

125. Until his death, we felt safe.: Hohenberg, Georg Duke of.

125. constitutional monarchy headed by Otto Habsburg.: Millard, 137.

126. "hope was associated with his name.": Schuschnigg, Kurt. *My Austria*, 20–21, Knopf, New York, 1938.

126. teetered on the brink of chaos.: Messersmith Papers, January 18, 1935.

126. "have to take a Habsburg into bed with them.": Ibid.

126. "Europe with no illusions about Hitler.": Ibid.

127. "no war in Europe as long as Mussolini is alive.": Vanderbilt Jr., Cornelius. *Farewell to Fifth Avenue,* 174, Simon & Schuster, New York, 1935.

127. dictator's position on the Habsburg restoration.: Hohenberg, Prince Gerhard.

127. "one set of people, but govern with another.": Mussolini, Benito. *My Autobiography*, 30–31, Charles Scribner's Sons, New York, 1928.

127. and the daughter of the King and Queen of Italy.: Brook-Shepherd, Uncrowned Emperor, 84.

128. "institution of monarchy can guarantee its permanence.": Geddyr, G.E.R. "Restoration of Habsburg's Within Year Predicted," *New York Times*, 1, November 21, 1934.

128. "in the newspaper he founded, Popolo d'Italia.": *New York Times*, "Vienna Celebrates Birthday of Otto," 1, November 21, 1934.

128. memorials were being removed from monuments there.: Ibid.

129. and estates would be returned to them.: Messersmith Papers, October 7, 1935.

129. "question of restoration of the monarchy.": Ibid.

129. by an overwhelming vote of 1,491,992 to 43,454.: Eade, Philip. *Prince Philip: The Turbulent Life of the Man Who Married Queen Elisabeth II,* 104, Henry Holt and Company, New York, 2011.

129. "return to Austria as private citizens.": Messersmith Papers, October 7, 1935.

129. "lead to a serious European conflagration.": Brook-Shepherd, 103.

129. to annex Austria would be met by force.: Ibid., 104.

129. who were at odds with one another.: Ibid.

130. "will ruin himself in twelve months.": Middlemas, Keith, and John Barnes. *Baldwin: A Biography*, 34, Weidenfeld & Nicolson, London, 1969.

130. once belonged to the Empress of Russia.: Ileana, Princess of Romania-Archduchess of Austria. *I Live Again*, 20, Rinehart & Co., New York, 1951.

130. and her Hungarian Countess mother.: Illustrated London News, Personalities of the Week: Ernst von Hohenberg, 7, April 25, 1936.

131. she was also a masterful lip reader.: Hohenberg, Princess Sophie de Potesta, March 25, 2011, interview.

131. and their efforts to restore the monarchy.: Hohenberg, Prince Gerhard.

131. ITALY TAKES UP WHITE MAN'S BURDEN IN AFRICA'S LAST NATIVE-RULED LAND.: *New York Times*, February 18, 1935, 4E.

131. Races, I know, are difficult to meld.: Mussolini, 151.

131. become more alluring to him.: Hauner, 112. Hitler's intolerance, racism, and plans were no secret and available for anyone to see who wanted to see.

132. "not interfere in Austria's internal affairs.": Riefenstahl, 183–184.

132. will be destroyed by the Nazis.: Hohenberg, Georg Duke of.

CHAPTER THIRTEEN
ONE BLOOD DEMANDS ONE REICH

133. "the greatest news story since the resurrection.": Gunther, John. *Inside Europe*, 297.

133. abdicated his throne to marry his mistress.: Rasmussen, Fred. "King Gave up His Throne for Love of Baltimore Girl: Sixty Years Ago Edward VIII Abdicated to Marry… Wallis Warfield Simpson," *Baltimore Sun*, December 15, 1996.

133. belief in royalty itself was being undermined.: Nicolson, Harold. *Diaries and Letters: 1930–1939*, Atheneum, London, 1966.

134. "concerned that he doesn't make her the queen.": Smith, Amanda. *Hostage to Fortune: The Letters of Joseph P. Kennedy*, 261, Viking, New York, 2011.

134. His wife would be his consort, but never queen.: Schad, Martha. *Hitler's Spy Princess: The Extraordinary Life of Stephanie von Hohenlohe*, 63, Sutton Publishing, Gloucestershire, 2004.

134. "in England who is ready to play with us.": Hauner, 118. Hitler's confidence in King Edward VII is revealing.

134. "because of the American newspapers, I am here today.": Messersmith Papers, December 6, 1936.

135. "and even peeped into windows.": Ibid.

135. was retitled the Duke of Windsor.: Sebba, 194.

135. where Benito Mussolini treated them royally.: Ibid.

135. assigned to protect and spy on them.: Ibid.

135. "keen intelligence and wide interests.": Messersmith Papers, February 23, 1937.

136. tea with Deputy Führer Rudolf Hess.: Sebba, 216.

136. "a firm nail in the coffin of monarchy.": Ibid., 201.

136. and her orphaned brothers from Konopiste.: Nostitz-Rieneck, Count.

136. "surprise and swiftness of our action.": Hauner, 125.

137. other book was Adolf Hitler's *Mein Kampf*.: Albright, Madeline. *Prague Winter: A Personal Story of Remembrance and War 1937–1948*, 53, Harper Collins, 2012.

137. the daily blood of future generations will grow.: Hitler, 1. No one need read beyond the first page of *Mein Kampf* to recognize Hitler's determination to destroy Austria. He was quoted in Gunther's *Inside Europe*, 1940 edition: "I did not take this decision (to acquire Austria) in the year 1938, but immediately after the Great War. I have never made a mystery of it," p. 109.

138. the largest mass circulation journal in Europe.: Hohenberg, Prince Gerhard.

138. world the most frightful of all slaughters.: Ibid.

138. "the preparation of the Sarajevo assassination.": Ibid.

138. and growing numbers of Nazis in Austria.: Ibid.

138. "Four Italians were severely hurt.": *New York Times*, "Mussolini Expels Austrian Soccer Team," July 12, 1937.

138. Central European cup tournament being held in Italy.: Ibid.

139. Duke and Duchess of Windsor honeymooned.: Messersmith Papers, November 30, 1936.

139. leader of the region's anti-Nazi Home Guard.: Hohenberg, Prince Gerhard.

139. "face to face meetings with the Nazi leadership.": Gini, Al, and Ronald Green. *Ten Virtues of Outstanding Leaders*, 92, Wiley-Blackwell, Malden, 2013.

139. "check to the mad armaments race.": Ibid., 92. In the Gilbert and Gott book, *The Appeasers*, Lord Halifax told a German diplomat, "[He] would like to see, as the culmination of his work, the Führer entering London, at the side of the English king, amid acclamation of the English people," p. 132.

139. "can't feel that either is unnatural or immoral.": Ibid.

139. from her Maltese Square home, became her prayer sanctuary.: Nostitz-Rieneck, Count. Our Lady of Victories Church in Prague continues to be a popular pilgrimage destination for Catholics.

140. and the onetime owners of Konopiste.: Hohenberg, Georg Duke of.

140. on a rare visit he made to Vienna in January 1938.: Hohenberg, Princess Sophie de Potesta.

140. was promptly reported to Berlin.: Ibid.

140. "to any aggravation of the Austrian situation.": Documents on British Foreign Policy 1919–39, 2/19, no 50.

141. become perhaps the greatest German in history.: Hauner, 127.

141. Austria would forcibly be incorporated into the German Reich: Schuschnigg, Kurt von, and Janet von Schuschnigg. *When Hitler Took Austria: A Memoir of Heroic Faith by the Chancellor's Son*, 88–89, Ignatius Press, San Francisco, 2012.

141. "raved like a madman.": MacDonogh, 22.

141. the Habsburg who was not a Habsburg.: Documents on British Foreign Policy 1919–39, 2/19, No 50./ Meysels.

142. should stand or fall with my country.: Brook-Shepherd, *The Austrians: A Thousand Year History*, 311, Carroll & Graf, New York, 1996.

142. feared might thwart his lifelong ambition.: Ibid., 304.

142. no Hohenberg would be safe.: Nostitz-Rieneck, Count.

143. "except to have Schuschnigg eventually give in.": Smith, 240, 241. Ambassador Kennedy's avowed isolationism haunted him, and his sons, the rest of his life.
143. added to keep the crowds from rioting.: Weyr, 38–39.
143. and the children sent to bed early.: Hohenberg, Princess Sophie de Potesta.
143. "face a difficult and fateful situation.": Schuschnigg, *My Austria*, 221.
143. "invasion by the German Army, to offer no resistance.": Ibid.
143. villages and towns across the country.: Hohenberg, Prince Gerhard.
143. speech seemed like a death sentence.: Ibid.

CHAPTER FOURTEEN
WITCHES SABBATH

144. the war began that evening.: Hohenberg, Princess Sophie de Potesta.
145. "even if the whole world were against him.": Hauner, 128.
145. He could barely believe their luck.: Hohenberg, Prince Gerhard.
145. It was a long, silent ride home.: Ibid.
145. They had not escaped.: Ibid.
146. "and happier the people of Austria will be.": Hauner, 128.
146. "restore my dear homeland to the German Reich.": Ibid.
146. "Today we are *your* boss!": Hohenberg, Prince Gerhard.
146. could destroy a family overnight.: Kanter, Heidi. *Some Girls, Some Hats and Hitler: A True Story*, 43–44, Virago Press, London, 2012. This book captures the fear and limited options Viennese Jews had in 1938.
146. help all of them safely escape the country.: Hohenberg, Georg Duke of.
147. balcony seemed covered by Nazi swastikas.: Ibid.
147. never bellowed the Nazi slogans with such mania.: Shirer, William. *Berlin Diary: The Journey of a Foreign Correspondent*, 78–79, Knopf, New York, 1941.
147. pro-Schuschnigg graffiti written just days earlier.: Hohenberg, Prince Gerhard.
148. and at what time Herr Hitler will arrive.: Persico, Joseph. *Edward R. Murrow: An American Original*, 136–137, McGraw Hill, New York, 1998.
148. "found raging expression in broad daylight.": Ibid.
148. "an indescribable witches Sabbath.": Weyr, 27–28.
148. Belvedere Palace where Max had been born.: Hohenberg, Prince Gerhard.
148. waiting for some word from the Embassy.: Hohenberg, Georg Duke of.
148. placed under house arrest at Belvedere Palace.: Schuschnigg, Schuschnigg, 111.
148. to quickly move against the Hohenbergs.: Hohenberg, Georg Duke of.
149. with only one Ambassador: Britain's Michael Palairet.: Millard, 149.
149. been baptized Franz Ferdinand Maximilian Hohenberg.: Hohenberg, Georg Duke of.
149. was also Adolf Hitler's Vienna destination.: Ibid. The manager of the Hotel Imperial would soon be arrested and imprisoned by the Gestapo.
149. to a less public location.: Hohenberg, George Duke of.
150. "The universal jubilation was simply beyond belief.": Riefenstahl, 221.
150. "yet more murderous Second World War.": Horthy.

150. "mongrel" multicultural Habsburg Empire.: Illies, 18.
150. traveled to the Hotel Imperial to pay his respects.: MacDonogh, 64–65.
151. Nazi-bannered balcony of the Hofburg Palace.: Hohenberg, Georg Duke of.
151. shook the walls and windows where they hid.: Ibid.
151. we will follow! Heil my Führer!: Shirer, 337. In the Schuschnigg Archives at the St. Louis University Library, the former Chancellor kept all the 1938 copies of Austria's most popular weekly magazine. The covers, photographs, and stories capture the abruptness of the Anschluss. The weeks prior to the Anschluss feature Schuschnigg, patriotic rallies, and children waving the Austrian flag. Arthur Seyss-Inquart was featured the week of the Anschluss. The following week the cover and entire issue focused on Adolf Hitler, his entrance into Vienna, and his speech to three quarters of a million cheering Austrians from the Hofburg Palace balcony.
152. "The Sudeten Germans of Czechoslovakia greet the Führer.": Albright, 77.
152. "Tell Everyone in Prague Hitler Says Hello.": Ibid.
152. and the eternal mask of the Jew devil.: Toland, John. *Adolf Hitler*, 455, Doubleday & Company, Garden City, 1976.
152. "putting up resistance against Berlin.": Smith.
152. "working out their destinies is not our business.": Smith, Richard Norton. *An Uncommon Man: The Triumph of Herbert Hoover*, 258, High Plains Company, Simon & Schuster, New York, 1984.
153. the Habsburg-hating Dr. Leopold Pötsch.: Hauner, 129.
153. "this old gentleman" had not diminished.: Ibid.
153. "an influence on the destinies of the nation?": Hitler, 159.
153. I remain in the memory of our old friendship.: Hauner, 130–131.
153. must not be allowed to happen.: Ibid. MacDonogh, 124.
154. Bloch died there in 1945 at the age of seventy-three.: Hamann, Brigette. *Hitler's Edeljude. Das Leben des Armenarztes Eduard Bloch*, 427, Piper Verlag, Munich, 2008. Hitler referred to Dr. Bloch as "Edeljude, a noble Jew."
154. a city with a large German population.: Weber, Thomas. *Hitler's First World War*, 344, Oxford University Press, Oxford, 2010. Fest, Joachim. *Hitler*, 13, Harcourt, Brace, and Jovanovich, New York, 1974.
154. "and protection as per the Führer's wishes.": Hall, Alan. "The Single Jew That Hitler Wanted to Save," *Daily Mail*, July 2, 2012.
154. "Get rid of the rubbish.": MacDonogh, 124.

CHAPTER FIFTEEN
DUEL

155. through family feuds, assassinations, revolutions, and wars.: Hohenberg, Prince Gerhard.
155. and expertise of Maria-Theresa.: Ibid.
156. "with the highest possible authorities.": Ibid.
156. against her brother-in-law, Emperor Franz Joseph.: Ibid.

156. "a strong majority for the monarchists.": MacDonogh, 35.
156. Dr. Ernst Kalterbrunner, the Austrian-born Gestapo Chief.: Hohenberg, Prince Gerhard.
156. a gorilla was in charge of Austria's state security.: Kershaw, Alex, 72.
157. thrown *out* of Vienna's dreaded Gestapo Headquarters.: Hohenberg, Prince Gerhard.
157. "their families and personal character.": *New York Times*, "Habsburg Princes Arrested by Austrian Nazis," 1, March 23, 1938.
157. government ministers continued to be arrested.: *New York Times*, "University Purge Pushed—Restrictions of Jews Increased," 3, March 31, 1938. Some Austrian Jews escaped, but seven thousand that did not escape committed suicide according to John Gunther in *Inside Europe*, p. 110.
157. Many of the arrested were never seen again.: Sayers, Janet. *Mothers of Psychoanalysis: Helen Deutsch, Karen Harney, Anna Freud, Melanie Klein*, 166, William Norton & Company, New York, 1991.
158. the British Foreign Office might help locate the men.: Hohenberg, Prince Gerhard.
158. including Prague, would soon follow.: Hauner, 129.
158. READY TO SUPPORT ANY SCHEME TO KEEP PEACE.: *New York Times*, "Czechs See Blow to Autonomy: Italy, France and Britain Are Ready to Support Any Scheme to Keep Peace," 1, March 31, 1938.
158. independence and unification with Germany.: Ibid.
158. "without any danger to their lives.": Millard, 153. Heinrich Himmler was a physically small, bookish, racist bureaucrat who shared a love of German mythology and a hatred of Jews with Adolf Hitler. In Peter Longerich's biography *Heinrich Himmler: A Life*, he wrote Himmler divided people into two categories, humans (all Germans) and sub-humans (everyone else), p. 265.
158. "accord you my most special protection.": Zámečnik, Stanislav. *That was Dachau 1933–1945* (translated by Derek B. Paton), 16, Foundation international de Dachau le cherche midi, Paris, 2004.
159. for them and their children to Switzerland.: Ibid.
159. No one was to help the Hohenbergs.: Ibid.
159. he never spoke to Mrs. Wood again.: Hohenberg, Prince Gerhard.
159. not available to speak, did she reluctantly leave.: Ibid.
159. and humiliated by visiting Nazi dignitaries.: Millard, 152.
160. tried to help but were rebuffed.: Gilbert, Gott, 126.
160. "and the English government does nothing?": Hohenberg, Prince Gerhard. Dachau's commander during the Hohenberg brothers' internment, Hans Loritz, was removed from his post by Hitler in July 1939 for his brutality. He was arrested after the war and committed suicide in 1946.
160. "nothing we can do for these people.": Ibid.
160. Czechoslovakia itself was no longer safe.: Ibid.
160. anti-Semitism rocked nearly every village, town, and city.: MacDonogh, 53–57.

160. hope, and fear, to Elisabeth Hohenberg.: Ibid. Goering was instrumental in planning the Anschluss, and the confiscation of Jewish property in Austria. As Reichstag President he declared, "If God had intended men to be equal he would not have created races." (*Goering: Hitler's Iron Knight*, pp. 61–62).

160. she might have smiled.: Hohenberg, Prince Gerhard.

162. "send them to the gallows immediately?": Ibid.

162. Her cool response momentarily silenced him.: Ibid.

162. "Write your letters and all will be well.": Ibid.

162. in a small corner of her own home.: Ibid.

163. under the positive influence of her father.: Hohenberg, Georg Duke of.

163. dared tell him to turn his radio down.: Hohenberg, Prince Gerhard.

163. They never returned.: Hohenberg, Princess Sophie de Potesta.

163. the first Austrian "criminals" sent there.: OuSArchiv Document Id 4094964, / OuSArchiv Document Id 11741977, KZ-Gedenskätte Dachau, 85221 Dachau, Alt, Römerstr, 75.

164. In May, another 120 detainees arrived.: MacDonogh, 118–120.

164. "number of well-known journalists and authors.": Ibid.

164. "would almost be ashamed to be free.": Ibid.

164. "Your Imperial Majesties.": Millard, 152.

164. about when, where, and how their parents had died.: Dachau correspondence.

164. earned him the red badge of a terrorist.: Ibid.

165. ashes on the paths where Gestapo officers walked.: Millard, 152.

165. a spoon to assist them in their task.: Ibid.

165. "excrement into buckets and cart them away.": Ibid.

165. brothers' faces were splattered with excrement.: Ibid.

165. and were the most charming of companions.: Ibid.

166. were not looking down on anyone.: Pauli, 305.

166. and children attacked, beaten, and robbed.: Ibid. Austro-Jewish journalist Theodor Herzl, considered the father of political Zionism, lived most of his life in Vienna. In 1897, he predicted, "The people will let themselves be intimidated by the Viennese rabble and deliver up the Jews. There you see the mob can achieve anything once it rears up.... They will kill us."

166. The guard aimed his gun but did not fire.: MacDonogh, 268–273.

166. for the strength of their political beliefs.: Hohenberg, Prince Gerhard.

167. but small victories made Dachau bearable.: Meysel, Lucian O. *Die verhinderte Dynastie: Erherzog Franz Ferdinand und das Haus Hohenberg*, 172, Molden, Wien, 2000.

CHAPTER SIXTEEN
BARGAIN WITH THE DEVIL

168. to negotiate their release with Heinrich Himmler.: Nostitz-Rieneck, Count.

168. fearful as they were of the long arms of the Nazis.: Ibid.

168. but no time or place was ever found.: Ibid.

169. was Berlin's most feared address.: Ibid.

169. The Countess of Nostitz-Rieneck did not.: Ibid.

169. Himmler and his immediate subordinates avoided her.: Ibid.

169. to Nazi Germany were drawing to an end.: Ibid.

169. was a work of folly and ignorance.: Fort Myers News-Press, "Allies Give in to Hitler, Sudetens Attack Czechs," 1, Monday, September 19, 1938.

170. moment, than it did these strange days.: Kennan, George. "Letters of George Kennan," http:/traces.org/kennansletter.html. The Czech surrender before Hitler's threats.

170. saved the city from the annihilation suffered by other European cities.

170. "the great window looking out over Austria.": Gilbert, Martin, and Richard Gott. *The Appeasers: The Decline of Democracy from Hitler's Rise to Chamberlain's Downfall,* 144, Houghton Mifflin, New York, 1963.

170. finger turn back the clock from 1938 to 1914.: Gaddis, John Lewis. *George F. Kennan: An American Life,* 120, Penguin Books, London, 2012.

170. "such terms as are dictated to a defeated enemy.": Sheean, Vincent. *Not Peace but a Sword,* 276, Doubleday, Doran, and Company, New York, 1939.

171. funeral attended by half a million mourners.: Kennan, George. *Sketches of my Life,* 4–5, Pantheon Books, New York, 1968.

171. "armed banditry." Publicly he said nothing.: Ibid.

171. "No frontier stations existed.": Ibid.

171. threatened inhabitants neither refuge nor security.: Martin, Gott, 151.

171. family in Austria became nearly impossible.: Nostitz-Rieneck.

171. but the unwelcome emigrants had nowhere to go.: Kanter, 143.

171. "will get the best results.": Smith, 247. Ambassador Kennedy resigned his position as Ambassador amid accusations he was a Nazi sympathizer. The accusations were untrue, but he was a fierce isolationist in part because he did not want his sons fighting and dying in a European war. His firstborn son, Joseph P. Kennedy Jr., died four years later in the war his father opposed. John F. Kennedy turned his observations regarding appeasement into his honors thesis at Harvard. It later became the book *Why England Slept.* George Kennan described the Ambassador's son as "an upstart and an ignoramus." Twenty-five years later, President John F. Kennedy appointed Kennan Ambassador to Yugoslavia.

172. for signing treaties and military alliances.: Hamann, 197. The only palace Hitler painted during his years in Vienna was a watercolor of Belvedere when Archduke Franz Ferdinand and his family lived there.

172. would have been different had he lived.: Portland, Duke of (Cavendish-Bentinck), 328.

173. only empty streets and cold silence.: Gaddis, 127.

173. he once again stayed at the Hotel Imperial.: Nagorski, Andrew. *Hitlerland— American Eyewitnesses to the Nazi Rise to Power,* 258, Simon & Schuster, New York, 2012.

173. "military occupation of Slovakia by a German army.": Millard, 141.

173. "the new European constellation that is arising.": Sheheen, Vincent. *Not Peace but a Sword*, 276, Doubleday, New York, 1939. To this day, the Beneš legacy continues to divide many in the Czech Republic.
173. "good Czechs and good Germans.": Nostitz-Rieneck, Count.
174. with the theft of her nationality and country.: Ibid. A Catholic priest at one of the churches Sophie Hohenberg visited urged his congregation to "abandon all hope in the virtue of the human race and seek solace in a just, unbending, and stern God." Quoted in *George F. Kennan: An American Life,* by John Lewis Gaddis, 122.
174. collaborating with evil or committing heroic suicide.: Ibid.
174. and his family was the alternative.: Nixon, Guy. Finding Your Native American Ancestors, 183, Xlibis Corp., Bloomington, 2012.
174. and their family became prize hostages.: Nostitz-Rieneck, Count.
174. and die in concentration camps.: Albright, 281–282.
175. a "desecrator of Nazi iconography.": Nostitz-Rieneck, Count.
175. its gates never to be seen again.: Albright, 281–282.
175. ancient families were systematically plundered.: Nostitz-Rieneck, Count.
175. "decadent Franz Ferdinand," was an early target.: Ibid.
175. Sophie and her brothers were expelled.: Ibid.
176. to entertain distinguished visitors.: Ibid.
176. and private homes of Gestapo officials.: Ibid.
176. Deputy Reich Protector of Bohemia and Moravia, Reinhard Heydrich.: Ibid.
176. responsible for the genocide of millions of Jews.: Dederichs, Mario R. *Heydrich: The Face of Evil,* 43, Casemate, Drexel Hill, 2009. Hitler's hatred of Czechs never left him.
176. "We will Germanize the Czech vermin.": Ibid.
176. "Torture and killing were his daily occupations.": Ibid.
176. furniture and treasures stolen from Konopiste.: Bennett, Magnus. "Heir to Stolen Jewish Property Foiled by Czech Restitution Law," Jewish Telegraphic Agency, Inc., 2001.
176. by Edvard Beneš and his government in exile.: Olson, 239–241, Brožovwský, Miroslav, 22. Lina von Osten Heydrich joined the Nazi Party in 1929 (Nazi membership number 1,201,380). She persuaded her future husband, Reinhard, to join the party in 1931 after hearing Adolf Hitler speak. She continued defending her husband until her death in 1985. Nevertheless, she was the author of a book titled *Leben mit einem Kriegsverbrecher (Life with a War Criminal)*, a title that must have come from her publisher or accountant. On March 28, 2011, *The Daily Mail* reported, "Son of detested Nazi leader sparks outrage after announcing he wants to restore castle where 'Butcher of Prague' ruled. His request was denied."
177. Hitler lamented he was "irreplaceable.": Hitler, *Secret Conversations*, 415.
177. arrest, torture, and murder of five thousand Czechs.: Horvitz, Leslie Ann, and Christopher Catherwood. *Encyclopedia of War Crimes and Genocide*, 200, New York, 2006. Paces, Cynthia. *Prague Panoramas National Memory*

Sacred Space in the Twentieth Century, University of Pittsburgh, Pittsburgh, 2009.

177. eulogy at a massive state funeral in Berlin.: Ibid..
177. Czechs tried to survive by being invisible.: Ibid.
177. "complete what I have set out to achieve.": Hauner, 134.
177. amongst the greatest achievers the world has ever known.: Ibid.
178. "What now?": Ibid. Hitler's question may imply he believed he would once again outmaneuver his opponents and achieve his ends without war.

CHAPTER SEVENTEEN
THE ELEVENTH COMMANDMENT

179. conscientious objectors brought from Dachau.: Hohenberg, Prince Gerhard.
179. was to be removed with their hands.: Millard, 155.
180. they waited for everyone inside to die.: Ibid.
180. did not learn he was alive for several months.: Hohenberg, Prince Gerhard.
180. fellow prisoners slept around him.: Ibid.
180. He decided to bore them to death.: Ibid.
181. Ernst was to remain at Dachau.: Hohenberg, Georg Duke of.
181. survived his ordeal without Ernst by his side.: Ibid.
181. his family did not recognize him.: Ibid.
181. It was a bittersweet homecoming.: Ibid.
181. mind remained imprisoned with Ernst at Dachau.: Hohenberg, Princess Sophie de Potesta.
181. he was expected to spy on himself.: Ibid.
182. and France all fell to Hitler's armies.: Weyr, 175.
182. the beginnings of a new "intercontinental order.": Millard, 142.
182. to escape the invading Nazis.: Habsburg, HRIH Archduke Christian. "Otto von Habsburg, A Long and Courageous Life in the Service to Europe," St. Mary's Mother of God Church, Washington, DC, October 22, 2011. The Duke of Windsor, living in French Exile, also made his way to Paris. He had ordered a diamond, sapphire, emerald, and ruby broach from Cartier Jewelers as a gift for the Duchess. He wanted to be sure it was delivered before the city fell to the Germans. Much to his relief, it was.
182. not his willing collaborator.: Ibid.
182. "I am to have that dream fulfilled today.": Speer, Albert. *Inside the Third Reich* (translated by Richard and Clara Winston), 172, Simon & Schuster, New York, 1970. Hitler seemed to only be able to have one "friend" during each period of his life. The architect Speer fulfilled that relationship for Hitler until 1945.
183. "We aren't done yet.": Ibid. Hitler had earlier confided to Leni Riefenstahl, "I'd give anything to see Paris just once. But I'll probably never be granted that in my lifetime," 210, Memoirs.
183. when the wars were over.: Ibid.

183. in movie newsreels across occupied Europe.: Savich, Carl. "Sarajevo 1941," October 24, 2014, http://serianna.com.

183. to announce the entrance of the Emperor.: Bossy, Raoul V. *Recollections of a Romanian Diplomat: Diaries and Memories Vol II*, 401, Ed. by G.H. Bossy & M.A. Bossy, Hoover Institute Press, Stanford, 2003.

183. "It was truly a funereal meal.": Ibid.

184. or the Gestapo would do it for him.: Hohenberg, Georg Duke of.

184. but no tea was ever served.: Hohenberg, Prince Gerhard.

184. to surrender her sense of humor to the Nazis.: Ibid.

184. and sense of humor remained intact.: Radziwill, 172.

185. nothing else was more important.: Hohenberg, Prince Gerhard.

185. but persistently, inquire about restitution.: Ibid.

185. their sixth child, a boy they named Gerhard.: Ibid.

185. She refused to wear it.: Ibid.

185. Few people had such courage.: Ibid.

185. "had every reason to be lasting and firm.": Delaforce, 165.

186. a Habsburg princess, was born in Vienna.: Longo, James McMurtry. *Isabel Orleans-Braganza: The Brazilian Princess Who Freed the Slaves*, 1, McFarland, Jefferson, 2008. The Austrian architectural influence in Petropolis is unique for Brazil and surprising to visitors who do not know its history.

186. what was believed to be long forgotten barbarism.: Zweig, xiv.

186. never granted the Nazis this triumph.": Muhlstein, Anka. *New York Review of Books*, 1, May 8, 2014.

187. the invasion made her worst nightmare a reality.: Nostitz-Rieneck, Count.

187. sacrificed as cannon fodder to the Nazi war machine.: Ibid.

CHAPTER EIGHTEEN
APOCALYPSE

188. the country Franz warned Austria to never fight.: Nostitz-Rieneck, Count.

188. Russia to turn south toward the city of Stalingrad.: Ibid.

189. remembered they were Austrians, not Germans.: Hohenberg, Prince Gerhard.

189. eight hundred thousand of their fellow soldiers did not.: Ibid.

189. and raped their way to Berlin.: Ibid.

189. but she refused to leave without Ernst.: Ibid.

189. unwittingly endangered his own covert activities.: Ibid.

189. in the care of distant Hohenberg cousins.: Ibid.

190. read lips because of her increasing deafness.: Ibid.

190. compound twenty-four hours a day inside and out.: Ibid.

190. and many others, died within its walls.: Millard, 13, 104.

190. redoubled her efforts to free him.: Hohenberg, Prince Gerhard.

190. "the highest possible German authorities.": Hauner, 199.

191. but she was never seen again.: Hohenberg, Prince Gerhard.

191. became a non-person within his own family.: Ibid.

191. "Would you like to share lunch with us?": Ibid.
192. urged Maisie to write one more letter.: Ibid.
192. to Heinrich Himmler, he would pass it on to him.: Ibid.
192. "I embrace you and send you a thousand kisses.": Millard, 155.
192. convinced Heinrich Himmler to sign the release order.: Hohenberg, Prince Gerhard.
192. and his family scattered.: Ibid.
192. "A thousand hugs, Ernst.": Ibid.
193. sense of humor revealed his former self.: Ibid.
193. and stress of the city stole his remaining strength.: Ibid.
193. None of them knew who was alive or dead.: Nostitz-Rieneck.
193. began bombing Vienna day and night.: Ambrose, Stephen E. *The Wild Blue Yonder: The Men and Boys Who Flew the B-24s Over Germany,* 102–220, Simon and Schuster, New York, 2002.
193. the Academy of Fine Arts were all damaged.: Ibid.
194. but she was not there to see it.: Hohenberg, Georg Duke of.
194. twelve Habsburg emperors, including Franz Joseph.: Ibid.
194. capital of Poland was razed to the ground.: Nostitz-Rieneck.
194. village where he died was named Sophienberg.: Ibid. Olson, 369–370.
194. "died for the Führer and the Fatherland.": Nostitz-Rieneck.
195. didn't know whether he, too, was dead.: Ibid.
195. "mass of immigrants from many nations and races.": Speer, 121.
195. keep non-Germans from entering the country.: Trevor-Roper, Hugh. *The Last Days of Hitler,* 26–31, Pan Books, London, 1995.
195. dismissing the advancing Russians as "Redskins.": Jones, 326.
195. They were too busy fighting for their lives to read.: Hamann, 384.
195. "one way or the other.": Hauner, 188.
195. "unless I drive a bullet through my head.": Ibid.

CHAPTER NINETEEN
THE WHOLE COUNTRY WAS AS IF UNDER A SPELL

196. seize power, and end the war.: Hansen, Randall. *Disobeying Hitler: German Resistance After Valkyrie,* 25, Oxford University Press, Oxford, 2014.
196. and religious leaders were shot, hanged, or beheaded.: Ibid., 60–72.
197. escape on the twentieth of July was a miracle.: Trevor-Roper, 33, 166.
197. He turned to morphine.: Ibid., 139.
197. "annihilation and hatred will meet him.": Hansen, 1–2.
197. "without regard to rank and prestige.": Speer, 423.
197. "but we shall take the world with us.": Toland, 872.
197. "It is enough to make one lose faith in God.": Hauner, 199.
197. from his Chancellery office to the bunker.: Hamann, 3.
198. "into which we would gain entrance.": Ibid.

198. and it angered me immensely.: Toland, 877. This recollection recalls one of the several brief visits Hitler made to Vienna prior to his triumphal return in 1938.
199. tried very hard not to be too frightened.: Hohenberg, Georg Duke of.
199. Uncle Fritz had been given at its beginning.: Ibid.
199. die together, as a family.: Ibid.
199. Elisabeth refusing to leave his office.: Ibid.
200. and treachery were everywhere.: Ibid.
200. between one individual and another.: Ileana, Princess, 216–217. Princess Ileana eventually moved to the United States, became a nun, and founded an Orthodox convent and monastery in Elwood, Pennsylvania, where she is buried. She inherited the Bran Castle in Rumania traditionally associated with Bram Stoker's novel *Dracula*. The castle became the property of her son in 2006.
200. character of the man, not his political beliefs.: Hohenberg, Prince Gerhard.
201. the communists regarded with respect.: Hohenberg, Georg Duke of.
201. no electricity, and almost no food.: Ibid.
201. in the chaos of the Russian advance.: Ibid.
201. troops and were again forced to run.: Ibid.
201. kept them safe also trapped them.: Ibid.
202. if they would be killed.: Ibid.
202. the medical attention he needed.: The mother of Prince Franz Joseph II of Liechtenstein was Franz Ferdinand's youngest sister, Archduchess Elisabeth Amalie Habsburg. Prince Franz Joseph II was the only leader of a country to refuse to return German soldiers to the Soviet Union after the war. His refusal saved thousands from imprisonment and death.
202. a common grave two miles from Konopiste.: Hutchinson, James Lee. *The Boys in B7 8th Air Force.*
202. but then his dark mood lifted.: Bernadotte, Count Folke. *Last Days of the Reich: The Diary of Count Folke Bernadotte, October 1944–May 1945*, 115, Frontline Books, London, 2009. One German whose belief in Hitler and Heinrich Himmler never wavered was Gudrun Burwitz, Himmler's daughter, who remained an unrepentant Nazi until her death at the age of 88 in May 2018. She was called by friends and foes alike, a Nazi princess, and had "marvelous" memories of visited Dachau with her when she was twelve.
202. as the greatest German of them all.: Hauner, 206.
203. "proved itself unworthy of me!": Ibid.
203. "He was the victim of his generals.": Ryan, Cornelius. *The Last Battle: The Classic History of the Battle for Berlin*, 362–363, Simon & Schuster, New York, 1966.
203. and Europe will never be Russian.: Ibid.
203. mistress had been captured and assassinated.: Toland, 888. The death of Mussolini seemed to signal to Hitler the end.

204. "National Socialist movement in a truly united nation.": Ibid., 879, 888. In the last months of the war, Albert Speer found himself on the German front near the Rhine River caught in a night attack among ordinary German citizens. In the darkness he listened to their conversation. Their faith in Hitler was unshakable even as the Reich collapsed around them. They believed only he understood them and would be able "to work the miracle of their salvation from this forlorn predicament," Hugh Trevor-Roper, p. 72.

204. all nations, international Jewry.: Ibid.

204. exorcising demons from those possessed by the devil.: https://enwikipedia. org/wiki/Walpurgis_Nacht. Witches Night is featured in Act II of Goethe's *Faust*, in Bram Stoker's novel *Dracula*, and Edward Albee's play *Who's Afraid of Virginia Woolf?* Thirty-one years to the minute of Adolf Hitler's suicide, Bishop Lanyi also had his dream of Franz Ferdinand's assassination.

205. HITLER IS DEAD NAZI RADIO REPORTS FÜHRER KILLED FIGHTING RUSSIANS.: *Philadelphia Inquirer*, "Hitler Is Dead, Nazi Radio Reports Fuehrer Killed Fighting Russians," 1.

205. in victory an undiminished crisis.: Thompson, Joseph. "The Evil That Men Do Lives After Them," *St. Louis Post Dispatch*, 5B.

205. "Nobody believes Hitler is dead.": Lochner, Louis. "The End of Hitler's Mountain Hideout," *St. Louis Post Dispatch*, 1B.

205. suicide, his military blunders, or the Holocaust.: Rissell, Herbert J. Interview, November 7, 2016. Herbert Rissell and his brother were members of the Hitler Youth. His memories of the final days of the war and the shock of Hitler's suicide provide insights into both the isolation and denial of Germany's population during and after the war. Rissell moved to the United States and retired to Pennsylvania, 30, 2017. "A German Life," *New York Times*, December 22, 2017.

206. Well, very little anyway.: "Joseph Goebbels' Secretary, Brunhilde Pomsel, Dies Aged 106," *Guardian*, January 2017.

CHAPTER TWENTY
PHANTOMS AND PATRIOTS

207. The date was May 8, 1945.: Fuller, Samuel. Faukenau Vision de l'Lmpossible. "The Big Red One—The Last Battle" film, Michkan World Productions, 2009. This film provides an eyewitness account of the final battle of World War II in Europe.

207. death rather than a world without Hitler.: Ibid.

208. for the millions killed by the Nazis.: Ibid.

208. to a Russian slave labor camp.: Ibid.

208. their family, Erwein's safe return.: Ibid.

209. "in our republic once and for all.": Sebestyen, Victor. *1946: The Making of the Modern World*, 129–130, Vintage Books, New York, 2014.

209. provided that they become good Czech citizens.: Nicolson, Harold. *Diaries and Letters of Harold Nicolson*, Vol. II, 392, Atheneum, New York, 1967.

209. "a foreign ulcer in our body.": Ibid.
209. "'Love Thy Neighbor' does not apply.": Ibid., 131.
209. turned against his "master race.": Ibid., 131.
209. to be banished from Czechoslovakia.: Douglass, R.M. *Orderly and Humane: The Expulsion of the Germans After the Second World War*, 1, Yale University Press, New Haven, 2012.
209. ordered them out of the country.: Sebestyen, 131.
210. N for "Nemec" sewn into their clothes.: Douglass, 1.
210. were expelled from their homeland.: Ibid., 101.
210. and Fritz Nostitz-Rieneck with their children.: Nostitz-Rieneck, Count.
210. Beneš refused to return it.: Ibid.
210. full custody of their underage children.: Deneken, Ludwig von. *Prague Post*, September 21, 2009.
210. his wife of thirty-five years as the "Habsburg princess.": Ibid.
210. between a Habsburg and a Hohenberg.: Nostitz-Rieneck, Count. Members of the Czech government insisted Sophie Hohenberg was a Habsburg.
210. family would leave Czechoslovakia together.: Ibid.
211. safe conduct pass during their deportation.: Ibid.
211. as Czech police looked the other way.: Douglass.
211. leaving without Erwein and Franz.: Nostitz-Rieneck.
211. or committed suicide there.: Sebestyen, 131–133.
211. outside of Karlsbad—today Karlovy Vary.: Nostitz-Rieneck.
211. had become a city of ghosts.: Ibid.
211. died during the "evacuation.": Douglass, 3, 5.
212. as a prisoner of war to Russia.: Nostitz-Rieneck.
212. They never returned.: Douglass.
212. "Iron Curtain" descending across Europe.: Churchill, Winston. "The Sinews of Peace," Westminster College, Fulton, Missouri, March 5, 1946. A church designed by Christopher Wren destroyed in the London Blitz was later reconstructed on the campus of Westminster College in Missouri as a memorial to the famous speech Churchill delivered there.
212. about the castle's surviving paintings.: Hohenberg, Prince Gerhard.
212. Nicholas presented the portrait to him.: Ibid. This portrait of Empress Alexandra of Russia now hangs in the private home of Princess Anita Hohenberg at Artstetten.
213. length of the Soviet occupation of Austria.: Ibid.
213. homesick for their own children.: Ibid.
213. it was another of Hitler's parting gifts.: Ibid.
213. "do not eat" list of postwar hardship cuisine.: Ibid.
213. they had eaten since before the war.: Hohenberg, Princess Sophie de Potesta.
214. civil authorities remained in firm control.: Ibid.
214. but they refused to give up hope.: Hohenberg, Prince Gerhard.
214. but the family relished being together.: Nostitz-Rieneck.
215. at themselves or their fellow Austrians.: Hohenberg, Princes Gerhard.

215. accompanied by genuine laughter.: Ibid. The Hohenberg sense of humor remains one of their defining characteristics, but the point of their story holds true. On the fifth anniversary of the Anschluss, Baldur von Schirach and Joseph Goebbels spoke to a crowd of 100,000 cheering Viennese from the Hofburg Palace balcony. Goebbels wrote in his diary, "One need have no fears about Vienna. The passages of my speech that drew the loudest applause were the ones in which I spoke of the insoluble union of the city with the Reich. Vienna has indeed become a Reich city," p. 124, *The Goebbels Diaries*.

215. Max had joined his brother in jail.: Hohenberg, Prince Gerhard. Leni Riefenstahl wrote in her *Memoirs* of being in Innsbruck when Hitler entered the city: "The Innsbruckers were delirious. They stretched out arms and hands toward Hitler in almost religious ecstasy. Elderly men and women were crying. The universal jubilation was simply beyond belief," p. 221, *Memoirs*.

216. and we were not that judge.: Hohenberg, Georg Duke of.

216. Both men were hanged.: Hohenberg, Georg Duke of.

216. were each sentenced to twenty years in prison.: Smart, Victor. Holocaust Education & Archive Research Team, 2008, www.HolocaustResearchProject.org.

216. "will remain a blot on our history for centuries.": Ibid. Baldur von Schirach's father was a German aristocrat and his mother an American aristocrat descended from two signers of the Declaration of Independence. He traced his anti-Semitism to Henry Ford's hate-filled book, *The International Jew*. For many years, Schirach was the leader of the Hitler Youth. He died in 1994.

217. he also took his own life.: Ibid.

217. and unceremoniously dumped there.: Ibid.

217. to pay his debts after Sarajevo.: https://www.geni.com/people/Gustav-Krupp-von-Bohlen-und-Halbach. Gustav Krupp died at Schloss Blühnbach in 1950. His son Arndt, the last of the Krupps, died there in 1968. Gustav bought the estate in 1917. Arndt offered it as a sanctuary to the exiled dying Shah of Iran in 1979. In 1988, the castle was bought by Frederick Koch, the oldest of the Koch brothers best known in America for their wealth, and conservative political activism.

217. diverse than at any time in centuries.: Sebestyen, 140.

CHAPTER TWENTY-ONE
ANSWERED AND UNANSWERED PRAYERS

218. Italian dictator's fate had all come to pass.: Hohenberg, Prince Gerhard.

219. and estates returned to him.: Nostitz-Rieneck, Count.

219. that her firstborn son still lived.: Ibid.

219. and died in quiet retirement.: Ibid.

219. a healing experience for them.: Ibid.

220. of his death gave no details.: Nostitz-Rieneck, Count.

220. until his final breath.: Ibid.

220. the gift Erwein's friend had given her.: Ibid.

221. meet again in a better place.: Ibid.
221. for Franz Assisi Friedrich Ernst Nostitz-Rieneck.: Ibid.
221. Third Reich continued claiming victims.: Hohenberg, Princess Sophie de Potesta.
221. pain and suffering were never broken.: *Time* Magazine, March 22, 1954, Vol. LXIII, 23.
222. "He was a loyal, honest Austrian.": Pauli, 308.
222. twenty-five expecting her first child.: Nostitz-Rieneck, Count.
222. and the Hohenbergs a fresh beginning.: Hohenberg, Princess Sophie de Potesta.
223. as a second Christmas.: Hohenberg, Prince Gerhard.
223. treasure could have made her happier.: Ibid. Princess Anita Hohenberg has a glass case containing the collection of ceramic lambs in her home at Artstetten.
224. to the palace where he was born.: Hohenberg, Georg Duke of.
224. "facing the land of my birth.": Hohenberg, Prince Gerhard.
224. to end his cousin's Austrian exile.: Ibid.
225. French occupation authorities deported him.: Millard, 146.
225. "loyal citizens of the Republic.": Hohenberg, Prince Gerhard.
225. his quest to end his cousin's exile.: Ibid.
225. recent coronation had done in England.: Ibid. Max found neo-Nazi groups reorganizing in parts of Austria. Klagenfurt, Carinthia, the city where Hitler's favorite teacher retired, earned the reputation as the "El Dorado for former Nazis." In Robert Kaplan's book *Balkan Ghosts*, he writes, "In proportion to its size, Carinthia produced more death-camp guards than any other region of Germany or Austria," p. xxv.
225. an uncomfortable reminder of their past.: Ibid.
225. physical threats, he refused to give up.: Ibid.
226. a resolution to the stalemate.: Ibid.
226. opponents continued blocking Otto's return.: Ibid.
226. He died the following day.: Hohenberg, Princess Sophie de Potesta.
226. but his request was rejected.: Ibid.
226. "began at Belvedere Palace in 1902.": Pauli, 307–308.
227. lived their lives faithful to the law.: Millard, 156.
227. stay with us forever.: Pauli, 307–308.
227. welcomed her cousin home.: Hohenberg, Princess Sophie de Potesta.

CHAPTER TWENTY-TWO
THE GOOD FIGHT

228. to return to Czechoslovakia for a visit.: Nostitz-Rieneck, Count.
228. library had replaced it.: Ibid.
229. tourists shuffling through the castle.: Ibid.
229. soothing him with a smile.: Ibid.
229. "write what they want to write.": Ibid.

229. "next interview will print the truth.": Ibid.
229. he came to live with her.: Ibid.
230. what we do with them.: Ibid.
231. sisters-in-law would be together.: Hohenberg, Princess Sophie de Potesta.
231. beneath the chapel next to Ernst.: Hohenberg, Princess Anita.
232. forms of multilateral political organizations.: *St. Louis Post Dispatch*, April 7, 1989, editorial, p. 3.
232. eastern Europeans fled into Austria.: Habsburg, H.R.I.H Christian, October 22, 2011. My wife and I were having dinner with the director of the Zentrum für Friedensforschung und Frieden Spädagogik (Centre for Research and Peace Education) in Klagenfurt, Austria, on July 1, 2011, when we received a telephone call informing us Otto Habsburg had died. The next day, black bunting could be seen hanging from windows in the city center.
232. the expulsion of the nation's Sudeten "Germans.": Ibid.
232. and calls for European unity.: Ibid.
232. or the wars that followed Sarajevo.: Nostitz-Rieneck, Count.
233. who remained alive in her heart.: Ibid.
233. rooted in that faith and family.: Ibid.
233. died peacefully in her sleep.: Ibid.
234. I have kept the faith.: Ibid.

CHAPTER TWENTY-THREE
THE DESTINY OF ONE FAMILY

235. a decade of communist occupation.: Hohenberg, Princess Sophie de Potesta.
236. his brother, sister, and himself.: Ibid.
236. forty cases of artifacts from Konopiste.: Edsel, Robert M. *The Monuments Men: Allied Heroes, Nazi Thieves, and the Greatest Treasure Hunt in History*, 305–306, Center Street Hachette Book Group, New York, 2009. Robert G.L. Waite also discusses the treasure found in the Alt-Aussee mines in his book, *The Psychopathic God Adolf Hitler*, as designated for Hitler's "Linz Center," p. 67.
236. great-grandchildren they would never know.: Hohenberg, Princess Sophie de Potesta. Ironically the wife of Baldur von Schirach and widow of Herman Goering both attempted to have art works stolen by their husbands during the war from Jewish families returned to them, not their rightful Jewish owners. For the most part, they succeeded. See: "Looted by Nazis, and Returned, Art is Back in Wrong Hands," *New York Times* article by Doreen Carajai and Allison Smale.
236. were returned to Czechoslovakia.: Ibid.
236. Konopiste was reopened as a museum.: Ibid.
236. to visit the castle of his father's dream.: Ibid.
236. "Now I really don't understand our father.": Ibid.
237. reality began to almost haunt him.: Ibid.

237. could not steal the love from that house.: Ibid.

238. fight about justice and truth.: Ibid.

238. Cardinal Archbishop of Vienna, Christopher Schönborn.: Nostitz-Rieneck, Count.

238. one of the stained-glass windows.: Hohenberg, Prince Gerhard.

238. love that made their lives possible.: Nostiz-Rieneck, Count.

238. Austrians in Argentina sorted out.: Hohenberg, Georg Duke of.

239. a quiet laugh only he heard.: Ibid.

239. beyond the Seas, King, Defender of the Faith, Emperor of India.: Hohenberg, Prince Gerhard.

240. of the royal family spoke volumes.: Ibid.

240. worst during the worst of times.: Cooke, Alistair. *Six Men*, 82. Edward's secretary wrote, "The King was like the child in the fairy stories who had been given every gift except a soul." The *Houston Chronicle* wrote of the Duke and Duchess, "Two people whose sense of history began and ended with each other."

240. and Habsburg cousins were there.: Hohenberg, Georg Duke of.

240. The Hohenberg's cousin, Cardinal Schönborn, had been the principle sponsor of Otto Habsburg's beatification.

240. good Christians, Austrians, and Habsburgs.: Brook-Shepherd, *Uncrowned Emperor*, 216.

240. there is always hope.: Hohenberg, Georg Duke of.

241. How could we not believe in miracles?: Hohenberg, Prince Gerhard.

BIBILIOGRAPHY

_____*On Masaryk: Texts in English & German.* Novak, Josef, ed. Amsterdam: Rodori, 1988.

____*Diaries & Letters of Harold Nicolson: 1939–1945, Vol II.* Nicolson, Nigel, ed. New York: Atheneum, 1967.

Agnew, Hugh. *The Czechs and the Lands of the Bohemian Crown.* Stanford: Hoover Institution Press, 2004.

Aichelburg, Wladimir. *Erherzog Franz Ferdinand von Osterreich—Este und Artstetten.* Verlagsburo Mag. Johann Lebner Ges.m.b. Wien, 2000.

Albright, Madeline. *Prague Winter—A Personal Story of Remembrance & War, 1937–1948.* New York: Harper Collins, 2012.

Alexander, Prince Regent, H.R.H. *Serbia's Part in the War Vol. I: The Rampart Against Pan-Germanism.* London: Simkin, Marshall & Hamilton, 1918.

Allen, Martin. *Hidden Agenda: How the Duke of Windsor Betrayed the Allies.* New York: M. Evans & Company, 2002, 189.

Ambrose, Steven. *The Wild Blue: The Men and Boys Who Flew the B24s Over Germany.* New York: Simon & Schuster, 2002.

"Angry Aristocrats." *London Daily Telegraph.* 6 July 1914.

Arco-Zinneberg, Graf Ulrich. *Meine Reise um die Erde: 100 Jahre Weltreise des Thronfolgers.* Marbach, 1993.

Aronson, Theo. *The Crowns in Conflict.* Manchester, New Hampshire: Salem House Publishers, 1986.

Asprey, Robert. *The Panther's Feast.* New York: G.P. Putnam's Sons, 1959.

"Austrian Throne Support for Otto." *New York Times.* 24 September 1933.

Baeta, Juergen, and John-Thor Dahlburg. *Mourning Millions: EU Leaders Mark WWI Centennial.* AP: The Big Story. http://bigstory.ap.org/article/eu-leaders-meeting-ypres-mark-wwi-centennial (Retrieved 4 August 2014).

Beatty, Jack. *The Lost History of 1914: Reconsidering the Year the Great War Began.* New York: Walker Books, 2012.

Bernadotte, Count Folke. *Last Days of the Reich: October 1944–May 1945.* London: Frontline Books, 2009.

Bestenreiner, Erkia. *Franz Ferdinand un Sophie von Hohenberg Verboten Liebe am Kaiserhof.* Zurich: Piper Taschenbuch, 2005.

Bloch, Eduard. "My Patient Adolf Hitler: A Memoir of Hitler's Jewish Physician." *The Journal of Historical Review*, May–June 1994, (Vol. 14. No 3) 27–35.

Bogle, James, and Joanna Bogle. *A Heart for Europe—The Lives of Emperor Charles & Empress Zita of Austria-Hungary*. Herfordshire: Gracewing, 1990.

Bossy, Raoul. *Recollections of a Romanian Diplomat: Diaries and Memories Vol. II*. Stanford: Hoover Institute Press, 2003.

Bostridge, Mark. *The Fateful Year: England 1914*. London: Penguin Books, 2014.

"Boys in Austria Praying for Peace." *New York Times*. 8 July 1916.

Brook-Shepherd, Gordon. *Archduke of Sarajevo: The Romance & Tragedy of Franz Ferdinand of Austria*. Boston: Little, Brown and Company, 1984.

Brook-Shepherd, Gordon. *The Austrians—A Thousand-Year Odyssey*. New York: Carroll & Graf, Publishers, 1996.

Brook-Shepherd, Gordon. *The Last Habsburg*. New York: Weybright & Talley, 1968, 214.

Brook-Shepherd, Gordon. *Royal Sunset: The European Dynasties and the Great War*. Garden City: Doubleday & Company, 1987.

Brook-Shepherd, Gordon. *Uncle of Europe: The Social and Diplomatic Life of King Edward VII*. Harcourt, Brace & Javanovich, 1976.

Brook-Shepherd, Gordon. *Uncrowned Emperor, The Life & Times of Otto von Hapsburg*. London: Hambeldon & London, 2003.

Brooks, Tim. *Ferdinand Porsche—Famed for First Hybrid, Beetle, and Link with Hitler*. More Motoring, The National, 12 February 2012.

Brown, Mark. "Blood Swept Lands: The Story Behind the Tower of London Poppies Tribute." *Guardian*. Sunday, 28 December 2014.

Brown-Scott, James. "War Between Austria-Hungary and the United States." *American Journal of International Law, Vol 12*. Oxford: Oxford University Press, 1918.

Brožovskŷ, Miroslav. Konopiste Chateau, Prague, The Institute for the Care of Historic Monuments of Central Bohemia of Prague, 1995.

"Brunhilde Pomsel, Aide to Goebbels and Witness of Nazi Fall, Dies at 106." *New York Times*. 31 January 2017, A26.

Burns, John F. "Remembering World War I in the Conflict's Flash Point: The Vienna Philharmonic Recalls World War I in Sarajevo." *New York Times Online*. http://nyti.ms/1x1HJ4R (Retrieved 4 August 2014).

"Camilla Attends WWI Candlelight Vigil at Westminster Abbey." *Royal Insight*. 5 August 2014. http://www.royalinsight.net/forum/index.php?topic=71365.0 (Retrieved 5 August 2014).

Carney, Matthew. "Hiroshima Marks 69th Anniversary of Atomic Bombing." *India Today Online*. http://indiatoday.intoday.in/story/Hiroshima-69th-anniversary-of-atomic-bombing/1/275739.html (Retrieved 4 August 2014).

Carruthers, Bob. *Private Hitler's War: 1914–1918*. Barnsley: Sword & Pen Books Ltd, 2014.

Carvajal, Doreen and Alison Smale. "Looted by Nazis, and Returned, Art Is Back in Wrong Hands." *New York Times*. 16 July 2016, C1.

Cassels, Lavender. *The Archduke and the Assassin: Sarajevo, June 28th, 1914*. New York: Dorset Press, 1984.

Cavendish-Bentinck, William. *Me, Women, and Things—Memories of the Duke of Portland*. London: Faber & Faber, 1938.

"Charles of Austria Dies of Pneumonia in Exile on Madeira." *New York Times*. 2 April 1922.

Churchill, Winston. "The Sinews of Peace." Westminster College Lecture, Fulton, Missouri, 5 March 1946.

Churchill, Winston. *The World Crisis 1911–1914*. London: Thornton Butterworth Ltd., 1923.

Clare, Georg. *Last Waltz in Vienna: The Rise & Destruction of a Family 1842–1942*. New York: Holt, Rinehart & Winston, 1980.

Clark, Christopher. *The Sleepwalkers: How Europe Went to War in 1914*. London: Penguin, 2012.

Cooke, Alistair. *Six Men*. New York: Alfred Knopf, 1977.

Cornwell, John. *Hitler's Pope: The Secret History of Pius XII*. New York: Viking, 1999.

"Court Rejects Complaint of Franz Ferdinand d'Este Heiress." *Prague Daily Monitor*, 15 April 2011.

Crankshaw, Edward. *The Fall of the House of Habsburg*. London: Longmans, 1963, 285.

Cruickshank, Charles. *The German Occupation of the Channel Islands*. The Guernsey Press, 1975.

Cultural Attaché (name withheld upon request). Phone Interview. Austrian Embassy. Washington, DC: 26 June 2014.

Curtis, Richard, Ben Elton, and Rowan Atkinson. *Blackadder: The Whole Damn Dynasty: 1485–1917*. Westminster: Penguin Books, 2000.

Czernin, Count Ottokar. *In the World War*. Lexington: Forgotten Books, 2013.

Dacre, Nigel. "100 years Ago Today: Archduke Franz Ferdinand Assassinated." *Centenary News*. 6 June 2014.

Dallek, Robert. *Franklin D. Roosevelt & American Foreign Policy 1932–1945*. Oxford: Oxford University Press, 1995. 2nd printing.

Dederich, Mario. *The Face of Evil*. Drexel Hill Press, 2009.

Dedijer, Vladimir. *Road to Sarajevo*. New York: Simon and Schuster, 1966.

Delaforce, Patrick. *Adolf Hitler: The Curious and Macabre Anecdotes*. London: Fonthill, 2012.

"Descendant of WWI's Archduke Franz Ferdinand Seeks Czech Castle." *Deutsche Press Agentur*. 6 April 2006.

Douglas, R. M. *Orderly & Humane: The Expulsion of the Germans After the Second World War*. New Haven: Yale University Press, 2012.

Eade, Philip. *Prince Philip: The Turbulent Life of the Man Who Married Queen Elizabeth II*. New York: Henry Holt and Company, 2011.

Edsel, Robert M. *The Monuments Men: Allied Heroes, Nazi Thieves, and the Greatest Treasure Hunt in History*. New York: Center Street, 2009.

Eisner, Peter. *The Pope's Last Crusade: How an American Jesuit Helped Pope Pius XI's Campaign to Stop Hitler*. New York: William Morrow, 2013.

Evans, Richard J. *The Coming of the Third Reich*. New York: Penguin Press, 2004.

Fallodon, Viscount Grey of. *Twenty-Five Years, 1892–1916, Vol. II*. New York: Frederick A Stokes Company, 1925.

The First!: The Story of the 1st Infantry Division (GI Stories). Paris: Stars & Stripes, 1944–1945.

Feigl, Erich. *Zita de Hapsbourg: Memoirses d'un Empire Disparu.* Buckinghamshire, England: Criterion Publishing, 1991.

Fest, Joachim. *Hitler.* New York: Harcourt, Brace, and Jovanovich, 1974.

The Fighting First. U.S. Army Film, Department of the Army, A War Department Official Film, public domain, AVA 107VBN1, 1946.

"Former European Enemies Mark Centennial of World War I Beginning." *Associated Press.* 4 August 2014.

Fuller Falkenau, Samuel and Emil Weiss. "The Big Red One—The Last Battle." Film: Michkan World Productions, 2009.

Gady, Franz-Stefan. "The Scandalous Love Affair That Started World War I." *National Interest.* 22 August 2014.

Gareth, Russell. *The Emperors: How Europe's Rulers Were Destroyed by the First World War.* Gloucestershire: Amberly Publishing, 2014.

Gaillon, Eloise, and Jeffrey Post. "An Examination of the Napoleon Diamond Necklace." *Gems & Gemology Magazine,* 2007.

Geddyr, G.E.R. "Restoration of Monarchy Within Year Predicted." *New York Times,* 21 November 1934.

Gerd, Höller. *Franz Ferdinand von Österreich-Este.* Graz, 1982.

Gilbert, Martin. *The First World War—A Complete History.* New York: Henry Holt & Company, 1994.

Gilbert, Martin, and Richard Gott. *The Appeasers.* Boston: Houghton Mifflin, 1963.

Gini, Al, and Ronald Green. *Ten Virtues of Outstanding Leaders.* Oxford: Wiley-Blackwell, 2013, 92.

Goebbels, Dr. Joseph. *The Goebbels Diaries 1939–1941.* Ed. and Trans. Fred Taylor. Hamish Hammler: London, 1982.

Goebbels, Dr. Joseph. *The Goebbels Diaries 1942–1943.* Ed. Louis P. Lochner. Garden City: Doubleday & Company, 1948.

Gooch, John. *Mussolini and His Generals: The Armed Forces and Fascist Foreign Policy 1922–1940.* Cambridge: Cambridge University Press, 2007.

Grace Communion International. The Protestant Church in Hitler's Germany and the Barmen Declaration, https://www.gci.org/history/barmen (Retrieved 22 August 2016).

Gunther, John. *Inside Europe: 1940 War Edition.* New York: Harper & Brothers, 1940.

Habsburg, Christian, H.I.R.H. Lecture: "Otto von Habsburg—A Long & Courageous Life in the Service of Europe". St. Mary Mother of God Church: Washington, DC. 22 October 2011.

Habsburg, Christian, H.I.R.H. Interview with author. Washington, DC. 21 October 2011.

"Habsburg Princes Arrested by Austrian Nazis." *New York Times.* 23 March 1938, 38, col. 1.

Hall, Alan. "The Single Jew that Hitler wanted to save." *Daily Mail,* 5 July 2012.

Hamann, Brigitte. *Bertha von Suttner: A Life for Peace*. Syracuse, New York: Syracuse University Press, 1996.

Hamann, Brigette. *Hitler's Edeljude. Das Leben des Armenarrztes Eduard Bloch*. Munich: Piper Verlag, 2008, 427.

Hamann, Brigette. *Hitler: Portrait of the Tyrant as a Young Man*. London: Taurus Parke, 2010.

Haslip, Joan. *The Lonely Empress: Elizabeth of Austria*. London: Phoenix, 2000.

Hastings, Max. *Catastrophe 1914: Europe Goes to War*. New York: Knopf, 2013.

Hauner, Milan. *Hitler: A Chronology of his Life and Time*. Basintoke: Palgrave Macmillan, 2008.

Hayman, Ronald. *Hitler & Geli*. New York: Bloomsbury, 1997.

Hébert, John. "The Map That Named America: Library Acquired 1507 \Waldseemüllen Map of the World." *Library of Congress Information Bulletin, Vol 62, No.9*. September 2003.

Higham, Charles. *The Duchess of Windsor: The Secret Life*. New York: McGraw Hill, 1988.

Hitler, Adolf. *Mein Kampf*. Trans. Ralph Manheim. New York: Houghton Mifflin Company, 1999, 159.

Hitler, Adolf. *Hitler's Private Conversations*. Ed. H.R. Trevor-Roper. Farrar, Straus, & Young, 1953, 55.

"Hitler Is Dead. Nazi Radio Reports Fuehrer Killed Fighting Russians." *Philadelphia Inquirer*. 1 May 1945.

Hoffmann, Heinrich. *Hitler As I Saw Him, Records of His Personal Photographer, Herbig*. 1974.

Hohenberg, Georg Duke of. Interview with author. Vienna. 30 June 2011.

Hohenberg, Prince Gerhard of. Interview with author. 30 March 2011. Klagenfurt, Austria, 9 April 2011; Vienna, Austria, 18 May 2011, Maria Tafael, Artstetten.

Hohenberg, Princess Sophie de Potesta. Interview with author. 30 March 2011, Klagenfurt, Austria; 13 July 2011, Brussels, Belgium; 15 March 2013, Brussels, Belgium; 22 March 2013, Brussels, Belgium. Email: 29 January 2013; 22 December 2014.

Höller, Gerd. *Franz Ferdinand von Östterreich*. Graz, 1982.

Holzer, Hans. *The Habsburg Curse*. Garden City: Doubleday & Company, 1973.

Horthy, Admiral Nicholas. *Memoirs* (annotated by Andrew L. Simon). Safety Harbor: Simon Publications, 2000.

Hutchinson, James Lee. Ed. *The Boys in the B-17: 8th Air Force Combat Stories of World War II*. Bloomington: AuthorHouse, 2011.

Ileana, Princess of Romania. *I Live Again*. New York: Rinehart & Company, 1951.

Illies, Florian. *1913—The Year Before the Storm*. Trans. Shaun Whiteside and Jamie Lee Searle. Brooklyn & London: Melville House, 2013.

"Italy Back Serbia's Accession to EU." *European Post*. 25 May 2015, 1.

Jászi, Oscar. *The Dissolution of the Habsburg Monarchy*. Chicago: University of Chicago Press, 1971.

John Paul II, Pope. *Gift and Mystery: On the Fiftieth Anniversary of My Priestly Ordination.* New York: Doubleday, 1996.

Johnston, William M. *The Austrian Mind—An Intellectual & Social History 1848–1938.* Berkley: University of California Press, 1972.

Jones, J. Sydney. *Hitler in Vienna; Clues to the Future.* New York: Cooper Square Press, 2002.

Judah, Tim. "Sarajevo's Memories." *The Economist: Intelligent Life.* Jan.–Feb. 2014. http://moreintelligentlife.com/content/features/anonymous/street-corner-started-20th-Trove.nia.au.npd/del/article/37838421 (Retrieved 7 July 2012).

Kanter, Trudi. *Some Girls, Some Hats and Hitler: A True Story.* Great Britain: Virago Press, 2012.

Kaplan, Robert D. *Balkan Ghosts: A Journey Through History.* New York: St. Martin's Press, 1993.

Kellerhoff, Sven Felix. "Wie Hitler seinen jüdischen Kompaniechef schüzte." *Die Welt*, 7 July 2012.

Kennan, George. *Sketches of Life.* New York: Pantheon Books, 1968.

Kennedy, John F. John F. Kennedy Library and Museum Archives, Diary European Trip, 8 July 1937.

Kennedy, John F. "Honors Thesis: Appeasement at Munich." 128–129, 11 March 2014.

Kershaw, Alex. *The Envoy: The Epic Rescue of the Last Jews of Europe in the Desperate Closing Months of World War II.* Philadelphia: DaCapo Press, 2010.

Kershaw, Ian. *Hitler: 1889–1936 Hubris.* New York: W.W. Norton, 1999.

Kershaw, Ian. *Hitler: A Biography.* New York: W.W. Norton, 2008.

Kiegard, Karl von. "Frederick Wilhelm Exclusive Interview with the United Press International." 20 November 1914.

King, Greg, and Sue Woolmans. *The Assassination of the Archduke: Sarajevo 1914 and the Romance That Changed the World.* New York: St. Martin's Press, 2013.

Kogon, Eugen. *The Theory and Practice of Hell: The German Concentration Camps and the Theory Behind Them.* New York: Berkley, 1980.

Kroeger, Alix. "Sarajevo Reinstalls Memorials to the Past." *BBC News*, 29 June 2011.

Kubizek, August. *The Young Hitler I Knew: The Definitive Inside Look at the Artist Who Became a Monster.* Yorkshire: Arcade Publishing, 2011.

Kürenberg, Joachim von. *The Kaiser, A Life of Wilhelm II, Last Emperor of Germany.* New York: Simon & Schuster, 1955.

Kurlander, Eric. *The Perils of Discursive "Balkanization" Petronilla Ehrenpreis, Krieg und Fridenszible in Diskurs.* H-Net Reviews in the Humanities & Social Studies, February 2007.

LaFore, Laurence. *The Long Fuse: An Interpretation of the Origins of World War I.* Philadelphia & New York: Lippincott, 1965.

Lamar, Cecil. *Wilhelm II Vol. II. Emperor and Exile 1900–1941.* Chapel Hill: University of North Carolina Press, 1996.

Lonndale, Maria Horner. *Vienna and the Viennese.* Philadelphia: Henry T. Coates and Co., 1902.

Larisch, Countess Marie. *My Past: Reminiscences of the Courts of Austria and Bavaria*. New York: The Knickerbocker Press, 1913.

Lebert, Stephen, and Norbert Lebert. My Father's Keeper: Children of Nazi Leaders: An Intimate History of Damage and Denial. Trans. Julian Evans. Little Brown & Company, Boston, 2001.

Lengyel, Emil. *And All Her Paths Were Peace: The Life of Bertha von Suttner*. Nashville: Thomas Nelson, 1973.

Levine, Don Isaac. *Letters from the Kaiser to the Czar: Copied from Government Achieves in Petrograd*. New York: Frederick A. Stokes Company, 1920.

Lillie, Sophie. *Was Einmal War Handbuch der Enteigneten*. Wien: Kunstsammlungen, 2003.

Linsboth, Christina. *Two Rulers in an "Automobile,"* World and Worlds of the Habsburgs, A Schloss Schonbrunn Kulturand und Betreibsges, m.b.H. project, Wien 2007–2008.

Longerich, Peter. *Heinrich Himmler: A Life*. New York: Oxford University Press, 2012.

Longo, James McMurtry. *Isabel Orleans-Braganza: The Brazilian Princess Who Freed the Slaves*. Jefferson: McFarland, 2008.

Lower, Wendy. *Hitler's Furies: German Women in the Nazi Killing Fields*. Boston: Houghton Mifflin Harcourt, 2013.

MacDonogh, Giles. *1938 Hitler's Gamble*. New York: Basic Books, 2009.

MacMillan, Margaret. *The War That Ended Peace*. New York: Random House, 2014.

Mack Smith, Denis. *Mussolini: A Biography*. New York: Vintage Books, 1982.

Mager, Hugo. *Elizabeth Grand Duchess of Russia*. New York: Carroll & Graf, 1999.

Marek, George R. *The Eagles Die: Franz Joseph, Elisabeth, and Their Austria*. London: Hart-David, MacGibbon, 1975.

Mason, Paul. "The European Dream is in Danger: Prepare for another rude awakening." *Guardian*, 24 May 2011.

"Maximilian von Hohenberg to Marry." 8 July 1926. "Royal Musings: Royal Musings News and Commentaries About the Reigning Royal Houses and the Former European Monarchies as Well." https://royalmusingsblogspotcom.blogspot.com/2010/07/maximilian-von-hohenberg-to-marry.html (Retrieved 27 April 2011).

May, Arthur J. *The Passing of the Habsburg Monarchy 1914–1918, Vol One*. Philadelphia: University of Pennsylvania Press, 1968.

McCullough, David. *Truman*. New York: Simon & Schuster, 1992.

McGuigan, Dorothy Gies. *The Habsburgs: The Personal Lives of a Royal Family That Made History for Six Centuries*. New York: Doubleday and Company, 1966.

McMeekin, Sean. *July 1914: Countdown to War*. New York: Basic Books, 2012.

Menzies, John. *Keynote Address*. US Centennial Commission Meeting & Public Programs. National World War I Museum at Liberty Memorial. Kansas City, Missouri. 27 June 2014.

Messersmith, G. S. *The Papers of G. S. Messersmith*. http://dspace.udel.edu:8086/dspace/handle/d19716/6176. (Retrieved 3 March 2014).

Messersmith, G. S. *The Papers of G. S. Messersmith*. 23 February 1935. (University of Delaware) Box 430.

Messersmith, G. S. *The Papers of G. S. Messersmith*. 7 October 1935. (University of Delaware) MSS 0109_0589-00.

Messersmith, G. S. *The Papers of G. S. Messersmith*. 7 October 1935. (University of Delaware) MSS 0578_0538-00.

Messersmith, G. S. *The Papers of G. S. Messersmith*. 18 January 1935. (University of Delaware) MSS 0109_0464-00.

Messersmith, G. S. *The Papers of G. S. Messersmith*. 30 November 1936. (University of Delaware) MSS 1090_0784-00.

Messersmith, G. S. *The Papers of G. S. Messersmith*. 6 December 1936. (University of Delaware) MSS 0109_2017-00.

Messersmith, G. S. *The Papers of G. S. Messersmith*. 23 February 1937. (University of Delaware) MSS 0109_0860-00.

Messner, Johannes Fr. *Dollfuss: An Austrian Patriot*. Norfolk: Gates of Vienna Books, 2004.

Meysels, Lucien. *Die Verhinderte Dynastie: Erzherzog Franz Ferdinand un das Haus Hohenberg*. Vienna: Molden, 2000.

Middlemas, Keith. *Baldwin—A Biography*. London: Wiedenfeld & Nicolson, 1969.

Millard, Frank. *The Palace and the Bunker: Royal Resistance to Hitler*. Gloucestershire: The History Press, 2012.

Moorhead, Caroline. *A Train in Winter*. New York: Harper, 2011.

Muhstein, Anka. "His Exile Was Intolerable." *The New York Review of Books*, 8 May 2014.

Mussolini, Benito. *My Autobiography*. New York: Charles Scriber's Sons, 1928.

Nagorski, Andrew. *Hitlerland: American Eyewitnesses to the Nazi Rise to Power*. New York: Simon & Schuster, 2012.

Neef, Christian. "Stolen Triumph: Russia Revisits Pivotal Role in World War I." *Spiegel Online,* International. http://www.spiegel.de/international/world/Russia-revisits-its-role-in-world-war-i-a-942500.html (Retrieved 4 August 2014).

Nickolich, Jessica, and James Hurley. *Franz Ferdinand*. http://entertainment.uk.msn.com/music/galleries/gallery.aspx?cp-documentid=148013878&imageindex=8 (Retrieved 21 August 2015).

Nicoll, Father Leo A. S. J. *Anton Puntigam S.J.: Leben un Wirken eines Jesuiten in Bosnien*. Diss. Vienna: University of Vienna, 1970.

Nicoll, Leo A. S. J. Correspondence with author. 25 May 2011.

Nicolson, Harold. *Diaries and Letters: 1930–1939*. London: Atheneum, 1966.

Nobel Peace Prize 2012. NobelMedia 2014. Nobelprize.org. http://www.nobelprize.org/nobel-prizes/peace/laureates/2012/7 (Retrieved 29 August 2015).

Nostitz-Rieneck, Count Gutsverwaltung. Interview with author. Schloss Geyregg, Eisenerz, Austria. 1 July 2011.

O'Connor, Richard. *The Cactus Throne: The Tragedy of Maximilian and Carlotta*. New York: G.P. Putnam's Sons, 1971.

Olson, Lynne. *Last Hope Island: Britain. Occupied Europe, and the Brotherhood That Helped Turn the Tide of War*. New York: Random House, 2017.

Olson, Lynne. *Those Angry Days: Roosevelt, Lindbergh, and America's Fight Over World War II, 1939–1941.* New York: Random House, 2013.

Olson, Lynne. *Troublesome Young Men.* New York: Farrar, Straus and Giroux, 2007.

Overy, Richard. *Goering: Hitler's Iron Lion.* New York: Taurus Books, 2012.

Paces, Cynthia. *Prague Panoramas: National Memory and Sacred Space in the Twentieth Century.* Pittsburgh: University of Pittsburgh, 2009.

Painter, Heather. Correspondence with Albert Knoll, Dachau Archives. Re: Zugangsnummernbuch. 29 November 2011.

Pauli, Hertha. *The Secret of Sarajevo.* London: Collins Clear-Type Press, 1966.

Penfield, Frederick Courtland, United States Ambassador to Austria Hungry. *Correspondence with Secretary of State.* National Archives at College Park Maryland. National Archives Microfilm Publications. Records of the Department of State to Internal Affairs of Austria-Hungary 1910–1929, microfilm 295. 20 July 1914.

Penfield, Frederic Courtland, United States Ambassador to Austria-Hungary. *United States Department of State / Papers Relating to the Foreign Relations of the United States, 1917.* College Park Maryland: National Archives Microfilm Publications, Microcopy No. 695. Supplement 2, The World War. 30 June 1914.

Persico, Joseph. *Edward R Murrow: An American Original.* New York: McGraw Hill, 1988.

"Personalities of the Week—Prince Ernst von Hohenberg." *Illustrated London News.* 25 April 1936, 7–24.

Petropoulos, Jonathan. *Royals and the Reich: The Princes von Hessen in Nazi Germany.* Oxford: Oxford University Press, 2008.

Pitts, David. *Jack and Lem: The Untold Story of an Extraordinary Friendship.* New York: Carroll & Graf, 2007.

Pless, Princess Daisy of. *What I Left Unsaid.* Ed. Desmond Chapman-Huston. New York: E. P. Dutton & Co., 1936.

"Pope Beatified Last Emperor of Austria." *New York Times International Edition.* 4 October 2004.

"Pope Much Depressed—Spends a Long Time in Prayer." *New York Times.* 29 June 1914, 1.

Pope-Hennessy, James. *Queen Mary 1867–1953.* New York: Knopf, 1960.

Portland, Duke of. "Letter to Thomas Masaryk." 2 August 1919. http://sophie-hohenberg-czech-rep.eu/en/index.php.

Powell-Spring, Blanche. "A Visit to Castle Miramar." *New York Times,* 5 March 1925.

Prague Post. Deneken, Ludwig von, 21 September 2009.

Princess Stephanie H.R.H. *I Was to Be Empress.* London: Nicholson & Watson, 1937.

Quotations: "The Failures of Diplomacy." lphahistory.com/worldwar1/quotations-roadtowar.

Radziwill, Princess Catherine. *The Austrian Court from Within.* New York: Frederick Stokes, 1916.

Range, Peter Ross. *1924: The Year That Made Hitler.* New York: Little, Brown & Company, 2016.

Rasmussen, Fred. "King Gave Up Throne for Love of Baltimore Girl: Sixty Years Ago Edward VII Abdicated to Marry Girl Born on Biddle Street." *Baltimore Sun,* 15 December 1996.

Remak, Joachim. *Sarajevo, The Story of a Political Murder.* New York: Criterion, 1959.

"Restoration of Habsburg's Within Year Predicted." *New York Times.* 28 October 1934.

Ricks, Thomas E. *Churchill and Orwell: The Fight for Freedoms.* New York: Penguin Press, 2017.

Riefenstahl, Leni, *A Memoir.* New York: St. Martin's Press, 1992.

Rissell, Herbert J. *From Hitler's Oppression to American Liberty.* Mustang: Tate Publishing, 2015.

Roberts, Kenneth L. *Europe's Morning After.* New York: Harper & Bros, 1921.

"Royal Funeral Brings Attack on Hofburg's Cerberus." *New York Times, Section Magazine, SM1.* 12 July 1914.

Russell, Gareth. *The Emperors: How Europe's Rulers Were Destroyed by the First World War.* London: Amberley, 2014.

Ryan, Cornelius. *The Last Battle: The Classic History of the Battle for Berlin.* New York: Simon & Schuster, 1966.

Ryback, Timothy W. *Hitler's Private Library: The Books That Shaped His Life.* London: Vintage Books, 2010.

Savich, Carl. "Sarajevo 1941." http://serianna.com (Retrieved 24 October 2014).

Sayers, Janet. *Mothers of Psychoanalysis: Helen Deutsch, Karen Horney, Anna Freud, Melanie Klein.* New York: W.W. Norton & Company, 1991.

Schad, Martha. *Hitler's Spy Princess: The Extraordinary Life of Stephanie von Hohenlohe.* Gloucestershire: Sutton Publishing, 2004.

Schindler, John. "Disaster on the Drina: The Austro-Hungarian Army in Serbia, 1914." *War in History,* 9, (2).

Schmitt, Bernadotte E. *The Coming of the War 1914, Vol. I.* New York: Howard Fertig, 1966.

Scholler, Christiana. Wilkommen im Schloss Artstetten, 2001.

Scott, James Brown. "War Between Austria-Hungary & the United States." *American Journal of International Law, Vol 12.* Oxford: Oxford University Press, 1918.

Sebba, Anne. *That Woman: The Life of Wallis Simpson Duchess of Windsor.* New York: St. Martin's Press, 2013.

Sebestyen, Victor. *1946: The Making of the Modern World.* New York: Vintage Books, 1914.

Sempa, Francis. "The Bloodiest Century." *American Diplomacy, Foreign Service Dispatches and Periodic Reports on U.S. Foreign Policy.* January 2004.

Seton-Watson, R. W. *A History of the Czechs & Slovaks.* New York: Hutchinson & Company, 1943.

Seton-Watson, R. *Artstetten Archives.* (Retrieved 25 June 2011).

Sforza, Carlos. *Makers of Modern Europe.* London: Elkin Matthew & Marrot, 1930.

Shapiro, Ari. *"A Century Ago in Sarajevo: A Plot, a Farce, and a Fateful Shot."* NPR.org. http://www.npr.org/2014/6/27/325516359/a-century-ago-in-sarajevo-a-plot-a-farce-and-a-fateful-shot. (Retrieved 27 June 2014).

Sheehan, Vincent. *Not Peace but a Sword.* New York: Doubleday, 1939.

Shirer, William. *Berlin Diary: The Journal of a Correspondent 1934–1941.* Knopf, 1942.

Smart, Victor. Holocaust Education & Archive Research Team, www.Holocaust ResearchProject.org, 2008.

Smith, Amanda. *Hostage to Fortune—The Letters of Joseph P. Kennedy.* New York: Viking, 2011.

Smith, Craig S. "Princess & Heir of Franz Ferdinand Fights to Repeal a Law and Gain a Castle." *New York Times,* 19 February 2007.

Smith, Denis Mack. *Mussolini: A Biography.* New York: Vintage Books, 1983.

Smith, J. D. *One Morning in Sarajevo: June 28, 1914.* London: Weidenfeld & Nicolson, 2008.

Sondhaus. Lawrence. *Franz Conrad von Hotzendorf: Architect of the Apocalypse.* Boston: Humanities Press, 2000.

Special Correspondent. "Bishop Lanyi's Death Recalls 'War Vision'". *New York Times,* 18 October 1931.

St. Louis Post Dispatch. Editorial page. 7 April 1989, 3.

Starhemberg, Prince Ernst Rudiger. *Between Hitler and Mussolini.* New York: Harper & Brothers, 1942.

Stiller, Jessie. *George S. Messersmith: Diplomat of Democracy.* Chapel Hill: University of NC Press, 2011.

Stoessinger, John. *Why Nations Go to War.* Boston: Cengage Wadsworth, 2011.

Storer, Maria Longworth. "The Recent Tragedy in Bosnia: In Memoriam: A Personal Recollection of the Archduke Franz Ferdinand and His Wife, the Duchess of Hohenberg." *Catholic World,* Vol. 99, August 1914, No 593.

Taylor, A.J.P. *The Struggle for Mastery in Europe 1848–1918.* New York: Oxford, 1954.

Taylor, Edmond. *The Fall of the Dynasties: The Collapse of the Old Order, 1905–1922.* Garden City, New York: Doubleday & Co., 1963.

Thiele, Johannes. *Crown Prince Rudolph 1858–1889: Myth and Truth.* Vienna: Christian Brandstätter Verlag, 2008.

Thompson, Dorothy. *I Saw Hitler.* New York: Farrar & Rinehart, 1932.

Tolstoy, Nikolai. "Consider a Monarchy, America." *New York Times,* 6 November 2016, 11.

Trevor-Roper, Hugh. *The Last Days of Hitler,* 7th edition. London: Pan Books, 2012.

Trosclair, Wade. "The Limits and Conceptions of Austrianness: The Bohemian-German Press During Franz Joseph's Jubilee in 1908." Dissertation, Central European Nationalism Studies Program. Budapest, Hungary, 2013.

"Two Shots Fired 100 Years Ago Today Swept the World Toward War." *Wall Street Journal Online.* http://wsj.com/articles/two-shots-fired-100-years-ago-today-swept-the-world-toward-war-1403917105?tesla=y (Retrieved 28 June 2014).

"University Purge Pushed—Restrictions of Jews Increased." *New York Times*, 31 March 1938, 3, col. 6.

Unowsky, Daniel. *The Pomp and Politics of Patriotism: Imperial Celebrations in Habsburg, Austria 1848–1916*. West Lafayette, Indiana: Purdue University Press, 2005.

Unterreiner, Katrine. *Emperor Franz Joseph 1830–1916: Myth & Truth*. Wien: Christian Brandstatter Verlag, 2006.

Vanderbilt, Cornelius. *Farewell to Fifth Avenue*. New York: Simon & Schuster, 1935.

"Vienna Celebrates Birthday of Otto." *New York Times*. 21 November 1934, 1, col. 2.

"Vienna Monarchist Report on Progress." *New York Times*. 7 February 1935, 8, col. 3.

Viktoria Luise. *The Kaiser's Daughter, Memoirs of H.R.I Princess of Prussia*. Englewood Cliff: Prentice-Hall, 1977.

Villahermosa, Gilberto. "Lost Interview with Herman Goering, The Reich Marshall's Revelations." *World War II Magazine*, September 2006.

von Mensdorff-Pouilly-Dietrichstein, Count Albert. "COUNT VON MENSDORFF; Austro-Hungarian Envoy to London Before 1914." *New York Times*, 18 June 1945.

von Muller, George Alexander. *The Kaiser and His Court*. New York: Harcourt, Brace & World, 1959.

von Schuschnigg, Kurt. *Kurt von Schuschnigg Manuscript Collections, 1932–1978*. St. Louis University Libraries, Special Collections. MSS 693.3.35 Folder 35.

von Schuschnigg, Kurt. *Kurt von Schuschnigg Manuscript Collections, 1932–1978*. St. Louis University. Folder 28 MSS 69.3.28.

von Schuschnigg, Kurt. *My Austria*. New York: Knopf, 1937.

von Schuschnigg, Kurt, and Janet von Schuschnigg. *When Hitler Took Austria: A Memoir of Heroic Faith by the Chancellor's Son*. San Francisco: Ignatius Press, 2008.

von Wiegard, Karl. "Frederick Wilhelm Exclusive Interview with United Press." *United Press*. 20 November 1914.

Vovk, Justin. *Imperial Requiem: Four Royal Women and the Fall of the Empresses*. University L.L.C. Bloomington, 2012.

Vyšnỳ, Paul. *Neo-Slavism and the Czechs 1898–1914*. Cambridge: Cambridge University Press, 1977.

Waite, Robert G. L. *The Psychopathic God Adolf Hitler*. New York: Basic Books, 1976.

Walker, Andrew. "Profile: Edward VIII." BBC News Broadcast. 29 January 2003.

Washburn, Albert Henry. Envoy Extraordinary and Minister Plenipotentiary to Frank Kellogg, US Secretary of State. May 6–7, 1927. Microfilm #1387. Records of the Department of State Relating to the Internal Affairs of Austria-Hungry and Austria 1910–1927. National Archives Microfilm Publications, National Archives at College Park, College Park, MD.

Watson, Greig. "Could Franz Ferdinand Welbeck Gun Accident Have Halted WWI?" BBC News, 25 November 1913. November 2013. http://www.bbc.com/news/uk-england-nottinghamshire-25008184# (Retrieved 1 September 2015).

Weber, Thomas. *Hitler's First World War.* Oxford: Oxford University Press, 2010.

Welzler, Luis. Correspondence with author. 18 August 2013.

West, Rebecca. *Black Lamb and Grey Falcon.* New York: Viking Press, 1941.

Weyr, Thomas. *The Setting of the Pearl: Vienna Under Hitler.* Oxford: Oxford University Press, 2005.

Whittle, Tyler. *The Last Kaiser: A Biography of Wilhelm II German Emperor and King of Prussia.* New York: Times Books, 1997.

Winder, Simon. "If Franz Ferdinand Had Lived." *New York Times Online: Op Ed.* 27 June 2014. http://nyti.ms/TEWb45 (Retrieved 28 June 2014).

Windisch-Grätz, Prince Ludwig. *My Memoir.* Boston: Houghton-Mifflin Company, 1924.

Zámecnik, Stanislav. *That Was Dachau, 1933–1945.* Paris: Collection Documents, 2004.

Ziegler, Philip. *King Edward VIII.* New York: Knopf, 1991.

Zweig, Stefan. *The World of Yesterday: Memoirs of a European.* London: Pushkin Press, 2009, 213.

SELECTED RESEARCH SITES

Alpen-Adria-Universität-Library-Klagenfurt, Austria
British Library, London, United Kingdom
Castello di Mirmare, Trieste, Italy
Dachau Concentration Camp Memorial, Munich, Germany
Edinburgh Napier University Library, Edinburgh, Scotland
Franklin D. Roosevelt Presidential Library and Museum, Hyde Park, New York
Hillman Library, University of Pittsburgh, Pittsburgh, PA
Hitler Story Bunker, Berlin, Germany
Imperial War Museum (Heeresgeschichtliches), Vienna, Austria
Imperial War Museum, London, United Kingdom
Jewish Holocaust Memorial Museum, Vienna, Austria
Jewish Museum, Berlin, Germany
John F. Kennedy Presidential Library and Museum, Boston, Massachusetts
Konopiste Castle Museum Benešov, Czech Republic
Library of Congress, Washington, DC
National Archives and Research Administration, College Park, MD
National World War I Museum and Memorial, Kansas City, MO
Pius XII Library, St. Louis University, St. Louis, Missouri
Schloss Artstetten Museum, Artstetten, Austria
Sarajevo 1878-1918 Museum, Sarajevo, Bosnia-Herzegovina
Sigmund Freud Museum, Vienna, Austria
St. Louis Mercantile Library, University of Missouri–St. Louis
United States Holocaust Memorial Museum, Washington, DC
U. Grant Miller Library, Washington and Jefferson College, Washington, PA
Universitäts bibliotheck der Vetmeduni Vienna, Austria

INDEX

ABOUT THE AUTHOR

James McMurtry Longo is a native of St. Louis, Missouri, where he was educated and taught in public schools for over a decade. He graduated from the University of Missouri–St. Louis, earned his Master's degree from Webster University, and his doctorate from Harvard University. He is an award-winning Professor of Education and Chair of the Education Department at Washington and Jefferson College in Washington, Pennsylvania. As a Fulbright Scholar he served as the Distinguished Chair of the Gender and Women Studies Program at Alpen-Adria University in Klagenfurt, Austria. He has taught in Austria, Brazil, and Costa Rica, and lectured at Harvard, Oxford, Napier University in Edinburgh, Zlin University in the Czech Republic, and throughout the United States.